The Last Slave Market

The Last Slave Market

Alastair Hazell

Constable • London

Constable & Robinson Ltd
3 The Lanchesters
162 Fulham Palace Road
London W6 9ER
www.constablerobinson.com

First published in the UK by Constable,
an imprint of Constable & Robinson Ltd, 2011

A copy of the British Library Cataloguing in
Publication Data is available from the British Library

ISBN: 978-1-84529-672-8

Typeset by TW Typesetting, Plymouth, Devon

Printed and bound in the UK

1 3 5 7 9 10 8 6 4 2

PEFC
PEFC/16-33-111
CATG-PEFC-052
www.pefc.org

In memory of my father

CONTENTS

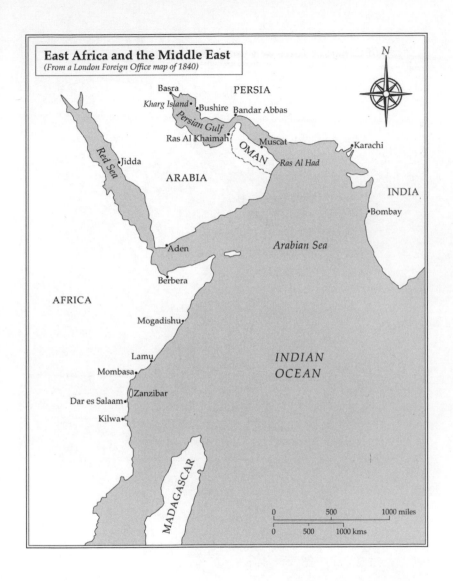

East Africa and the Middle East
(From a London Foreign Office map of 1840)

N

Basra

Kharg Island • Bushire

PERSIA

Bandar Abbas

Persian Gulf

Ras Al Khaimah

OMAN

Muscat

Karachi

Red Sea

• Jidda

Ras Al Had

INDIA

ARABIA

• Bombay

• Aden

Arabian Sea

Berbera

AFRICA

Mogadishu •

Lamu •

INDIAN
OCEAN

Mombasa •

Dar es Salaam •

◊ Zanzibar

Kilwa •

MADAGASCAR

| 0 | 500 | 1000 miles |
| 0 | 500 | 1000 kms |

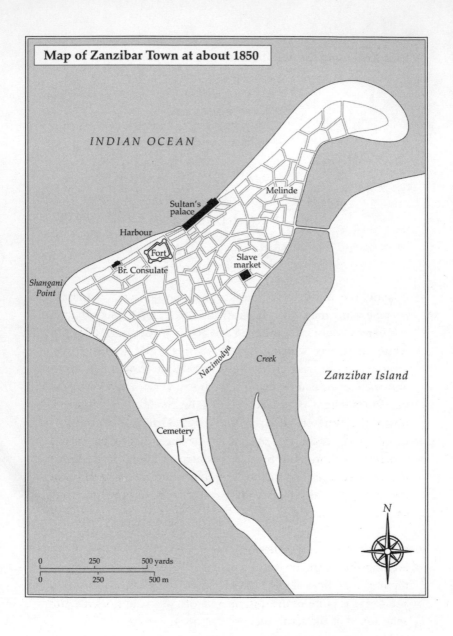

Map of Zanzibar Town at about 1850

PROLOGUE

One hot day in the early 1960s, a small motor launch containing a single white man and a number of African *askaris* set off across the narrow waist of southern Lake Nyasa in Central Africa. The white man was wearing a pith helmet and gleaming white uniform, his *askaris* were dressed in khaki, each wearing a red fez, and the launch had an awning to shield its passengers from the brilliant sunlight. The lake, which stretches for 570 kilometres down the southern end of the Great African Rift Valley, is exceptionally deep, and on either side high mountains cascade down to its shores, but here, at its narrowest point in the south, the distance from one side to the other is little more than twenty kilometres. By early afternoon, they were approaching the eastern shore, and at three o'clock the launch beached on a spit of land that projected into the water from the opposite side. The spit was mainly occupied by fishermen, who mended nets there. In the evening they brought in their narrow dug-out canoes, dragging them in long lines above the water line. There was also a village, and near the point of the spit, the remains of an old stockade, now abandoned in the scrub that grew above the shore.

The white man was the new Assistant District Commissioner from the lake's western shore. He was in his early forties, and had come out from England just a year earlier. He had crossed the lake in order to meet Makanjira, the Yao chief, who lived on the spit of land. In particular, he wanted to settle a difficult dispute concerning relatives of the chief's on the lake's western side.

Makanjira was waiting for him in the village. He was a portly man, often drunk, but he was proud that his influence extended over a large area of the eastern shore, and he was proud of his large number of wives, who were also portly and often drunk. Most of all, he was proud of his name, which went back many generations. He did not particularly like it when the British came over the water to interfere in his life, and disturb his slow routines. Nevertheless, district officials came and they went, they rarely stayed long, and in general it was good to keep them happy. So when the new white man arrived, Makanjira treated him politely, and they sat down in the village meeting place in the mid-afternoon and began to talk.

The conversation lasted a long time, and there was little resolution. On the eastern shore, someone had been killed, or perhaps had disappeared, and there was a question of responsibility. Compensation needed to be paid, but nothing was sure, and the chief showed little interest in reaching a conclusion. He sucked his teeth, and after the white man said anything, took a long time to consider his response. He was easily distracted by the comings and goings of a group of young men at the other end of the square. He was waiting for his visitor to leave, to take his boat back across the water. Long lines of white egrets were flying across the pale sky. Fires were glowing in the dusk, and the smell of cooking maize filtered up through the smoke. Then, unexpectedly, the white man said he would stay the night. He had a tent, and he would camp outside the village. They could talk again in the morning.

There was a pause when he said that. Slowly Makanjira climbed to his feet, lifting himself off his stool with great effort. With equally great politeness he asked the white man if he would accompany him on a walk outside the village. It was still early, and he liked to walk along the shore at that time of day. The visitor agreed, and together they took the path out of the village, between a long row of huts. The women were cooking over their fires, men were sitting smoking, and it was a peaceful scene. They walked slowly. The chief was accompanied by two of his wives and a number of young men. Soon they had left the village and were following the path above the shoreline. There was a strong smell of drying fish. Kingfishers were calling in the early dusk, and the evening wind, the *mvera*, which came down the Rift Valley at that time of year, was beginning to drive waves up on to the beach.

Finally, they approached the end of the spit. In the fading light, the remains of the stockade could still be seen, its wooden stakes half buried in the bush. They resembled crazy figures, half human, attempting to escape from the sand. Makanjira pointed to them. Through his interpreter he asked his visitor if he knew what these were, what they meant.

No, he did not.

The stockade had been built by one of his predecessors a hundred years ago, the chief said, nodding pensively. It had been a kind of enclosure, strongly fortified.

The white man, with sudden understanding, said, 'Ah, is this where the Makanjira of that time defied the British? Where he held his power.'

The chief clicked his lips and slowly shook his head. He looked out across the water. The other side of the lake could be seen in the sunset, a dark line of mountains on the western shore. The deep waters were pale, almost milky in the evening light. A fish eagle called, a long yelping cry, then was quiet.

'This was not to keep people out,' the chief said. 'It was to keep people in.'

Still the visitor did not understand.

'You see,' said the chief, 'that Makanjira was rich. He was very powerful.' He spoke almost sadly. 'More powerful than I am.'

'From trading, I suppose?'

'From trading.'

'Across the lake.'

'Yes. Across the lake. At its narrow point. This was where the boats came in. The dhows, with their big sails.'

The visitor was becoming restless. He, too, looked across the water. He was wondering where the best place would be to set down his camp, and he was not sure he wanted to hear any more. 'Bringing cloth,' he said. 'And ivory.'

'Not cloth,' said Makanjira heavily, with immense patience. This white man was new, he was inexperienced. He needed to understand. 'No, not cloth,' he repeated. 'The dhows didn't bring cloth.' He paused. 'They brought *people*.' He stared with yellow heavy lidded eyes. 'Do you see?'

But the white man did not see. Perhaps he was thinking of other things.

'They brought slaves,' said the chief. 'And we kept them here, in this stockade. So that they should *not* escape.'

Deliberately, he pointed at the arc of broken wood, and then at the lagoon on the landward side, separating the spit from the shore. And the white man, looking at the twisted pieces of wood in the half light, the water lapping at the shore on almost every side, and the mountains falling to the expanse of bush beyond, suddenly realized what the chief was saying. He understood just how hard it would be to escape from such a place. If you made it to the water, and then across the lagoon on the landward side, they would still be waiting for you, to re-imprison you or worse. You might even die if you tried. It came to him with a shock.

'Slaves were good,' said the chief quietly. The two men were about the same height, and he looked his visitor directly in the face. He had dull eyes, unblinking, expressionless. 'They brought money, they brought power. Yes, they were very good.' He wrinkled his nose. 'Many died, of course, but there were still enough to make money. The village had a *mwalim* then, an educated man, who taught us religion. Before you British came.'

The white man looked again at the high escarpment to the east behind them. The mountains were utterly black, like a wall against the sky.

'Yes, we sent them over there,' said the chief nodding, pointing to the east, across the lagoon. 'Through the mountains to the coast. The road is hard, but Swahili merchants came for them, and we sent them to the coast, to Zanzibar.' He looked back at the white man. 'Many of them died,' he said again. He had a habit of repeating himself. 'But there were enough.' Unexpectedly, he smiled.

The white man was unsure what to say. He suspected he was being mocked. The place made him uncomfortable, and he wished he were not staying the night, but it was too late now to leave.

'You come here to talk to me of one man who has disappeared,' said the chief quietly. 'Maybe he was sold. Maybe he was killed. I don't know. It happens. But in those days, many were sold and many died, and no one cared.' He wrinkled his nose again. 'Go up the lake, farther north, and you will see. The dhows are still there, they still cross the lake. You can see them. Big boats . . .'

'But no slaves . . .'

'No,' said the chief. 'No slaves. These days, we don't take slaves.' He chuckled almost like a child then, as if at some private joke, before turning. Slowly, he walked back up the track towards the village, and his wives and young men followed. A black and white kingfisher, landing on one of the broken stakes, began to trill in the half light.

Next morning the district officer left in his boat, and the problem of the missing man was never settled; nor did he ever meet Chief Makanjira again. But years later, he told his son the story, and that story led to this book.

INTRODUCTION:
THE BLACK COAST

It should be remembered that from time immemorial the traffic in slaves on these coasts has been considered equally just with any other.

POLITICAL AGENT IN ADEN TO SECRETARY OF THE
BOMBAY GOVERNMENT, DECEMBER 1841

In May 1873, prices for slaves were high on the East African coast, and the dealers on the Zanzibar waterfront made no secret of the good season they were having. Slaves were coming in to the island in large numbers that year, conveyed from the mainland in small, shallow-draft *mtepes*, the open-decked sailing craft of the Swahili coast. Most of them came from the little town of Kilwa, 170 miles to the south of Zanzibar, since that was where the main route from the great slave-hunting grounds of the interior finally reached the sea.

The journey north usually took two days, and the slaves, packed in tight rows, were given water but little else, and often arrived in desperate condition. The long march to the coast had taken months and had left its mark. Afterwards, cooped in barracoons in the marshy, malarial country at Kilwa, many became sick, and when they were delivered at the Zanzibar waterfront, they were emaciated, and often traumatized by the long ordeal. Wrenched from their homes, physically abused, sold and bought many times, they had little sense of where they were or what was expected of them. They had witnessed and experienced terrible violence. The women, deprived of their children, were constantly raped on the trail. The men, often summarily beaten, had seen many of their companions mutilated and killed.

These were *bagham*,[1] the raw, untrained slaves from the interior. The higher born Arabs of Zanzibar considered them to be barbarians, pagan Africans who spoke no Arabic or Swahili, and regarded them with aversion and contempt. Thought of as little more than beasts, sometimes branded like animals, they were disembarked at the Customs House, a collection of shacks and yards above the quay, which extended out into the stinking mud. There, the importer paid two dollars per head in duty before herding the slaves through the streets of the town to his compound. Once inspected, they would be separated into categories: the healthy divided from the sick, the young from the old, and the women from the men. Some – the oldest, the unwell and the least desirable – he dumped on the public market quickly for whatever he could get. The more valuable – the young women and men, and above all the children – he would fatten up and train over several months until they understood the rudiments of what was required of them in their new life. They might be brutally treated in this grim rite of passage. The women would be casually abused, the men beaten by other slaves specially employed to 'season' the latest purchases – men who perhaps themselves had been through this very process years before. Finally, when the new captives were ready, they too were brought to market, and the best ones sold for a handsome profit.

These early months of the year were a time of great activity in Zanzibar. The harbour was packed with high-sterned *bugalas*, the huge, triple-sailed, ocean dhows that came down from the Persian Gulf with the north-east monsoon every year to trade goods before returning with the changed winds. They brought dates, salt fish and ghee, and they returned with ivory and hides, beeswax, some gold dust and slaves – just another commodity, but one which was increasingly valuable in the countries of the north. For during the last two seasons, along the Somali coast of Africa, on the Red Sea and in the Gulf ports of Persia and Arabia, demand had been unusually high. Between 1869 and 1870, a cholera epidemic had scythed through the cities and towns of the Middle East, and the slave populations of the region had been reduced by up to half. As the households and factories, the palm estates, fisheries and stoneworks of the area attempted to rebuild their workforces, prices had soared. And Zanzibar, one of the last major sources of slaves in the world, was having a good year. That season, over 20,000 slaves were exported from the island, and most of them went north.

Among the throng of merchants and sea traders filling the yards and sheds of the Customs House that May, haggling and arguing over the price of goods, the cost of shipping and the settling of accounts, there were very few westerners. Perhaps the occasional naval captain would appear in the crowd of Swahilis, Arabs and Indians, or one of the few European or American traders in town – pale, overdressed in the heat and suffering from the climate. But in the deafening noise and stench of the city's packed streets, these were infrequent sights. However, one European was seen along the front almost every day early that year. He was not a trader, and took no part in the arguments, but he knew everyone. He was a doctor and a botanist, a slim, bearded man with a slight stoop. When he looked at a man, he tended to do so with a straight, impersonal stare. He said very little, but he listened a great deal, and often he could be seen taking notes in a small, leather pocket book. He observed and he counted, and there were few things he did not make it his business to inquire about.

This man was the acting British consul, and slave trading was something he was interested in. Standing outside his office on Shangani Point, he watched the *mtepes* coming into port, and as the packed vessels came round on the surf, heading for the harbour, he noted the numbers. He did it with an earnest and unflagging interest. It was almost academic, his interest, for he brought to it the same intensity and energy that he applied to his botany, and to the collecting of plants. Information, classification and knowledge fascinated and preoccupied John Kirk. He tried to understand what he observed around him. It was how he had been trained as a medical student in Scotland many years before.

Yet he was not a passive man by temperament, and he represented a country for which slave trading was a particularly loathsome and immoral activity. There was, therefore, a reason why he did and said nothing as the boatloads of slaves were disembarked on the quay that May. For even though he was acting consul, and slave trading had been illegal in the British Empire for over sixty years, in 1873 the selling and buying of human beings were both still perfectly legal within the territories of the sultan of Zanzibar. And although Zanzibar was an old and loyal ally of the British, along the East African coast that season, the trading in people continued almost exactly as it had done for thousands of years.

The final link in the chain of trade from the African coast to the Persian Gulf had actually been forbidden by treaty for over thirty years, and was technically disallowed. Nevertheless, policing that link was almost impossible, and the small group of Royal Navy cruisers intermittently detailed to enforce the law was seldom successful. The treaty was a weak one; in fact, it was almost a pretence, since it actually provided cover for the smugglers. It allowed them openly to embark slaves, and then ship them legally far up the African coast, with papers that stated they were destined for the tiny island port of Lamu at the northern-most extent of the sultan's domains. From there it was still a long voyage of several hundred miles up the coast of Somalia and across the Gulf of Aden to the ports of Arabia, but the slave smugglers timed their operations carefully. They knew the winds, and they knew the movements of the British ships, and few of them were ever caught.

Everyone was aware that the treaty was a sham, that it even protected the illegal trade. The sultan knew, although he pretended not to. The British authorities in India, who had responsibility for policy over the Indian Ocean, knew, but the slave trade was of no interest to them. In London, the politicians professed to be concerned, but did little beyond paying for the few warships necessary to keep public opinion happy. Most of all, the acting consul in Zanzibar knew, for he more than anyone had studied where the dhows went each year and how many slaves they carried. But there was a kind of conspiracy to allow this secret trade to go on, to pretend it was under control, because it was in everyone's interest to do so, and to leave the status quo undisturbed.

Nevertheless, because under law the trading of slaves was forbidden throughout the British Empire, in 1867 a Vice Admiralty court had been set up by treaty in Zanzibar to adjudicate over dhows caught smuggling slaves. Yet at times that, too, was little more than a masquerade. Instead of catching slavers, all too often the naval cruisers harried ordinary shippers. Tempted by a bounty on each ship caught, they attacked vessels on the slightest pretence, and the dhows were condemned and burnt on the most trivial evidence. Papers that were out of date, a couple of boys discovered hidden beneath a sack, or a woman taken on board with a consignment of hides, perhaps to be sold at some northern port – to the sailors of the Royal Navy it was all the same, an excuse for pillage and sport. The maritime traders of the African coast came to hate the cruisers for the way they harried their ships, plundering their meagre wealth, and destroying their boats – just as the naval cruisers hated them, for were not all Arabs slavers, they said.

Perhaps they were, for to the people of the Indian Ocean, slaving was no sin. Their customs excused it. Their religion justified it. But for John Kirk, presiding over the court on the Zanzibar waterfront in 1873, British justice sometimes seemed a futile process, an ironic comment on the might of the British Empire, which destroyed a poor fisherman whose papers were not in order, yet permitted in the full light of day the embarking and disembarking of thousands of slaves only a few yards along the shore. He did his job, read out the law and pronounced judgement, although at times he wondered if he were not a fool to do so.

The act that abolished the slave trade had been passed in Britain in 1807 after a long struggle that had convulsed the nation. For nearly thirty years the abolitionists had fought their cause in the press, in parliament and in public meetings the length and breadth of the country. They had waged an extraordinary campaign, addressing packed halls in every city and town, printing hundreds of thousands of leaflets, and bringing relentless pressure to bear on their parliamentary representatives. For the first time, they exploited the power of the popular press and in so doing aroused the deep religious instincts of the Victorian middle classes, mobilizing public opinion in a way that had never occurred before. When finally they triumphed over the entrenched interests of mercantilists, shippers and Caribbean planters, the abolitionists believed they had begun to extirpate a dreadful evil from the world. Even so, the fight continued until 1833 when a further act was passed forbidding slavery itself throughout the British Empire and its colonies. Treaties followed with virtually every other nation involved in the trade, and the Royal Navy was detailed to patrol the shores of Africa to prevent slaves being shipped across the Atlantic to the plantations of the New World.

For over three hundred years, Europeans had used slave labour from Africa to develop their colonies in North and South America and the Caribbean. Britain during that time had become the greatest beneficiary and the most extensive practitioner of the traffic. But it was also the British who first developed an intense moral repugnance against what they most of all had encouraged and practised. They felt a particular guilt about this 'of all evils, the monster evil',[2] and the abolitionist interest in Parliament, under heavy pressure from voters, became a powerful one. Governments were forced to respond, and by the early nineteenth century, prevention of slave trafficking had become a central principle of British foreign policy.

Yet in the Middle East and parts of Asia where Britain's imperial arm, the East India Company, ruled supreme, a different moral climate prevailed. Although few were aware of its scale, in the Indian Ocean a trade not dissimilar to the Atlantic traffic went on virtually unimpeded. Throughout the nineteenth century, tens of thousands of Africans continued to be taken each year and exported via the Red Sea and the ports of the Persian Gulf into Muslim Asia. It was even suggested that the East India Company was complicit in allowing this business to survive and prosper.

Among those who knew 'the East' it was widely considered that slavery in Asia was somehow different, and that the trade from eastern Africa was unlike that from the Atlantic seaboard. The Indian Ocean trade was conducted not by British or even, usually, other Europeans, but by Muslim shippers, Arab merchants who had traded with the African coast for thousands of years. And the people they purchased were not destined for the brutal, industrial-scale plantations of Brazil or the Caribbean, but for the households and cities of Persia, Arabia and Turkey. Once incorporated into the Muslim world, these slaves became part of long-established societies, and were generally treated well. They were deeply integrated into family life and into the wider community.

Throughout Persia, Turkey and Arabia, cities and towns traditionally depended on slave labour, and had done so since ancient times. Slaves were used in households, they provided the artisans, craftworkers, masons and builders in the cities; they furnished concubines for the harems, and eunuchs to guard the holy places of Mecca and Medina. Soldiers and warriors, the *nakhodas* or sea captains of ocean-going vessels, and pearl divers in the Gulf, were all predominantly slaves. Some slaves rose to positions of great eminence in military forces. They were considered indispensable to the functioning of established societies, which could not survive without them. Slavery was even mentioned in the Koran and in other holy texts, where the practice was explicitly condoned.

For the British and their empire in the East, this created confusion and disagreement. Evangelicals and abolitionists never ceased to agitate, attempting to persuade their rulers to take the struggle on to this new frontier, and intermittently politicians in London and their representatives in far-flung places would seek to fulfil their moral pledges. However, in the East the situation generally appeared differently. Officers of the Company and others who travelled in the region saw slaves being treated well, often better than labourers in the cities of Britain, and there was a reluctance to interfere in the workings of traditional cultures. Many officials admired the social structure of the places where they spent their lives, and excused the situation by referring to Britain's own feudal past. Among those whom they were least comfortable in criticizing was Seyyid Said *bin Sultan*, ruler of the Gulf state of Oman.

Seyyid Said had traditionally governed Oman from his capital, Muscat, but his empire encompassed large tracts of the African continent, and by 1840 he ruled from his southern capital, Zanzibar. He was greatly admired by the British, who for years had relied upon him as their chief ally in negotiating the difficult sea lanes that controlled the route to India. Among officers of the East India Company, he was especially esteemed for his bravery and his loyalty. Yet, embarrassingly, he was also rumoured to be the world's greatest slave trader.

Slaves had been exported from the East African coast for thousands of years, and Zanzibar had long been a major source of the traffic, but in the early nineteenth century, the island's importance grew. Over the centuries, Muslim scholars had proscribed an extensive body of rules governing the manner in which slaves should be treated, and historically many slaves received their freedom, an act held to be blessed by God. Inevitably, this created a constant need for further supplies. In the past, new slaves had been acquired by warfare, for it was not permitted under Muslim law to enslave other Muslims. But as the European powers advanced to the north of the Islamic world, depriving it of traditional sources in the Caucasus and elsewhere, only Africa remained as a supply of new labour. The region stretching from Sudan through Abyssinia down to the Zambesi valley became the largest and most lucrative source of new slaves.

From the southern Nile, substantial numbers were taken and transported up river to Egypt, or brought by caravan across the desert to the Red Sea ports, and then exported to Arabia. Abyssinian women were in great demand for the harem, and they too were taken across the Red Sea. But one of the single most important hubs remained the island of Zanzibar. There slaves were collected from a vast area of southern and eastern Africa, before being shipped north. Even the name suggested an ancient association with the traffic – the word 'Zanzibar' was thought to mean 'black coast'. The island was the outlet for a whole subcontinent.

Several attempts had been made to restrict the Zanzibar trade. In 1822, Seyyid Said had finally agreed to cease selling slaves to European or American vessels for export to their plantations, and a treaty was signed prohibiting the traffic outside Said's 'dominions and dependencies'. But as the then governor of Mauritius, wrote: 'We by no means wish to innovate on any of his religious practices or observances relative to Slavery, which is recognized and encouraged by the Mahometan faith.'[3] Slave trading into the Muslim world was still reckoned to be acceptable, and as Said's territories extended from the Persian Gulf down to tropical Africa, the export of Africans into the Middle East remained undisturbed.

However, a year later a stern, evangelical British sea captain called Owen paid Said a visit in Muscat. During a mapping expedition along the East African coast, this geographer had been appalled at the evidence of slave shipments he had come across. The two men exchanged gifts. Said courteously presented the captain with a fine sword of Omani steel. Owen responded bluntly with a Bible translated into Arabic. Then, abruptly breaking protocol, he issued Said with a threat: unless he gave up slaving immediately, Owen told his host, he would personally interfere within Said's southern territories, supporting a rebellion on the African coast.

The captain held to his threat, declaring a British protectorate at Mombasa, but it did not last long. Said, calling in favours with friends in Bombay, protested vehemently at such curt behaviour to an old ally, calculating that his friendship and influence in the Gulf were more important to the Company than curtailing his predeliction for slave trading. He was right. A year later, Owen's ineffectual colony collapsed, the enthusiastic captain was posted far away and Said was allowed to continue developing his African empire.

When he finally settled in Zanzibar in 1838, Seyyid Said was at the height of his power. For over two decades this enigmatic and complex man had involved himself intimately with British policy in the Persian Gulf. The British had been drawn to him by force of circumstance – he was virtually the only dependable ruler in a vital and turbulent region – but Said was skilled at persuading his allies of his goodwill and loyalty. They rewarded him with military support, and protection, and when he moved his court to Zanzibar, they were less than pleased. Tied to him by links of friendship, treaty and mutual dependence, the Company was not prepared to let him go and, two years later, sent one of their most experienced political officers down to Africa to watch over him. They considered Said to be their man, and so Zanzibar, in effect, became another client state of Britain's vast empire in the East.

By the 1840s, Said had transformed his new capital in Africa from a mere backwater, a slave market with a fort, to the largest and most prosperous trading city of the western Indian Ocean. In the process, it had become a unique mixture of cultures and races, African, Arab and Indian. Several thousand Omanis had settled there, coming south with Said from Arabia, and occupying positions of privilege and wealth. They owned large clove estates, as well as substantial town establishments. Nearly a thousand Indian traders drove the country's commerce, financing the trading caravans that journeyed inland, as well as much of the shipping to the Gulf and to India. Many of them were also rich, although they lived simply, and their leading merchant, as Customs Master, ran the Zanzibar economy.

Behind the grand buildings along the seafront, in the town's squalid and crowded hinterland, lived a very different population. Maritime Arabs from the Persian Gulf mixed with Swahili natives of the coast, Comoro islanders and African traders from the interior. But the bulk of this population were not Arabs, Indians or Swahili, nor were they mainland traders. They were slaves, Africans imported from far inland, bought and sold many times, and bound to labour in one of the many occupations that kept this city alive.

Out of a total population of around 100,000, perhaps over half were slaves.[4] They were the backbone of the city and the surrounding countryside. Graded into categories, they provided for everything that was required: the *mahamali* laboured in the port; the *wazalia* worked on the large clove estates; domestic slaves worked in the houses and, in the larger establishments, own slaves; trusted slaves captained dhows, or managed caravans into

15

slaves; trusted slaves captained dhows, or managed caravans into the interior, and had as much authority as free men; slaves were used as porters for the caravans; concubine slaves 'worked' in the harems of the rich; and the poorest and least valuable slaves, purchased from the market for the meanest task, were sold on when they were finished with.

In Zanzibar, slaves were a commodity, cheap to obtain and abundantly available, and the city depended on them. They were a common form of investment, and slaves who made money would purchase other slaves to hire out for income. They were goods to be exported, but they also provided for everything in a world where luxury and indolence were the right of the ruling class. The possession of slaves and of concubines were the measure of a man's wealth, a true indication of his power and status. They were more important than money. Some of the wealthier Arabs in Zanzibar possessed establishments of over a thousand people, showing just how rich the Omanis in Africa had become.

They had become rich through trade. Perched on the edge of Africa, Zanzibar was a gateway to a dangerous and violent continent, but the energy of the place was prodigious. Gum copal, which was used for coach varnish in Europe,[5] and ivory, as well as slaves, were shipped in quantity from the mainland, arriving at the Customs House almost daily. There, on a rude terrace in front of the building, traders of all kinds gathered in the morning to settle and discuss the day's commercial and political business.

[It] is an Arab bourse, [wrote the traveller, Richard Burton,] where millions of dollars annually change hands under the foulest of sheds, a long, low mat-roof, supported by two dozen rough tree-stems . . . It is conspicuous as the centre of circulation, the heart from and to which twin streams of blacks are ever ebbing and flowing, whilst the beach and waters opposite it are crowded with shore-boats . . .[6]

Here, Arab, Indian, African and European met, haggled and exchanged money. The ivory, the copal and the slaves were disembarked, or re-shipped, and the quantities noted. Outside its gates, transactions took place to raise the money to meet the customs dues. It was the centre of the city's economic power.

In these early years, Zanzibar was a vital but also a violent city. Ceremonial battles between slave armies were held in the open squares, and armed champions fought bloodthirsty and sometimes fatal bouts while the crowd watched and laid bets. Colourful wedding processions were preceded by terrifying imitation animals with carved heads and bodies of undulating cloth. Half-naked men with painted faces enacted mock fights, while masked performers capered and grimaced before the crowd. Adulterers were beaten through the streets with clubs and sticks. More serious crimes were punished by mutilation, imprisonment or public execution. Death was ever present and funerals were frequent, their torchlight processions winding regularly through the town to the shore at night, pursued by packs of dogs. 'Scarcely an hour in the day passes that I do not hear the wild, mournful ... wail ...'[7] wrote an early visitor.

Human life was held in low regard, perhaps because of the terrible diseases for which Zanzibar was notorious. In the streets, the sight of maimed beggars and rotting corpses was common, but human lives were also cheap for a more literal reason – any day of the week, a man, woman or child could be bought or sold as easily as a donkey or a dog.

The public slave market was the oldest institution on the island. Its origins went back to the eighteenth century, if not before. It had existed before the town itself, and to the Arab conquerors, it was a symbol of what Zanzibar was. Situated in the centre of the town in an open square, close to the creek, it was surrounded by a number of sheds and tethering posts. There, throughout the year, thousands of *bagham*, untrained slaves, were displayed and publicly auctioned. Prices varied considerably, depending on market demand and on the readiness and quality of supply; slaves were sorted and valued by category. In the mid-1850s, able-bodied young men were priced at between four and twelve dollars each – about the price of a donkey. Prices for young women varied also, and the more expensive females, destined for the harem, were often groomed and decorated to show off their finer points.

Children were always in high demand but usually plentiful, and a five-year-old child was valued at two dollars, or the price of a goose. A slave above middle age, worn out and not destined to live long, fetched a mere dollar.

Many descriptions of the mid-nineteenth century slave market exist – it was thought to be one of the last of its kind in the world, and every European visitor to Zanzibar felt compelled to inspect it. The place was tawdry and rundown, but at the height of the season it was crowded, noisy and chaotic, with competing traders shouting out prices for the latest deliveries. It was not unusual for several hundred captives to be available at any one time. The slaves stood or squatted in a miserable semicircle in the dust, in groups of over a dozen, each attended by an auctioneer singing out prices in an endless monotonous chant.

The market was also a place for recreation. Zanzibaris of every kind would stroll through there in the early morning or evening to survey the slaves and comment. An ancient superstition held that if the slave trade was going well, the city would prosper, and in the midst of the din, popular entertainers juggled swords and daggers for the amusement of the crowd. But in the low season, or when the mainland trade routes were closed by war, the place was half empty, dejected and deserted.

The procedures for sale do not appear to have varied much over the years. A British naval captain visiting as early as 1811 described how women for the harem were specially prepared, 'having their skins cleaned, and burnished with coconut oil, their faces painted with red and white stripes, which is here esteemed elegance, and the hands, noses, ears and feet, ornamented with a profusion of bracelets of gold and silver and jewels . . .'[8] By the mid-century, these women were kept apart in a special section of the market, veiled and decorated, as befitted luxury and costly items for wealthier patrons. At the other end of the scale were those who had suffered most on the long journey from the interior. Emaciated, often sick, stunned by abuse and starvation, they were dumped in large numbers on the market for a quick sale at any price, and often sold in job lots, they were considered so expendable.

Again and again, horrified European spectators made the comparison with an English stock fair – how the slaves were inspected and forced to run through their paces to demonstrate their fitness, their parts touched, prodded, felt, examined. 'An Arab approaches, and cattle dealer-like, pokes the girls in the ribs, feels their joints, examines their mouths, fingers their teeth, trots them up and down to see their pace, then, after haggling about their price, takes one and leaves the other.'[9] The manner in which younger women were led off behind a rough awning for a fuller and more detailed inspection never failed to excite comment.

What strikes us today, though, is not the brutality or even cruelty of the place so much as its apparent ordinariness. The auctioneer, droning out prices for the latest batch of captives, often seems half asleep. The slaves themselves, when not exhausted or emaciated beyond caring, appear indifferent to their surroundings. The Arab, Indian or Swahili purchasers, strolling round the market, engaged in conversation, or merely passing through, show little interest. When finally a purchase is made, the haggling over, the buyer walks briskly on to his next point of business. This was evidently not a big deal, and yet the market still occupied a special place in the mythology of the country. Slaves may have been a commodity to be bought or sold like any other, but the market represented the subjugation of a continent. It demonstrated the imposition of an alien culture on the 'barbarians' of the interior. It lay at the heart of Zanzibar.

The British did not give up easily. They continued to put pressure on Said, attempting to achieve their ends by treaty and with due consideration.

Then, in the early 1840s, the foreign secretary, Lord Palmerston, a committed antislave trader, read of the traffic taking place on the western shores of the Indian Ocean, and peremptorily demanded an account of his Indian colleagues. Reluctantly, the Company complied with his request, and for the first time evidence was compiled on the full scale of the trade in human beings into the ports of the Middle East. During the following year, as letter after letter arrived in Bombay recording shipments into the Gulf and along the Arabian coast, the extensive evidence became impossible to ignore. The quantities varied from as little as twenty slaves to several hundred in a boat, but clearly this was a significant business. The prices obtained for the human cargo were also cryptically noted.

> September 27, 1840 ... Slaves ... brought from Zanzibar by a Lingar boat ... Price of a boy of eight years of age – 17 dollars. Do. of a young man without a beard full grown – 21 dollars. Man about thirty years of age, beard full grown – 10 dollars. A woman stoutly made – 35 dollars.[10]

Even so, various Company agents tried hard to show the matter in a sympathetic light. Slavery was intrinsic to the societies of the region, they wrote, and to interfere would be to upset the fragile stability upon which the Company relied for its security. Some questioned whether slave trading was even that immoral.

The political agent in Aden tried to put the matter most clearly. 'It should be remembered that from time immemorial the traffic in slaves on these coasts has been considered equally just with any other,' he wrote. It was an old and established custom. People's wealth was derived from the numbers of slaves they owned, and indeed the British over the years had never argued or remonstrated with them about this practice. As a result, they still regarded 'the trade of their forefathers' as a perfectly legitimate right. He then got down to the detail.

> And further, slavery provides them with food, and attached servants, those from the higher classes select their bodyguard. The care of their domestic economy, the tutors of their children, and frequently the *nacodas* [i.e. captains] of their vessels, are slaves. Their harems are filled with chosen beauties from the Galla tribes and Serwahil; and much of their domestic satisfaction arises from the idea of possessing an ample establishment of the kind, an attractive slave girl being considered the most complimentary present that can be offered ...

He rounded off his argument with a passionate plea to his masters to leave the matter alone. 'From time immemorial these customs have existed . . . sanctioned by all they have loved and honoured . . . as yet unquestioned by any other power.'[11]

This was the benign, tolerant view of slavery and slave trading, frequently heard among officers and travellers in the Gulf. Few of them had been to the African coast where the trade began, or had seen the horrors of its early stages, and if they considered slavery an evil, then it was a necessary one, a price worth paying to sustain the ancient societies upon which British rule depended.

Nevertheless, in London, Palmerston was not to be put off. Among all the documents he had read was one sent by Atkins Hamerton, the Company's agent in Zanzibar, which, perhaps for the first time, set out the extent and detail of the trade at its African end: the caravans arriving at the coast, the Indian merchants who went to the mainland to haggle and bargain for captives, the exchange of human beings for beads and cloth. In this one document, the tone was different. Hamerton refused to disguise the sufferings of those who were transported across half a continent to fill the bazaars of Arabia and Persia, and his dispatch, given the constraints of the day, was harrowing.

> I fancy, in no part of the universe is the misery and human suffering these wretched slaves undergo, while being brought here and until they are sold, exceeded . . . They are in such a wretched state from starvation and disease, that they are sometimes not considered worth landing, and are allowed to expire in the boats to save the dollar a head duty, and the bodies of these poor people are eaten on the beach by the dogs of the town; none will bury them . . .[12]

The quantity of slaves imported into Zanzibar from the mainland averaged between 15,000 and 20,000 each year, he estimated, three-quarters of whom were sent on to the Red Sea and the Persian Gulf.

The foreign secretary responded with characteristic force. In 1843, he sent a letter to Hamerton, who, as well as being Company agent, was nominally consul to the British Crown. In it, Palmerston instructed him to inform Said immediately that this disgusting traffic must cease. 'The British Government is determined at all events to put this slave trade down,' he declared, 'and is conscious that it has the means of doing so.'[13] The letter was intended as an obvious and explicit threat to the ruler of Zanzibar but it was also a direct challenge to the Indian government, which had protected him for so long.

The Governor General of India was a grand and powerful man, and he did not consider himself especially bound by the demands of the British foreign secretary. Under point of law, he reported through a Board of Control in London to the British cabinet. However, in India, his authority extended over a vast empire and the lives of many millions of people, and London was a very long way away. Even so, his reaction to the reports on slave trafficking had so far been balanced, and worded with care. He had deplored the evidence of inhumanity with which he had been presented, and accepted that any civilized person must deeply regret such a situation. Nevertheless, he had informed London that his resources were still limited, and under the circumstances, therefore, the government of India was in favour of doing nothing about the matter.[14]

Palmerston's letter changed all that. Since its inception, the East India Company had always resisted any attempt from London to impinge on its power and authority in the East. It was the official government of India, and control of policy in the Gulf and Indian Ocean was a jealously guarded privilege. Now London threatened to intervene, and the Company was well aware that once the wall was breached, it might be difficult to keep the home authorities out. Officials in India suddenly became very serious about slave trading. In 1843, Hamerton, on returning on leave to Bombay, was told there was unfinished business for him to do in Zanzibar. He had to go back to Africa and get to work. The Company now wanted Said to curtail his unfortunate habits and a treaty was needed to stop their Omani friend from embarrassing them further. They wanted no more interference from Britain.

Said did not compromise easily. During the next two years, he resisted every attempt the agent made to control his activities. Repeatedly, he reminded Hamerton that slavery was intrinsic to Islam itself. 'The Koran, the word of God . . . sanctioned it; and the Arabs, of all Mahomedans, the people considered by the Almighty as most deserving of favour, had a right to enslave infidels,' he told him.[15] For Arabs to enslave Africans was a prerogative, and it had been conferred by God. Yet Hamerton was a painstaking and hardy negotiator, and he had the might of his Company behind him. In 1845, a treaty was finally signed, committing the Zanzibaris to cease exporting slaves from Africa. It was a triumph, because at one stroke it gave both the British government and the Company what each badly required. Slave exports to the Gulf would cease, and London would henceforth refrain from meddling in the region.

So the matter was settled – except that the treaty was a sham. It gave everyone what they wanted, including the Zanzibaris, and it changed nothing. Once it was signed, the Company lost interest in the trafficking of slaves, and the new treaty was left unpoliced and unenforced. Along the western shores of the Indian Ocean the slave trade did not cease; on the contrary, it grew, unimpeded, tolerated, even half protected within the shadows of the law. The numbers of black Africans exported from Zanzibar increased as the century advanced. It seemed that nothing could stop the traffic.

Hamerton died in his post, a cynical and disillusioned man. He was succeeded by consul after consul during the mid-years of the century, 'Indian' men, appointed as agents from Bombay. Civilized men, unprepared for what they would find in Zanzibar, each one of them was horrified at the systemized scale and violence of the slave trafficking into the island and strove to use his power and influence to mitigate the horrors. Inevitably, they all failed, because the authorities in India had no interest in the matter and refused to support them, and the government in London exerted no authority. Also, each one quickly succumbed to the diseases that plagued the island, and was forced to leave before he could cause any serious disturbance to the continuing trade in people.

To the Zanzibaris, this was no matter of chance. Each consul's failure was evidence to them of the unchanging nature of the universe, and the inability of man to affect it. Slave trading had gone on since the world began, they said, and like the monsoons, and the succession of the seasons, the harvesting of men from the interior was part of the order of things. It would never change or cease. Even the most powerful empire in the world could do nothing. The westerners came and went, but Zanzibar and its trade endured.

However, in 1873, the British consul was not an 'Indian', trained in the service. John Kirk was not even a real consul or administrator, but a medical officer temporarily occupying the post while the real consul, laid low by disease, was away on sick leave. Moreover, unlike his predecessors, he was not horrified at what he saw daily at the Customs House, for he had witnessed far worse. During the five years he had spent travelling in the interior he had seen slavers at work and so he knew what they were capable of. He was entirely unemotional about it but yet had no tolerance for the institution of slavery, which often confused the typical officer from the Gulf. For Kirk, the slave trade was like the other diseases that infected the city of Zanzibar, which he saw daily around him. But this was one he could do nothing about, and that was what angered him.

Zanzibar was not the only slave market in the world to be open for business during the last decades of the nineteenth century. Although in Istanbul, and even as far away as Khartoum, most of the great slave emporiums of the past had been closed, the effect was often merely to drive the business elsewhere. Throughout the African continent, there were countless local markets, and in Marrakech in Morocco a large market received slaves from the African interior until early in the twentieth century.

But Morocco was a kingdom virtually closed to the outside world, and the African interior was far from the sight of western eyes. Zanzibar, on the other hand, by the 1870s had come to assume a peculiar significance. Not only was its trade sanctioned by the country's lawful ruler, the island also functioned as an entrepôt, a centre for the export of slaves from Africa across the oceans to other countries and continents. To many British, with their obsessive interest in maritime commerce, this was particularly offensive. In 1870, the foreign secretary in London wrote that Zanzibar's ruler was 'now the only sovereign who openly permits the traffic in slaves by sea, with all its attendant horrors, to be carried on . . .' Along the coast of West Africa, British naval efforts had closed markets and successfully prevented the shipment of hundreds of thousands of slaves to the New World. Yet in the Indian Ocean, where Britain alone ruled the waters, it seemed impossible to eradicate this seaborne traffic. Slave shipments apparently continued undisturbed as they had done for millennia.

In that sense, Zanzibar had come to embody the last manifestation of an ancient evil. It was the final market, the one that had to be closed.

Part One

INTO AFRICA

When they went to the coast they were told, 'Next year you must bring ivory and slaves . . . and you will make your fortune . . . You will get anything you want if you bring these two things, ivory and slaves.'

ABDALLAH ('THE YAOS' QUOTED BY ALPERS P.63)

1 : THE RIVER

The kite has come . . . The slave trade has brought about this miserable state of things.

JOHN KIRK'S JOURNAL, 3 AUGUST 1859

Slowly, the steamer was coming apart. For almost two years, between 1858 and 1859, the expedition had been moving up the Zambesi river and back down again to its headquarters in the estuary – moving, not steaming. At times the river was so low and blocked by so much sand, they had to haul the vessel along the shallow bottom by winches and ropes, its hull scraping and rasping through the rocks and mud. It was savage, back-breaking work in the intense heat. Damp and teredo worm had attacked the steamer's body structure, so that rust was peeling off its hull in great black cakes, and the woodwork was deteriorating fast.

According to John Kirk, the expedition's botanist and medical officer, it had been badly designed and badly built. 'The engine is good but too weak and no expense has been put in which it was possible to avoid . . .' he wrote.[1] Along the valley, no coal was to be found, and so they were forced to spend time searching for wood, which lasted them just a day or two. 'The boiler is good,' wrote Kirk. 'But not made for wood, the tubes are too far apart . . . I don't know who designed her and what she was designed for

29

... The men who approved the plans ... were such fools ...'[2] It was clear the ship would not last them much longer.

Moreover, in late 1859, famine had struck the Zambesi valley. Food became very scarce, and the Portuguese colonists who lived along the river's edge were no longer prepared to sell them provisions. Kirk, who was a good shot, spent long hours on shore hunting for meat, and the ivory from an elephant he killed was sent to the coast to raise money. The river valley was desolate and empty from the effects of famine and slave raiding, and at night they could see fires on the horizon. Farther into the interior Portuguese and African rebels were fighting. They heard news of the conflict, and occasionally saw armed men on the shore, but the war was far away.

For the men on the steamer, there was only the river, with its sandbanks, its crocodiles and its flocks of wild birds, a huge stream that wound on and on without end into the far interior. It carried them, but it obstructed and isolated them, too. Kites circled for carrion above the deck, and the desolation surrounding the disintegrating ship was affecting the party badly. Relations between the men broke down. Three of the original party from England had already left or been sacked. David Livingstone, the expedition's leader, was increasingly frustrated and angry at the poor progress. Obsessively refusing to accept any reversal, he retreated into himself, communicating with no one.

Kirk, almost alone among members of the expedition, had maintained cordial relations with their leader, but he too had begun to lose faith in the expedition's purpose, and had even begun to doubt Livingstone himself. Their chances of success seemed remote since their efforts were constantly frustrated by the enormity of the forces against them: the punishing effects of weather and famine, the diseases that never ceased to debilitate them, but most of all the vast river upon which they depended for everything. It was their means of transport into the interior, it was their lifeline to the coast and the outside world, and yet slowly it was destroying them. Shifting its course, plunging through deep gorges, or leaving them stranded for weeks on its shoals, it had a personality of its own. Against its capricious strength, everything they did seemed futile and destined for failure.

Kirk's respite was his work, most of all his botany, to which he dedicated himself with almost religious intensity. But the river again was the enemy, and many of his most precious specimens had been destroyed by the water. Now, in late 1859, the steamer had clearly reached the end of its useful life, worn away by heat and damp, by the insects and the rocks, and without it they could not continue. Kirk did not wish to. When he left England, he had signed up for a two-year contract, and in January 1860 his term would expire. He did not consider he was needed any longer, and he had received no sign from his leader that his skills were still required. He began to think about his return.

The expedition had set sail from Liverpool on 10 March 1858, bound for the Zambesi estuary via Cape Town. Led by Dr David Livingstone, its purpose was to explore the upper reaches of the great river in order to increase geographic and scientific knowledge, and to assess the country's potential for growing sugar, wheat and cotton. It consisted of seven Europeans, including an economic botanist, a geologist, a naval officer and a moral agent, and it was supported by ten natives. Livingstone had absolute power to dismiss any member he wished. He was the reason for the expedition's existence, and the driving force behind it. When the undertaking had been announced in the British House of Commons, the statement was greeted by cheers from both sides of the House.

In 1857 Livingstone was a national hero. Between 1853 and 1854, with only a small number of African companions and few resources, he had walked across the African continent from east to west, the first white man ever to do so. His feat was hailed by Sir Roderick Murchison of the Royal Geographical Society as 'the greatest triumph in geographical research which has been effected in our times.'[3] But to the general public, Livingstone's achievement was far more astonishing for its physical endurance, bravery and Christian heroism. Africa was unknown, remote, barbarous, but also terrifying and exotic. The account of his travels published in November 1857 sold 70,000 copies, made him moderately rich and increased his fame. The RGS gave him its gold medal, he was granted the freedom of several cities, and Oxford University made him an honorary doctor. He had an audience with the Queen. He toured the country lecturing to packed halls, and people crowded the streets to get a view of him.

Livingstone was a hero special to the Victorian age. Brought up in abject poverty in a slum near Glasgow, he had educated himself through long nights of hard study. Then, as a doctor and missionary, he had gone to Africa to bring the truth to heathens oppressed by superstition and slavery. Hatred of the slave trade was Livingstone's passion all his life, and although the abolition debate had cooled by the middle of the century, the subject still had power to arouse great emotion. The public loved the modest man with his idiosyncratic cap and rough speech, and the government was soon persuaded to back his proposed expedition to the Batoka Plateau, high above the Zambesi river, where the Makololo tribe, who had befriended him on his earlier travels, resided. There, claimed the famous doctor, conditions were ideal for European settlement. Cotton could be grown in quantities to rival those produced in the southern states of America. He had been there and he was sure of it. The cultivation of crops combined with peaceful trade would drive out the hideous trafficking of men and women. Christianity and commerce would work together. The message appealed immediately to British self-belief, and Lord Palmerston gave it his public support.

John Kirk first heard about the chance of working on the Zambesi expedition when he was walking down Prince's Street in Edinburgh, and ran into his former botany professor. The old man dryly informed him that Sir William Hooker of Kew had been asked to recommend a botanist to accompany Livingstone to Africa. Kirk replied that he could start the next day.

Like Livingstone, Kirk was a Scot. Born in December 1832, he was the son of a church minister from the little village of Barry in Fife. Although poor, Kirk's father was an educated man, a graduate of St Andrew's University. He was also intensely dogmatic. During a schism that had split the Scottish church in the early nineteenth century, he followed a breakaway group, resigned his living on a point of principle, and set up a rival church in the ruins of a local castle. The family's subsequent financial struggles affected John Kirk all his life. He was continually anxious about money. He was also always suspicious of the dangers of sticking to an absolute principle, and where that might lead. Kirk was a pragmatist. But after studying botany, qualifying as a medical doctor, and spending some months as resident physician at Edinburgh Royal Infirmary, he craved adventure.

In early 1855, he volunteered with several friends to enrol for medical duties in the Crimea, but they arrived too late for service in the war and instead travelled through Turkey and Greece, where Kirk spent some of his time improving his shooting skills. He became interested in the Muslim world, and started experimenting with his new hobby, photography. He collected a number of rare plants, at least one of which was an unknown species, and on his return to Britain presented some of the new specimens to the Royal Botanical Gardens at Kew. There he met the director, Sir William Hooker, who was engaged in one of the foremost scientific enterprises of the nineteenth century – using the resources of the British Empire to build a great centre of botanical knowledge.

Botany was Kirk's passion, and Hooker needed people like him wherever he could find them. So he proposed Kirk for the job with Livingstone on the Zambesi, and Kirk took it without further thought. He was twenty-five years old. To be chosen to go to Africa, to follow this extraordinary man back beyond the borders of the known world, and to collect plants that had never been seen before – it was an extraordinary offer. Livingstone accepted him at once, just as he took the others on his expedition with little or no personal validation. This was, Kirk soon discovered, the way 'the Doctor' worked. He didn't particularly like travelling with other Europeans, and he didn't communicate well with them. He spent as little time checking their suitability as he did that of the vessel that they brought with them. It was his way. He had walked through Africa on his own. He didn't really need other people. He was self-sufficient.

Once embarked, though, the demands he made were exacting, and he was very specific in his requirements. Developing the country and directing its inhabitants towards industry and cultivation were the objectives of the expedition, he wrote, and his deepest hope was that this would lead to the end of the slave trade. Kirk was to assist by devoting his efforts towards the discovery of plants and other produce that might be of economic use. He was also to make extensive scientific observations, and he was to consider strongly the 'moral influence which may be exerted on the minds of the natives by a well regulated and orderly household of Europeans'. Arms were not to be used, the chiefs of native tribes were to be treated with respect, and the members of the expedition were to bear in mind that they arrived as 'members of a superior race' travelling among 'the more degraded portions of the human family'. Kirk was also advised to pay special attention to the dangers of constipation.[4]

However, the 'household of Europeans' proved to be neither well regulated nor orderly. By mid-1858, they had reached the Zambesi estuary, assembled their steamer, the *Ma Robert*, and begun their first ascent of the river. The disagreements and arguments between a group of men so arbitrarily selected began at once. Livingstone and the ship's captain, Bedingfield, were constantly at loggerheads, and their quarrels were interminable. Baines, the expedition's storekeeper and artist, worked hard but went down regularly with fever. Kirk liked him, but Baines fell foul of Charles Livingstone, the leader's brother. The younger Livingstone had been appointed in the position of moral agent, a job he regarded seriously, although its responsibilities were ambiguous. He was an arrogant and vindictive man. He despised the Portuguese colonists on whom the expedition often depended, and he used his influence with his brother to divide the party. The young geologist, Thornton, was reprimanded early on for not working hard enough. Rae, the engineer, soon wanted just to serve out his contract and leave.

Kirk, the expedition's botanist as well as medical officer, attempted to keep out of the quarrels. He was there for his botany, and he had work to do, which overrode all discomfort. But he was also there because of Livingstone, and the man perplexed as well as fascinated him.

They appeared to have much in common, although Kirk was younger than his leader by nineteen years. Both were Scots, doctors and had intense religious influence in their background, but all this masked great differences. Kirk had known some hardship, but his father was educated and had sent him on to university, where he had mixed with clever worldly men – Joseph Lister, the future pioneer of sterile surgery, was a friend and classmate. Kirk didn't look back; he didn't need to. Livingstone, however, had suffered a life of real poverty. As a child, he had worked in the mill, and he had fought harsh conditions to study by night. He had created himself from nowhere. His was a real accomplishment, done out of pure will and self-belief. He had come further than other men, but to get to where he was, he had had to sacrifice much. Kirk knew that, and would never have compared himself with the other man. Nevertheless Livingstone's struggle and success had created its own demons, and they tormented him – and around his personality the life of the enterprise turned.

Forty-four years old, of short build and stern in his expression, Livingstone was an awkward man, often ill at ease with himself. Despite his huge powers of endurance, he was physically clumsy – when one of his arms had been broken, he had set it himself, and now it hung limply by his side. After spending years on his own, travelling in the bush, his speech was slow and did not come easily. Often he was morose and turned in on himself, and his ability to communicate with his team was poor, sometimes disastrously so. Early in his journal, Kirk wrote: 'The doctor might be more careful in speaking and express himself so as to shew better what he wishes, so that those under him might be able, if they wish, to carry out his plans . . .'5

Livingstone continued to be silent for long periods, forcing his companions to interpret the slightest signs as indications of his wishes. Insistent humming, they discovered was a bad omen, as was an emphatic clearing of the throat. When he sang to himself, the tune was the only clue of what was to come, and when things were bad, it was as well to give him a wide berth. He was much preoccupied by the state of his bowels, which he discussed with Kirk obsessively.

The Doctor also changed his mind continually. His attention to detail was poor, leading to inadequate preparation at every stage. Kirk had been astonished at the chaotic arrangements when they left England. 'Things turn up in queer places . . . there are several things the want of which we now regret.'[6] Yet Livingstone also had an exceptional fixity of purpose, which, allied to his strong religious sense, made him an indomitable and compelling presence. His will-power never gave way. Yet this waterway – 'his pet river' as Kirk called it – upon which he had placed such store, severely challenged him. He had badly underestimated it.

Reports on the Zambesi from the Doctor's earlier travels had quickly proved catastrophically inaccurate. By the dry season of 1858, the current was far lower than they had expected, and at times there was only a foot of water. For days they were forced to haul the *Ma Robert* over the sand and rocks by means of its anchor. The vessel itself was a terrible disappointment. It would only fire on the hardest kinds of wood, and was slowly breaking up beneath them. Nevertheless, throughout 1858 and 1859, the small party of seven Europeans and twelve Africans steamed and hauled and dragged their difficult vessel up and down the broad river, repeatedly going hundreds of miles into the interior, and then returning to their base at Shupanga near the sea. Intermittently, they were supported by naval cruisers bringing letters and supplies from the outside world. Meanwhile, they attempted to understand the Zambesi's movements, to calculate conditions when it might become more amenable to travel, and to find out where it led.

Then, late in the first year, the Zambesi dealt the expedition its crushing blow. Some three hundred miles from the sea, as the river came off the high plateaux of central Africa, it became a torrent, pouring through a chasm hundreds of feet deep and extending for several miles. These were the cataracts of Kebra Basa.[7] During an expedition several years earlier, Livingstone had been warned by Portuguese about the falls, but he had disregarded their advice, and talked airily of blasting his way through the barrier to reach his destination on the Batoka Plateau beyond. It was not until November 1858 that he saw the rapids for the first time; entering the mouth of the gorge, the sight was chastening.

The rocks and cliffs were massive, the river an enormous boiling torrent that no boat could ever navigate. Kirk wrote: 'The Doctor changes his appearance completely from the first time he saw the rocks . . . and in the shaking of his beard, we could see that things were not working well.'[8]

Livingstone had toured Britain talking of a high plateau in Central Africa, a place ready for missionary endeavour, and suitable for trade and agiculture. He had raised funds and secured government support on a promise that the Zambesi would provide access to this region. The rocks and chasms of Kebra Basa now told him he had been wrong, and yet the Doctor refused to accept what he saw.

Nevertheless, when disaster struck, Livingstone looked for scapegoats. It was his nature. Always full of dark suspicions, he turned on people without reason. Bedingfield, blamed for the early failures of the ship, had already been dismissed; now it was the turn of Baines. Thirty-eight-year-old Thomas Baines had worked and travelled in South Africa. He was hard working and committed to the expedition's success, but he had offended the moral agent, Charles Livingstone. The day they first encountered the rocks at the entrance to the rapids, Livingstone rounded on the unfortunate artist and storekeeper, accusing him of neglecting to provision the porters, and of being deficient in his duties. Kirk watched the quarrel with misgiving. He understood that the porters were to have provided for themselves. 'I do not know of any orders having been given to Baines to have them rationed.'[9] Once again, Livingstone had failed to communicate what he intended. Baines attempted, unsuccessfully, to defend himself, but the accusations festered, unresolved.

Meanwhile, Livingstone, angry and frustrated, decided he would go back to the rapids and investigate them further on his own. Perhaps he thought they might still be navigable, but this was a judgement he wished to make alone, and he told the rest of the party he did not want anyone else to come with him. He did not trust them, nor did he need them. Kirk was furious. He refused to accept this, and told the Doctor it was an insult to leave the rest of the party there just to 'smoke their pipes and wait for his return.'[10] Livingstone, surprised to be confronted in this way, reluctantly agreed to take Kirk with him up the gorge.

The march turned out to be the worst either man had ever made. Between mountains 2,000 feet high, a channel seventy yards wide plunged over enormous rocks, disjointed and pitched against one another like 'all the sphynxes and statues of Egypt'. The hot, broken ground that wound between the cliffs and the torrent was terrible to walk on – 'the heat now is like hell if that place is what I imagine it – you cannot hold on any time by the rocks.'[11] When they finally emerged from the ascent, the local people were astonished to hear where they had come from. No one ever went that way, they said, not even the elephants took that path up the river. Finally, some weeks later, the two men returned, meeting the rest of the party and falling back to their temporary base at the little Portuguese settlement of Sena. They were exhausted and in terrible shape.

There Livingstone put together his report for the British government, and he let Kirk read it before sending it off. The rapids of Kebra Basa were a problem, he wrote, but not an insurmountable one. In the rainy season, he believed, 'a steamer of light draught and capable of going 12 or 14 knots an hour would pass up ... without difficulty when the river is in full flood.'[12] Kirk was astonished. It was quite clear to him that no boat would ever make that passage. However, although he was concerned, he kept his doubts to himself, because yet another vessel plus more supplies was what the Doctor was requesting.

Sena, the expedition's base for much of 1859, was a dejected place of two thousand people living in a scattering of stone and lime houses and reed hovels along the river bank. Once, it had been a more substantial settlement, and a chapel still remained, but the bells were cracked and broken. The fort was weak, and between the dwellings, deep pits were filled with rubbish. During the rains, these became a terrible health hazard. Slaving was endemic the length of the Zambesi valley, and Sena was one of its centres. Livingstone thought the Portuguese were addicted to the practice since they had been shipping people from East Africa to the New

World for generations, and local governors had grown rich on the business. Along the river, it had become part of a way of life that was corrupt, superstitious and cruel. Isolated in their small towns, after generations of indifference and isolation, the settlers had acquired many of the customs of the Africans they attempted to rule. They dealt in slaves, they took concubines, and when the rains failed, 'they make processions like the rain makers of the interior, at full and change of moon.'[13] They suffered terribly from syphilis, so that many of their children were born malformed and blind.

Strangely, Kirk liked them. They were humorous and generous, and when the expedition needed help, they offered it. 'The hospitality of these poor traders cannot be too much admired . . . I might have come off much worse in an English colony . . .' he wrote.[14] Trapped in a precarious existence on the edge of this huge river, oppressed by a vicious government, and caught in the midst of almost continuous warfare, they seized the few pleasures available. They ate and drank voraciously, were sexually promiscuous and died early from disease.

Kirk did not condemn them. When their troops were brought in, wounded and dying from the war inland, he assisted at one of their primitive hospitals. He did not take sides. One of his friends, Sr Vienna, 'bought his young wife and used her until she was about 18, when . . . he tired of her and purchased two others . . . naturally much younger.'[15] Kirk made no judgement. The slave trade was ruining the country, but it was like a disease, a terrible social ill, a vice. Africans and Portuguese practised it indiscriminately. Individuals made what accommodations they could, and he did not despise them for it.

Instead, he turned to his botany, collecting and cataloguing with intense dedication. It helped to give him a detachment and discipline that saw him through the crises plaguing the expedition. Yet even that was hard, the conditions were so bad. In Sena early that year, he wrote: 'Of all the miseries [so far] the worst is that of being alone in the cabin for four months with millions of cockroaches and not a single companion to speak to.' Nevertheless, botany kept him sane. It allowed him to forget his growing doubts about the expedition. He worked at it 'like mad, in desperation'.[16]

The discovery of the rapids had produced a crisis. The Portuguese had established rights in the Zambesi valley, and the expedition was there only with their permission. Blocked by Kebra Basa from ascending the river into territory beyond the control of the Portuguese, Livingstone was trapped and frustrated at being unable to fulfil his ambitions. However, not far from Sena another large river, the Shire, flowed into the Zambesi from the north, and in December 1858 Livingstone decided to follow it.

In January the next year, they took the *Ma Robert* slowly up the broad, flat waters of the new stream, entering an enormous swamp they named Elephant Marsh, an alluvial plain of isolated lagoons covered in reeds, lotus and water lily. The people who lived in this remote, isolated place survived by fishing and hunting the hippos and elephant herds that inhabited the marsh, and they were unused to strangers. The swamp also blocked the slavers from the Zambesi penetrating farther north. Beyond it lay tantalizing glimpses of the highlands of the Great Rift Valley, and here Livingstone thought he might find the land he sought – a country suitable for settlement, beyond Portuguese control.

So in March they returned, and Kirk and Livingstone trekked alone into the highlands above the Shire. The Mang'anja inhabitants they met were peaceful, industrious farmers, who planted cotton. The country seemed ripe for settlement, and Livingstone believed he might be within reach of his goal. He wrote enthusiastically to London, claiming he had finally discovered a land ready for English colonization, 'cotton producing districts of Africa' large enough to rival those of the Americas. Kirk, travelling with the Doctor on his own, discovered how different he was now. Amusing and inventive, he related to Africans easily, persuading them to help him. On their way to meet a local chief they were confronted by a 'dice doctor', who threw stones and shells on the ground to divine how dangerous these strangers were. Livingstone chatted to the man, getting him to throw his charms repeatedly until they came up with the right answer, and they went on to meet the chief.

This was the man who had tramped across Africa, at ease with its inhabitants, surviving on his own in the bush, at times so private and self-sufficient as to be almost like a wild animal. He and Kirk got on well as they trekked through the high mountains of the Shire that season. At one point, Livingstone was ill and Kirk nursed him back to health. The Doctor, maybe for the first time, recognized he was dependent on another, and later he named a range of local mountains after his companion as an honour.[17]

It was not until their next visit later that year that they discovered other people were also interested in this land of plenty. They began to meet small parties of Yao Ajawa,[18] a tribe who were advancing from the country to the east. Travelling into the highlands above the Shire, they were coming for a reason.

For generations the Yao had been long-distance traders across south-eastern Africa, taking goods from the far interior as far as the Indian Ocean. They liked to deal in ivory, but in recent years they had discovered an increasing appetite for another commodity among the merchants of the coast – slaves – and on the Shire highlands, the settled agricultural communities offered plentiful opportunities for acquiring them. The Yao were traders, and they were looking for goods to sell.

At first, the evidence was slight. In one village, Livingstone and Kirk came across a pile of thick beams, about nine feet long with a fork at one end. They were slave forks, for shackling reluctant captives. They also heard for the first time of Arab merchants active on the great lake of Nyasa to the north of the Shire. The Yao spoke of them as masters of the slave trade in the region, but later when he met them, Kirk realized they were not true Arabs. They were Swahili from the coast, trading malachite and copper purchased in the land of the Kazembe, deep in the centre of the continent. They travelled with many slaves, they carried guns and their presence this far into the continent was a recent phenomenon. They were men from Zanzibar, the coastal city far to the north, and they had not been seen down here before.[19]

As soon as Kirk and Livingstone returned to the boat, the divisions within the expedition flared up again, and they were bitter and destructive. The Doctor was easily influenced by his brother's opinions, and the moral agent seemed determined to show his power. He was a dilettante who hated physical work. He fancied himself as a photographer, but that too required more effort than he was prepared for. He was dangerous handling a rifle, and when he ventured out into the sun it was not 'without an umbrella and felt hat, with all the appurtenances of an English gentleman . . .'[20]

Kirk soon came to despise him, and Charles Livingstone, picking up the other's dislike, took it upon himself to demonstrate his power. One day, after collecting plants on the river bank, Kirk returned twenty minutes late to find the boat had been deliberately started without him. He ran down the river bank and caught up with it. On board, he learnt he had been accused of absconding on a sporting trip, and the Doctor had been persuaded to leave him in the bush as punishment.

Thomas Baines was not so lucky. There had been continual rumours that he pilfered stores for his own benefit, and in October 1859, Livingstone instructed Kirk to return to Tete on the lower Zambesi to check their supplies. The Doctor had been convinced that Baines was 'guilty of gross breaches of trust in secretly making away with large quantities of public property . . .'[21] Kirk was told to convey the artist and storekeeper to the coast, where he would be dismissed.

When Kirk got to Tete, he found their stores were chaotic, but there was no evidence of theft. He inspected the storebook and found only a cask of sugar and some butter missing. Baines was disorganized and vague, having been suffering constantly from fever, and when Kirk told him he was about to be sacked, he went to pieces. Together they went down river to the estuary where Livingstone met them. There, at Shupanga, Baines was interrogated in their building on the river bank. The storekeeper was barely coherent, and the only evidence against him came from the younger Livingstone. Despite this, the Doctor still found him guilty, and Baines was deliberately isolated from the rest of the party. When he finally left for England, disgraced, Kirk and Rae gave him money; otherwise he would have been destitute.

Baines' humiliation and expulsion shocked Kirk. He was disturbed at the Doctor's readiness to believe mere rumours, and sacrifice a companion on the flimsiest of evidence. Baines had not deserved such treatment, but the episode was a warning, and Kirk began to be wary of saying or doing anything that might possibly be misinterpreted. When he wrote to his brother Alick about a small financial disagreement between himself and Livingstone, he said he would pay the bill regardless:

> I shall tell Dr Livingstone that it has been settled . . . [for] if he once takes an ill opinion of anyone, [he] makes up into a devil very soon . . . He would at once, if we had a quarrel make out that I attempted to cheat him.[22]

His trust in their leader had been dealt a serious blow.

Meanwhile, the *Ma Robert* was disintegrating piece by piece. They had spent almost two years travelling up and down the Zambesi and the Shire, attempting to establish a base in the highlands, and then being forced to return for supplies. Many of the crew who remained were stricken by sickness, and some had to be taken to the river mouth for evacuation by cruiser. By January 1860, it seemed to Kirk that the enterprise was finished. His own contract was up, and the boat itself had become a liability.

> This is an awful place to live in, I mean the ship. My specimens, the result of five months . . . are all wet and run the risk of utter destruction. The water floods the floor from the windows, while the roof leaks at every joint . . . Many a pig lives in a better house than we do . . .[23]

He waited for Livingstone to tell him he was discharged, and yet the Doctor refused to say so.

For two months, as they made preparations at the mouth of the Zambesi for another trip inland, Livingstone gave no hint whether he wished Kirk to stay or leave. In March, Kirk asked whether a botanist was required any longer, but Livingstone would not commit himself. He was neither prepared to ask Kirk to remain, nor would he ask him to go. It was as if he would not admit to any need for the other man. So Kirk waited for a decision, and Livingtone said nothing, and Kirk said nothing either. Neither would give way.

For weeks the tension remained. Livingstone was completely intolerant of the failings or the needs of others; they did not matter to him. He had no use for companions unless they were prepared to assist him in his personal mission. Kirk couldn't stand that. He would stay, if he were asked. He would follow Livingstone, but only if he recognized that there were others involved in this crazy, desperate venture, and Livingstone wasn't accustomed to that. He was sullen and uncommunicative.

Finally, the older man gave way. He wanted to make a last trip to the Batoka Plateau, he said, travelling overland beyond the Kebra Basa, and he wanted Kirk to go with him. He was forced to admit it. 'He desired me to go and I did not choose to decline,' as Kirk put it.[24] But the question now was no longer whether Livingstone needed a botanist. It was whether he needed someone reliable with whom to travel. He must have known the hold he had over the younger man; he had only to ask and Kirk would come along. Yet Livingstone hated having to ask. It was almost as if he were humbling himself when he did it.

That May, they set off together with Charles Livingstone, leaving the rest of the expedition behind with the slowly foundering *Ma Robert*. Kirk couldn't say why he went, and he wrote to his brother that it was a waste of time and effort. He was a rational, logical man, yet now he was embarking on a journey fraught with peril, for reasons he did not agree with, following a man whose motives he doubted. Yet he couldn't say no.

They were away for several months, and during the trip Kirk witnessed a total breakdown in the relationship between the Doctor and his brother. At one point, Livingstone accused Charles of destroying an old and rotting pillow, and Charles responded with a stream of hysterical accusations on the mismanagement of the expedition. Both men lost control of themselves, the Doctor abusing his brother in such foul language that Kirk could hardly believe it was the man he knew. A few weeks later, Charles Livingstone lost his temper again, assaulting one of Livingstone's Makololo followers, and was saved from being immediately killed only by the Doctor's personal intervention.

Shortly after that, as they returned to the coast, the Doctor insisted that once again they had to visit Kebra Basa. He was obsessed with the rapids and could not leave them alone, but this time he wished to travel down by water, taking the gorge by canoe. He was determined to show that the river had no power to obstruct him, as though what he had seen could be dismissed, almost proved not to exist. If he could have willed the rapids away, he would have done so.

But Kebra Basa did exist, vast and impassable, and the passage turned into a terrifying ordeal. Halfway down the gorge, their canoes collided with rocks and they were thrown into the maelstrom of water. Kirk never forgot the experience, for he almost lost his life. He lost everything else – his rifle and chronometer, his journals and all the plant specimens he had carefully collected on the journey. He was bitter.

> Of all losses the loss of notes was the greatest – 8 volumes of notes and about 100 drawings of plants, these new ones and of interest, all botancial notes, in fact everything to keep me in mind of the trip, all was gone.[25]

For him, that last attempt on the gorge had been a disaster.

Without equipment, medicine or supplies, the remainder of the journey was a desperate one. They limped back into the Portuguese settlement of Tete in November, in rags and exhausted. By the end of the year they managed to rejoin the rest of the party near Sena, where the *Ma Robert*, its hull under water, was finally sinking beneath the Zambesi. Kirk went to the town to get canoes to take down their baggage, and when he returned only the mast and funnel of the 'infernal ship' were visible. It was late December, and the rain was torrential. Their resources were depleted and they had achieved very little. It seemed to mark the end of the expedition.

2: THE MISSION

It is curious how all agree in the wickedness in selling people,
although they still do it.

JOHN KIRK, 29 JULY 1861

It should have been the end, and yet it was not. In early February
1861, a Royal Navy cruiser arrived at the mouth of the Zambesi,
bringing a new river vessel from Britain and a party of six
missionaries. Inspired by Livingstone's call to bring Christianity
to Africa, and by his optimistic accounts of the interior, they had
come to plant a church in the country high above the waters of
the Zambesi.

Livingstone's speeches, and his letters back to England, had
galvanized a renewed movement dedicated to fighting the African
slave trade. The mission, sponsored by the Church of England and the
universities of Oxford, Cambridge, Dublin and Durham, was led by a
clergyman, Charles Frederick Mackenzie, who had been ordained
'Bishop of the Mission to the tribes dwelling in the neighbourhood of
Lake Nyasa and the River Shire'. With him were his deacon, Henry
Rowley, two other clergymen, Lovell Procter and H.C. Scudamore, as
well as layman Horace Waller, plus a carpenter and an agriculturist.
After much discussion, in May the party set off in the new boat, a
schooner 115 feet long and rigged with paddles. Called *Pioneer*, it
sailed up the great Zambesi towards the mouth of the Shire.

Mackenzie was an idealistic, naive man. A mathematics don from Cambridge, he was impractical, impulsive, indecisive and a poor planner. He was also emotionally dependent on his elder sister, and on taking the job, he had insisted that she join him in Africa. Kirk liked and admired him for his enthusiasm and his energy. Nevertheless, from the arrival of the missionaries, the expedition took on an unreal and slightly quixotic air. Mackenzie's companions were a mixture of high and low church, and disagreed on matters of doctrine. As they progressed slowly up the Zambesi, through the flat African plains, Rowley and Waller had furious theological discussions over the apostolic succession, and the divine right of European kings. Mackenzie had a knack of getting into trouble.

On Sunday morning the worthy prelate got into the wheels for a bath, putting cassock &c on the upper floats. By and by the force of current made the wheels revolve, and the right reverend gentleman was seen hanging on to the floats like a squirrel. After great exertion he gained a footing and rushed on deck, quite forgetting nakedness, shouting out, as his cassock &c floated astern, 'Save my cassock! Never mind the trousers. Save my cassock.'[1]

Kirk, always ironical, saw the amusing side of their troubles. Perhaps he had to, because he could guess what lay ahead. The *Pioneer*, designed to carry twenty people, was hugely overloaded with forty-eight passengers, and its deck was jammed with boxes, bales of material and coal. But within days the coal ran out, and once again they were reduced to daily wood cutting on shore.

In late May, they entered the Elephant Marsh, but this time it was very different. The swamp was almost dry, its channels narrow and low in water. Kirk was appalled, for it was now their only route to the interior, yet day after day they were forced to drag the heavily weighted ship by rope and anchor. He had been through this before, and he knew where it led. On 7 June, he wrote that 'since coming to this marsh, I believe we have laid out with the boats forty anchors'.[2] After endlessly dragging the *Pioneer* through the mud, the feeble current sometimes carried them back to where they started. On 26 June, Kirk wrote his brother: 'At present we are on one of the banks, having dragged [the ship] through forty yards of sand and still 15 off the deep on the other side.'[3] The number of Africans and Europeans going down with sickness increased, and by early June they had ten cases of fever.

However, the missionaries, earnest and idealistic, were merely frustrated by these delays. Africa was new to them, its conditions arduous and vexing, but as yet unexciting. With their high-minded principles, their knowledge and their resources, they felt they should have prevailed with ease. Instead, this waterway, which was intended to be their ally, prevented them from reaching their goals. Nevertheless, by July they were at their temporary base, Chibisa's, the village of a friendly chief, and there they heard that there was warfare to the north. Parties of Yao were constantly encroaching into the region, burning villages, killing older people and taking the young off as slaves.

They left the boat and continued by land, and on 16 July, in a village high above the Shire, the expedition ran into a slave gang with eighty-four captives.

> The slaves were . . . tied by the neck with ropes, in gangs,
> some refractory ones had beams of wood as thick as a man's
> thigh and six feet long with a fork at one extremity in which
> the neck was secured by an iron pin.

It was the party's first direct encounter with slavers. As they advanced into the village, the guards ran off and the slaves, mainly women and children, were immediately liberated. They had been horribly treated. Two women had already been shot when attempting to escape, and 'one woman who was unable to carry both her load and her young child, had the child taken from her and saw its brains dashed out on a stone.'[4]

After weeks of dragging the ship through the marshes, it was an inspiring occasion for the missionaries. This was the reason they had come to Africa, and their struggle to reach these highlands had now proved worthwhile. Freeing the slaves had been easy; their enemies had fled at the first sight of Christian courage. There were reports of further slave gangs to the north, and the party at once set off in pursuit.

As they went deeper into the Shire highlands, they began to meet groups of Yao and come across burnt-out villages. Finally, at the end of July, the inevitable conflict occurred, when they were attacked and fought back. The missionaries had guns and were supported by Livingstone's personal Makololo followers.[5] When the Yao attackers fled, Livingstone ordered their village to be burnt in revenge. It was a dramatic, even a symbolic, act. In a country already torn apart by tribal conflict, the newcomers had demonstrated their superior power.

From the beginning, the missionaries could not help but see slave taking and slavery itself in the simplest, most dramatic terms. To them, it was a stark issue: good versus evil, right versus wrong. Yet slavery in Africa was a much more complex matter; its origins and functions were not easy to understand, and few of these early explorers and missionaries even attempted to do so. In one form or another, the practice was deeply entrenched within almost every African community, but it was a very different system from the bondage that had become established in the plantations of the New World.

African society itself was utterly different from the societies of the West. People were first and foremost members of a group rather than individuals. They lived in complex networks of debt and obligation, extending across families into larger communities. The rights of one person over another were multifold, and often binding. Men had rights over wives, parents over children, elders over junior members of the group, and these rights could be transferred. Individuals might be handed over to pay for crimes committed by the family, children could be pawned for loans, men and women handed over as trophies in war; and such transactions, though cruel, were accepted practice. Inevitably, at the bottom of any group were the most disenfranchised who, for any number of reasons, had few rights at all. Whether they had been acquired in war, or were criminals, or were penalized in some other way, they joined the ranks of the exploited, passing into a status that could be termed slavery.

Sometimes such people were 'sold' to other groups who needed them more – the women to bear children, the men for labour or to fight. People rather than land meant wealth. In the more hierarchical groups, when a ruler wished to gratify his whims or demonstrate power, these 'slaves' might be sacrificed as part of elaborate rituals. Everywhere they were exchanged for alternative goods – copper bars, agricultural implements, ivory. Some tribes even sold their own people when they had to.

Contact with the outside world increased the traffic, since there was demand from beyond the seas for this human commodity, and from the trading centres of the coast came new items, imported cloth being particularly sought after. The exchange of people for goods intensified. When slaves could not be purchased, they were invariably taken by other means. They became a reason for conflict, as well as a result of it.

Into this hard and complicated world, well-meaning missionaries and explorers often unknowingly stumbled. They were intruders bearing an alien morality, which was regarded with suspicion or even derision, and they were judged not by what they said but by how they acted.

The mission was finally founded at Magomero, a place shaped like a bowl in the hills. Mackenzie and his companions were left there with the freed slaves, while Livingstone, Kirk and Charles Livingstone continued north, travelling along the shores of the great inland sea, Lake Nyasa. They found the country in chaos. Slave raiding was everywhere, and not only by the Yao. Another tribe, the Maviti, also attacked their neighbours ferociously, but their motives were entirely different. 'The Maviti,' Kirk noted, 'are said to kill all over the age of ten. Those under, they carry off to increase their tribe.'[6] He was beginning to realize that slavery in Africa was a difficult matter to understand.

Nevertheless, the result was wholesale destruction. From the slopes of Zomba mountain, Kirk could see burning villages dotted across the plain all along the lakeshore. 'The whole country is deeply engaged in the slave trade. They sell their own people and help dealers to purchase their own neighbours.' Cloth was in constant demand. 'They give four fathoms for a man. They give this to the head man [in a village] who shews them whom to catch.'[7] Along the shores of the lake, the beaches were crowded with people constantly offering slaves and ivory to the travellers. 'The banks are black with people. If the slave trade is to continue, this is the best locality; for all the slaves in the world would make no impression on the numbers.'[8] On the lake itself they met Swahili from the coast, who were buying people and shipping them across the deep, narrow waters by dhows constructed specially for the purpose. At crossing points, Yao chiefs had established trading posts and stockades to collect the slaves and hold them for onward transport to the coast, from where they would be shipped north to Zanzibar. The peaceful prosperous country that Livingstone had first explored had completely changed.

While Livingstone and Kirk were away, the missionaries found themselves in increasing difficulties. Mackenzie had been constantly beset by local Mang'anja asking for help to fight the Yao intruders and, finally persuaded that the cause against the slavers was a righteous one, he had agreed. Leading parties of Mang'anja, he made a series of chaotic sorties against Yao villages. Helped by their guns, the missionaries and their allies easily won the battle. Taking inspiration from this triumph, the bishop now saw himself as a latter-day crusader. His success went to his head, and he wrote that when he closed his eyes, he imagined himself in combat on the ancient plains of Troy.

Afterwards, however, he was distressed to find that his allies were no better than their enemies, the Mang'anja having captured as many Yao children as they could to sell. Success carried its penalty, and having started down this path, Mackenzie found it impossible to pull back. By October, he was leading a force of over a thousand men. He continued his campaign against the Yao, and as he marched, repeated aloud to his followers, 'The battle is the Lord's, and he is the Governor among the people.'[9] But the people did not see it that way at all. For them, the battle was about guns and plunder. Idealistic, romantic and inspired, Mackenzie was out of his depth, seemingly unaware that the mission had become involved in a tribal war, where both sides were now active slavers.

The missionaries themselves were regarded as little more than another gang, raiding to acquire people.

Kirk, returning with Livingstone in November, heard the bishop's account with deep misgiving. He thought 'the policy . . . questionable'. The attacks had been confused, with a 'total absence of any head, the Bishop giving up to Waller all direction while Waller was little seen.'[10] However, that month two more missionaries arrived at Magomero from the coast – Henry de Wint Burrup from Oxford and Dr John Dickinson from Durham – plus Richard Clark, a tanner and shoemaker, and at the estuary, naval vessels were expected, bringing the bishop's sister, Miss Mackenzie, her maid Sarah, Mrs Burrup and Mrs Livingstone, the Doctor's wife, as well as two further missionaries. There could be no going back.

Mackenzie, on hearing this news and desperate to welcome his sister, immediately said he wished to go down river to meet the new arrivals, but the Doctor was cool. The missionaries' job was to stay where they were, he told the bishop, and he wanted no passengers going the other way. He would go to the mouth of the Zambesi and bring the ladies back himself, and he arranged to meet Mackenzie in the Elephant Marsh on his return. They would be there on the first of January 1862 at the confluence of two rivers. In December, he and Kirk set off, leaving the missionaries on their own.

The return to the coast that year was punishing, with the boat barely moving. 'Although we progress at about 3 yards a day, it is by taking the sand bank before us,' wrote Kirk. 'And not only the bank we are on but the whole mass of sand which cross the river has moved down . . .'[11] They spent five days hauling their way through one bank alone. One of the paddles shattered; once mended, the engine sucked in mud. The incidence of fever became worse. The African men began to die. Livingstone, deluding himself on the depth of the water, refused to believe what he saw. In late December, the boat hit a sandbank and remained stationary all evening. They continued leveraging the vessel along with two capstans and four-inch ropes, pulling on anchors fixed to the shore, with over forty men tugging at the ropes, which then broke. Day after day, Kirk recorded 'the old work of out anchors, anchors don't hold well, lift them, lay them again, anchors come lower still . . .'[12] Crab fashion, they crawled down the great river, moving from bank to bank, while steadily the fevers got worse. The carpenter was suddenly seized with vomiting and, despite all treatment, died a day later. No one seems to have thought it necessary to communicate with the missionaries high above the Shire just how severe their delay was.

In January it was no easier. The river continually changed its course. When the rains arrived, great floating islands of earth and vegetation broke from the banks, borne by the current downstream, trapping the vessel. They found these fragments of land occupied by snakes, rats and other creatures, and were forced to hack themselves free before being invaded by vermin. 'This is disgusting work,' wrote Kirk. 'Here we cannot keep her afloat even during a flood . . .'[13] Finally, in late January, they reached the coast, where a cruiser, HMS *Gorgon*, came in to meet them.

The *Gorgon* had brought yet another river vessel for them to use, the *Lady Nyasa*, which was to be conveyed in parts and reassembled farther upstream. The cruiser had also brought five more missionaries, together with Mrs Livingstone, Mrs Burrup and Miss Mackenzie, Miss Mackenzie's maid and her donkey, as well as vast quantities of luggage and equipment. Slowly and in great disorder the entourage was disembarked at the river mouth. All were bound for the mission at Magomero far away in the highlands.

The naval officers delivering this assembly were horrified at the plan to take these unprepared women deep into the wilderness. Preparations for setting forth up river were chaotic. The new missionaries disagreed on most things, but particularly on matters of religion, and they bickered and fought incessantly. Huge quantities of equipment were unloaded, and then had to be abandoned to rot on the shore. The paymaster of the *Gorgon* was appalled at the waste.

Nearly every conceivable kind [of] . . . wearing apparel, household furniture, provisions, agricultural instruments, cooking utensils, knick knacks of every kind, including necessaries and luxuries lavishly furnished by the mission, are to be seen half buried in sand, lying about in every direction, exposed to chance and weather . . .

As they prepared for the journey up the Zambesi, the women insisted that all their vital necessities were taken on board, including at the last minute two handsome saloon chairs. 'I never saw people so superfluously provided,' wrote the outraged officer. 'They are gorged with luxuries regardless of expense.'[14]

The *Pioneer* was by now totally overloaded. Nevertheless, it was also required to convey its as yet unassembled sister, the *Lady Nyasa*, up to the Shire. As the boilers of the smaller ship were placed on the *Pioneer*'s deck, the deck beams moved by almost half an inch, and gaps appeared between the planks. Livingstone, aghast, vaccillated, loading then unloading, and finally loading again the various parts of the second vessel. Finally, Captain Wilson, the commanding officer of the *Gorgon*, agreed to assist with additional craft. So in mid-February, the overburdened *Pioneer* moved slowly back upstream, trailing two smaller boats with the *Lady Nyasa* distributed variously among all three. The additional gear weighed 45 tons in all, and whenever the *Pioneer* lurched to the side, she remained fixed with one paddle totally immobilized, the other lifted high out of the water until her balance could be forcibly restored.

Progress was slow. Every inch of deck was covered in luggage. Miss Mackenzie's donkey plus two mules and a farm cart were also on board. Catering for the ladies proved difficult, and in order that they might change discreetly and in private, a cover was hung across the upright smokestack of the *Lady Nyasa*, forming a secluded tent. Miss Mackenzie, a good-humoured but elderly hypochrondiac, was unable to walk without help.

Mrs Livingstone presented graver problems. She was overweight and unhealthy, and Kirk was surprised at her coarse manners. She was greedy and continually borrowed money, although no one was entirely sure what she did with it. 'There must be some queer game up,' he wrote to his brother. The ivory they had been holding against hard times had also disappeared, 'and who got the money, I don't know.'[15] The truth came out gradually. Mary Livingstone was a distressed and unhappy woman. For years she had been, effectively, abandoned by her husband while he travelled in Africa, and she had no real interest in the Zambesi enterprise. She only wanted to be with him, and not left on her own any longer. In Britain, she had turned to alcohol to ease her pain, and she continued with the habit as they went up the Zambesi. Stewart, one of the new missionaries, privately admitted to Kirk, 'that she drank very freely, so as to be utterly besotted at times'.[16] The money had apparently gone to buy liquor from the Portuguese.

The discovery of his wife's alcoholism was deeply distressing to Livingstone. He had scarcely viewed any of his companions with consideration, and it embarrassed him that his closest helpmate should have become this coarse drunken woman. He knew how it must disparage him in the eyes of his comrades. Saving people from the ravages of the slave trade accorded badly with such private weakness, and he retreated more into himself and became increasingly difficult to communicate with.

The voyage up river was becoming more and more dangerous. Except for Mary Livingstone, none of the new arrivals had travelled in Africa before. The Portuguese were hostile to a British settlement on the Shire. As Kirk tried to point out to Livingstone, they considered they had prior rights there, but the Doctor would have none of this. He was obsessed with establishing his settlement on the Nyasa highlands, and oblivious to any risks they took. Once more, they began to run out of coal. The two mules had died almost immediately, making the wagons redundant. The feedpipes of the boiler burst, sending scalding water in every direction. The country around them was deserted, although at night they could see great fires in the distance. And they were over a month late for the meeting with Mackenzie at the confluence of rivers in the marsh.

Captain Wilson of the *Gorgon* had accompanied the party, together with two of his ship's light boats and a team of fifty 'blue jackets'. In mid-February, he and Kirk finally decided to press on ahead to meet the bishop, travelling with the women and eleven sailors in the lighter, smaller vessels. Kirk, aware just how desperate matters were, recorded their progress with grim irony. As they moved up the stream . . .

> . . . we had the stern completely occupied by the Bishop's old invalid sister who had followed him through some sort of fanatical infatuation. She was unable to place one foot before the other. If she decided to shift her position, she had to get assistance and to have herself supported with pillows. The daily laundry was a serious job. A bower or shelter had to be constructed and she carried to it . . .[17]

By late February, they had entered the great marsh again. The currents were strong, and on one occasion a boat was flooded. Groups of elephants watched them from the water's edge as they passed, and at night clouds of mosquitoes deprived them of any sleep. They moved through lagoons covered with water lily, and inhabited by vast flocks of geese and whistling duck. But by the time they arrived at the meeting point where the two rivers joined, they were almost two months late and, unsurprisingly, no one was there to meet them. So they pressed on, and on the 4 March came up under Chibisa's village. There, as they searched for a landing place, Kirk spotted a man on the dark heights above them. They called out to him and when he replied, Kirk recognized the Makololo dialect of Livingstone's followers, who had been left with the mission. The man came down to them, and 'on enquiring after the Bishop, to my horror I got the answer "O Shuile, he is dead."'[18]

Slowly, the story came out. While they were away, the mission had continued its conflict with the Yao. In December, two of the missionaries had been attacked and robbed by another chief to the south. Mackenzie decided to punish the man, and leading a small force of African allies, the missionaries had marched out, praying for God's blessing as they went. In a haphazard way, they burnt their enemy's village while their followers plundered the country for goats and sheep. Confusion followed, and Mackenzie, unsure of his next step and desperately worried that he might miss his appointment on the river, eventually continued south, with Burrup, to the meeting in the marsh. Burrup was physically tough, and capable of hard travel in the bush, but neither man was certain of the route, and soon they became lost. They sang hymns for encouragement and finally found the river.

A few days later, while travelling in the dark, their canoe was overturned by the strong current, and all their medicines lost. Soon both were suffering from ill health, and reaching a small island near the confluence of the two streams, they decided to camp and wait for Livingstone. But he did not come, and there they remained for nearly a month, frightened of missing Livingstone's return. Their health continued to deteriorate. Obsessively watching the river, and plagued by mosquitoes, they read the Bible to each other in Greek for comfort. Mackenzie, delirious, told Burrup how he longed to see his sister again. He was becoming weaker every day, and bleeding at the nose and mouth. Eventually, on 31 January, he died. Burrup was carried back by porters to Magomero where he fell into a coma before he also died.

Morale at the mission disintegrated. The remaining missionaries, frightened and leaderless, felt themselves abandoned. Rowley and Waller, belonging to different churches, did not get on and argued interminably. They were running out of cloth to purchase food and other supplies. The mission was badly infected with disease, and thirty of their African followers had already died. Some of the mission boys, in desperation, had sold themselves as slaves to outside chiefs. One morning, to their horror, the body of another boy was discovered, eaten by ants. They were incapable of dealing with the conditions of African life. Livingstone, their only contact with the outside world, was far away. They felt isolated, afraid and unsure what to do. Finally, they sent a letter down to the river at Chibisa's, begging for help. Kirk received it the day he arrived, 4 March.

Although he knew it was dangerous, he felt he had no choice but to go to assist them. The journey to Magomero was difficult, he was unequipped with sufficient medicines and the rain was torrential.

He wrote:

> Nothing but what seemed an absolute necessity would have
> induced me to go off thus without medicines, proper food,
> sufficient supply of cloth during the wet season and with a
> large body of untried Englishmen. But it was an act of
> humanity from doing which there was no escape.[19]

Next day, he and Wilson set off with half a dozen sailors. Both
Kirk and Wilson soon went down with malaria, and for two days
they lay in a hut in the bush unable to crawl. Finally, despite their
illness and the constant rain, they made contact with the
remaining missionaries at Magomero. To their surprise, they
found them healthy and well stocked with provisions, but they
were panicky and desperate, and one of them, Rowley, was bitter
at the way they had been seduced by Livingstone with false
reports, then left to their own resources. Kirk, exasperated, told
them that, unfortunately, they had better get used to it. They
would have to depend on themselves, he said, for they were
unlikely to see the *Pioneer* soon, and Livingstone had other
matters to attend to. Waller, whose view of Livingstone was close
to adulation, seemed intent on getting out as soon as he could.

Livingstone himself heard of the disaster after he had returned
to Shupanga near the Zambesi's mouth, but he showed little pity
for the foresaken missionaries. England would send out better
men, he chillingly remarked when he heard of Mackenzie's and
Burrup's deaths. He was more concerned about the impact on his
expedition. 'This will hurt us all,' he commented, then went on,
'but I shall not swerve a headbreadth from my work . . .'[20] Refusing
to take any responsibility for initiating the fight against the Yao, he
began consciously to distance himself from the mission. Writing
back to England, he openly blamed Mackenzie for the disaster.

Then in April, while they were at Shupanga putting the second
ship together, Mary Livingstone became seriously ill. She had
been getting increasingly stout, Kirk observed, and 'her indiscre-
tions in eating and drinking . . . have been such as to undermine
her health.'[21] In late April, she fell into a coma, injections proved

unavailing and on 27 April, she died. For Livingstone, this was yet another blow and he became even more introverted. The additional deaths were badly affecting morale. The engineer, Rae, complained bitterly at the way the Doctor had led them. Hardistry, another engineer, announced he would leave. The African men became insubordinate and were often found drunk. The expedition threatened to fall apart in recriminations. Waller later said that only Kirk's steadfastness held the party together.

During the next three months, there were repeated attempts to get both ships up the river, and in June the second vessel was finally launched. The main vessel, the *Pioneer*, like her predecessor, was now wearing away, eaten from outside by teredo worm and ants. She was beset with fevers, 'a beast for sickness', Kirk wrote. The group continued to argue interminably. The tedium of endlessly moving up and down the river without evident purpose, the obstinate refusal of the Doctor to acknowledge any defeat, the difficulty of obtaining supplies and the constant ill health, were grinding them down. Kirk himself felt disillusioned and ready to go. He wrote to his brother that he'd finally had enough.

He had completed as much of his botany as he was able, and he didn't have Livingstone's blind faith. He thought the expedition done up, finished. It had failed to all intents and purposes, and he was a pragmatic man. Yet he still could not walk away. Although he hated Livingstone's inconstancy and selfishness, his obsessive refusal to acknowledge failure and, above all, his disloyalty, Kirk would not leave him. There seemed no point in staying, yet until Livingstone said otherwise, he would remain. In a strange mixture of pride, doggedness and refusal to be beaten, he would test himself to the end.

The Doctor still did not want Kirk to leave. Together with Charles Livingstone, he was the only other member of the original team who had remained. It was as if, while he persisted, Livingstone could still persuade himself that the venture was not futile, and that he was not deluding himself. By now, the Doctor was almost desperate. During the past three years he had changed, cutting himself off from anything but minimal communication with his companions. He seemd to hate their company and was at home only with Africans. He appeared to have forgotten about the mission, although reports coming downstream told them that the violence was getting worse, and the missionaries were in a desperate state.

In September 1862, Livingstone abruptly announced that he was going to attempt the ascent of the Rovuma, another river that flowed into the Indian Ocean far to the north of the Zambesi. It was a bizarre, even a crazy, idea. The mission was failing and its crisis should have been his priority, but Livingstone as always attributed failure to the faults of others. He thought ascending the Rovuma might offer him alternative access to the interior, and that this new river would be the answer to his problems. He had no evidence for his optimism, but he was dogged and insistent, and the commander of a visiting cruiser, HMS *Orestes*, eventually agreed to provide support, lending him two light boats and a party of seamen.

Once more, Livingstone asked Kirk to come with him, and once more Kirk agreed – as though he needed to keep pace with this unpredictable, compulsive man for as long as he could; or it may have been Kirk's own fear of failure, of not coming up to the mark and being discarded, as others had been. Despite the inevitable presence of Charles Livingstone, he went along.

They entered the Rovuma on 9 September 1862. Narrow gorged, shallow and rocky, it was evident early on that this was no alternative route. Yet obsessively Livingstone took the two small boats on up through the shallow rapids day after day. Kirk's journal notes become increasingly fatalistic, as though now he recognized he was tied to a man who, in the end, might destroy him. 'Still there is no change in Dr L's plans,' he wrote several days into the gorge. 'He is going on still, regardless of the return. His determination seems to amount to infatuation.' The river got worse, and there were reports of serious rapids ahead. They passed slave-trading parties on their way from the interior to the northern coast. People were unfriendly, and with the falling water levels they ran a risk of being trapped, yet Livingstone refused to turn back, and Kirk began to think he had lost all sense of reason.

He was now deeply disturbed by the man he was following. 'I can come to no other conclusion than that Dr. L. is mad.'[22] The Doctor was prepared to risk everything – the mission left on the Shire, their companions at Shupanga – for the sake of this whim.

Days of steering against brilliant light reflected from the water started to make Kirk lose his sight. Between notes on his blindness – 'the feeling of sand in the eyes' – he tried to comprehend the man leading their expedition, an incredible man with a will of iron and a vision that would let nothing obstruct it, but was he worth following to destruction?

On 18 September they were attacked. Asked to come close in to the bank to trade cloth, they were ambushed from both sides of the river at a narrow point in the gorge, with arrows and with guns. Kirk was a good shot. He saw two men coming down towards them, heading off the boat, and one had a gun. Kirk shot first, and killed him. This was not what he had come to Africa to do, and it disturbed him badly. As they went farther up this river, so different from the Zambesi, narrow and dangerous in totally different ways, he knew they were vulnerable and desperately wanted to go back, to escape. There was nothing ahead, except some slaving town in the hills above. They had to return. Finally, Livingstone agreed.

Not for the first time, Kirk felt that he had avoided disaster and possible death by the narrowest of margins, and he doubted the judgement of his leader more and more.

By 1863, they had been in Africa for nearly five years, and Livingstone was no longer the man he once was. The experience had affected him as profoundly as anyone. Kirk thought that deep down he had been sorely disturbed by what he had discovered about his wife, and her death may even have been a relief. That year, a last attempt was made to ascend the Zambesi and the Shire. They lashed the two river boats together to prevent them colliding, and then took the strange double vessel, veering and shuddering, up the stream. For Livingstone, all depended on this final throw.

After the Rovuma, the tension between Livingstone and Kirk was now always present, beneath the surface. Livingstone must have realized the doubts Kirk had, yet it was still Kirk he wanted to accompany him. And still Kirk somehow kept himself clear of the older man's ability to upset and damage him, but the balance broke down as they passed Mount Morambala before the entry to the Shire in January 1863.

The only reason Kirk could now give himself for his continued stay in Africa was his botany. Collecting plants was his own private cause, and he held it dear. It was abstract, unemotional, and it gave him a point of reference, but it also framed his character. Adventure and risking danger were so much a part of him, he used his botany as a form of control, a discipline that made his risk taking allowable, even justifiable. He did it in the pursuit of science. Botany gave him a purpose.

They had often passed the mountain, which rose thousands of feet above the river valley. It was a unique environment, and Kirk wanted to search it for plants. He had agreed with Livingstone that this time they would remain there while he made the climb, but when they got to Morambala, the Doctor said he would not permit it. He did it deliberately, denying Kirk the men he needed. He said there was no time.

Kirk was bitter. 'He chooses to expect everyone to sacrifice for his own special work, their own . . .' Livingstone had struck at him where it hurt most, and after years of doing the Doctor's bidding, he felt let down. 'Since he shews such a narrow selfish mind, he will find that if I don't do botany, I do little else with a will and orders obeyed as duty only are worth little on this sort of service . . .' It was a petty quarrel, but the relationship between them was intense. Kirk was the only man Livingstone had allowed himself to depend upon. He had exerted a powerful influence over the younger man, but after so many blunders and miscalculations that influence was failing. He knew it, and Kirk thought he hated knowing it. 'His . . . conduct on changing plans which completely tied us to the vessel, must have been simply some sort of . . . revenge, knowing what must be thought of him by me . . .'

The day was a Sunday, and Livingstone asked Kirk sarcastically whether he was aware of this. 'I told him I did not know what day it was and so ended the palaver.'[23] Sunday labour had never mattered before to Livingstone, and they both understood that. For Kirk, the Doctor had broken a key understanding between them, and he would never trust him again. After these five years, a point had been passed in their relationship. In this way, they entered once more the Elephant Marsh for the sixth time in four years, and yet again the swamp had changed. This time it was like a morgue.

The country upstream was suffering from famine, and in the highlands there had been harrowing scenes of starvation with people dying in large numbers. Kirk wrote: 'The country is in a miserable state . . . and the natives drag out their existence on various grass seeds . . .' Only the slavers had prospered, as people in desperation sold their families and even themselves to the traffickers. The dead bodies they left behind were carried away down river and into the marsh. On 24 January, Kirk noted:

> While coming up we saw 4 or 5 dead bodies made up in the sleeping mats or with reeds floating down daily. How many pass us unobserved or by night, we cannot tell or how many the alligators dragged aside among the reeds as they floated past, but a dozen a day would be a small allowance for the numbers cast into the river daily.[24]

The boat, too, was suffering. Although they had been warned of the famine, Livingstone had refused to take on extra rations. Now they were paying for it. Kirk, angry at yet another example of the Doctor's lack of foresight, advised him to return for fresh provisions, but Livingstone would not alter course. The two vessels continued slowly, but now the party had split. Rae, the engineer, and two others refused to remain with Livingstone on the main vessel. One of the stokers had an attack of fever – his urine was almost black – and the blacksmith suffered in the same way.

In late January, they were stuck for almost a month in the middle of the marsh, becalmed in the low channels, without fuel and unable to advance. 'We are prisoners to the ship,' Kirk wrote. 'All about is marsh and without a boat, no bird can be shot.' The channels were full of crocodile, and when Kirk shot a hippo they gathered on the carcase. He watched fascinated as they competed for the food. The following day, a corpse was attacked.

> Today a dead body floated past. As it came to the place where so many alligators lay, one made a rush swimming swiftly for it. He seized it and struggled. Then all the alligators within half a mile came up and one after another snatched it and tried to tear off limbs as it floated down. The water was lashed up by the beasts, each one trying to tear it and no sooner had a limb gone and the remains left by one beast than it was caught up by another.[25]

The isolation, sickness and desperate surroundings were affecting everyone. Rae and his two companions in the *Lady Nyasa* were living in a miserable state. 'It is like stepping into a death chamber to go and see the faces of the three who inhabit that vessel . . .' Rae would not come on board the *Pioneer*, his antagonism to Livingstone was so intense, and the Doctor himself was increasingly unpredictable. One Sunday, Kirk and a companion went out in a small boat for a change of scenery. On their return, they were told savagely by the Doctor that leaving the ship on a Sunday was not to be permitted. 'Cant piety,' Kirk remarked. 'We are suffering from long confinement to ship on poor diet . . .'[26]

Meanwhile, the news from the mission was becoming worse. Another missionary, Scudamore, a good, strong man, had also died. Livingstone's Makololo followers who had remained there had taken to terrorizing the neighbourhood, stealing provisions, animals and women from all around. Livingstone, when told, refused to believe such lies of his faithful companions. However, for the first time, his will failed him and he was unsure what to do. He was 'sadly puzzled and many schemes float through his mind', Kirk wrote, with a note of sympathy, for failure now seemed inevitable. In March, they received another letter from the mission. The doctor, Dickinson, was critically ill, and Clark, the tanner and shoemaker, was 'in a state of mania with epileptic fits which had supervened on fever with dysentery . . .'[27] The mission followers continued to terrorize the neighbourhood, and finally Livingstone decided to go up there to find out for himself. He took Kirk with him.

At Magomero, the remaining missionaries had spent the previous months arguing and debating whether they should stay or leave. In the midst of the escalating tribal war, the small party was isolated, with few resources and short of provisions. Communication down the river was difficult and they had little sense of where Livingstone and his expedition was, or indeed whether he cared about them. With the exception of Waller, who still believed in the Livingstone magic, the missionaries were now all disillusioned. The country was nothing like they had expected. The wide miles of cotton fields that Livingstone had written of did not exist.

Stewart, a recent arrival, was the bitterest of all. On the death of Scudamore, with whom he had formed a close friendship, he took his copy of Livingstone's *Travels* and hurled it into the river. 'His cursed lies have caused much toil, trouble, anxiety and loss of life . . .' he wrote.[28] Other disasters followed. In mid-March, Dickinson died. The following month, young Richard Thornton, who had been at the mission intermittently, also died. Another medical doctor, Meller, asked to leave.

By now, news of these failures had filtered back to England, and they were beginning to cause concern. Attempts were made to suppress a journal sent by Rowley to his sick wife, in which he described the chaos and mismanagement. In July 1862, at a large public meeting in the Sheldonian Theatre in Oxford, an account of the mission's activities, including letters from Mackenzie, was read aloud. Descriptions of missionaries marching into battle at the head of a small army, burning villages and capturing stock, were heard in appalled silence, and a wave of condemnation spread through the English church. Key people dissociated themselves from the enterprise, and Livingstone himself was criticized. Accounts of piled stores lying wasted by the banks of the Zambesi upset those who were trustees for the contribution of public funds. In February 1863, a new bishop was consecrated to take over from the ill-fated Mackenzie.

William George Tozer was a practical, down-to-earth Lincoln-shire rector, with flaming red hair, who believed in order, strict accounting and non-interference, even if that meant tolerating slavery. He arrived at the mouth of the Zambesi in June 1863 on the cruiser HMS *Orestes*, which also conveyed Foreign Office papers informing Livingstone that his expedition was to be recalled, and all naval support would now terminate. Tozer knew that left on its own without any regular communication with the outside world, the mission could never survive. He proceeded up the Zambesi, holding aloft an umbrella against the sun, deter-mined on its withdrawal.

Kirk had reached the same conclusion when he and Livingstone arrived at Magomero in mid-March. He thought the station was 'quite untenable'. The land had not been sufficiently cultivated to support the population. The missionaries had not thought to put in place proper drainage, and he was not surprised at the appalling ill health. Very little in the way of the local language had been mastered. Dickinson had died, but Kirk's arrival saved Clark's life. 'Dr. Kirk with a kindness which will never be forgotten, watched by his side night and day and promised to remain as long as he could be of any service.'[29] Livingstone seemed more concerned at the rumours concerning his Makololo. It must have been evident to both of them that they were near the end of the road.

Then that month, Kirk, whose health had been robust for most of the previous five years, came down with a bad attack of dysentery. It would not leave him, and in late April, he told Livingstone he was planning his return.

Livingstone took it badly. They disagreed about money. Livingstone told Kirk that if he wanted to go the direct way back, via Aden, he could finance it himself. He did not want Kirk to leave, and Kirk wrote that for several days . . .

> . . . his manner is still very distant, in fact there is no doubt but that he will help me only if he thinks that I . . . will do so to him. He is savage at being jammed up here, the more so as it is his own doing . . .[30]

There was further disagreement on Kirk's specimens, which Livingstone suggested could be brought down river once Kirk had left. But Kirk did not trust him. He said he would make his own arrangements for them to be brought back if he could not take them himself.

Yet despite everything, he still had sympathy for the Doctor. 'Poor fellow, he is sorely perplexed how to save money and keep up the appearance of being honest.' Then, at this crucial moment, Livingstone, too, fell ill. He had fever and pain in the bowels, his tongue was foul, he was passing mucus and blood and vomiting. So once again, Kirk held on, nursing him back to health. He was amused that, sick, Livingstone experienced the weaknesses he had despised in others. 'This afternoon we got a supply of native beer for which Dr L craves sorely . . .' And two days later: 'He is well, only shaken a little, craves for sardines which now are not. He laughed at others having a wish for something tasty and now finds it out [himself].'[31] But the hold that Livingstone had exerted over him for so long had dissolved. Although he felt genuinely sorry for the Doctor, he was quite clear about his departure.

By then, they had returned to the Shire, and when Kirk said farewell, Livingstone was laboriously supervising the dismantling of the smaller boat, preparing to drag it overland by wagon up to Lake Nyasa. Stones and tree roots were being hacked out of the bush in a desperate attempt to create a road. Kirk was no longer prepared to take part in such a quixotic, futile enterprise. He left Livingstone alone, without regret, taking a small boat on 19 May back down to the Zambesi. From there, he went on to the coast. He was reduced almost to a skeleton by his illness, and it was not until July, when he was resting at Quelimane on the Mozambique coast, that he learnt of the expedition's recall.

A boat had been finally sent up river to rescue the Doctor. Frustrated by the difficult waterways, blocked by tribal conflict, yet driven on by his own desperate fury, Livingstone was trapped, but he would not give up, and would not admit failure. Instead, he continued to blame others for the expedition's disasters. He accused Tozer of cowardice, for withdrawing the mission and ensuring the failure of the whole enterprise. The new bishop, on arriving at Magomero, had quickly decided the entire venture had been a waste of money and of lives. No one had been taught even the barest essentials of Christian belief, and 'the waste of mission property . . . [was] prodigious'. His view of the Doctor was equally critical. The plan of a colony of commerce, agriculture and Christianity on the upper Shire he considered a 'chimera of the wildest kind'. 'I believe [Livingstone] to be a good man,' he wrote, 'but to use the phrase of one of our party, a "very dangerous one".'[32]

Kirk, waiting for a ship at Quelimane, was exhausted. He felt he had been lucky to get out with his life and his integrity intact. He was, perhaps, the only one who had, but he was determined, once back in England, not to talk about what had happened. His journals were for his own use, he wrote, and not for publication. He was not disillusioned, for he had had few illusions to start with, but he had learnt much.

Confronted by the conditions of Central Africa, the powers and energies of modern man had proved worthless. Science and optimism, bravery, faith, idealism and conviction had all failed. Worse, stuck on the high Zambesi or in the hills above the Shire, the missionaries and explorers had behaved no more admirably and with no more discipline than the slavers they came to oppose. Their efforts had been futile, their claims to come from a superior culture derisory.

The town of Quelimane Kirk found to be run down, violent and filthy. Fever was endemic. The town still exported slaves in small numbers to the islands of the Indian Ocean and the Americas, but the colonists themselves seemed to have no self-belief, and the mercantile culture of the Mozambique Portuguese appeared to be in terminal decline. Kirk had come across one of the reasons on the shores of Lake Nyasa months before. The traders from the interior were increasingly taking their custom farther north to another ocean port, one that was far more vigorous and enterprising. The island state of Zanzibar.

Part Two

DEVOTED TO THE TRADE

On arriving at Zanzibar they are frequently in the last stage of lingering starvation, and are unable to stand; some drop dead in the custom-house and in the streets, and others who are not likely to recover are left on board to die, in order that the master may avoid paying the duty which is levied on those landed. After being brought on the shore the slaves are kept some time in the dealers' houses until they gain flesh and strength, when they are sold by auction in the slave market. The Arab regards the slaves as cattle; not the slightest attention is paid to their sufferings; they are too cheap and numerous to be cared for.

With a population to govern wholly devoted to the trade, and an executive equally involved in it, Syud Majeed may be said to hold the reins of power by sufferance . . .

CHRISTOPHER RIGBY, MUSCAT ZANZIBAR COMMISSION, 1860

3: COWRIES, COPAL AND ELEPHANTS' TEETH

*It is a very striking, though most humiliating, sight to observe one of
the Zanzibar rakish looking crafts arrive . . . crammed with naked
slaves for the market – all as silent as death. The Arab owners, gaily
dressed, stand at the stern, and one holds the colours, in seeming
defiance of the Consulate as he sails past.*

J.A. GRANT, *A WALK ACROSS AFRICA*

The city of Zanzibar was the largest entrepôt in the whole western
Indian Ocean. Positioned at the southernmost end of the
monsoon winds, it was the supply point for slaves out of East and
Central Africa into the wider world. And there in 1866 came John
Kirk.

He arrived on the island in early June. He had not intended to
go back to East Africa. His experience on the Zambesi had been
punishing, and on his return to England he had kept out of the
controversy surrounding the expedition. It had been much
criticized and Kirk was almost the only person to emerge with his
reputation enhanced. But when Livingstone invited him to
contribute to the account of the venture, he declined. He thought
it advisable to keep his opinions to himself. Nevertheless, he was
now known as a minor explorer and geographer, and a friend of
Livingstone's. A photograph of him taken about that time, shortly
before he left again for Africa, shows a slim man with dark

receding hair, a full beard and moustache, regular features and a direct, confident gaze – poised, relaxed and sure of himself.

Botany remained Kirk's passion. He had spent much of the time following his return working in Edinburgh on the plants he had brought back from Africa, and he had also assisted at Kew, classifying other specimens. He was beginning to feel a part of something much larger than a single expedition. The work that Joseph and William Hooker were engaged upon – collecting and classifying many of the world's plants – was hugely ambitious, an enterprise at the forefront of scientific endeavour, and Kirk felt privileged to be able to take part.

He needed money though, and jobs were hard to come by for a doctor who had spent the last five years on an obscure African river. Kirk could not afford to occupy his life merely as a collector of plants, and he was forced to consider other options. At one time or other he contemplated joining a scientific expedition to the Galapagos Islands, then a position managing the Botanic Gardens in Mauritius, as well as a similar opening in Bombay. He even thought of taking a job as consul in Mozambique, but all were poorly paid, and Kirk by now had another matter to take into account. In 1864 he had met Helen Cooke, the daughter of a Worcestershire doctor. She was just twenty years old and had lived a quiet English provincial life. Kirk called her Nelly, and she fell for the intense, slightly eccentric doctor and botanist who had just spent half a decade in one of the most desperate regions on Earth. His lack of money and poor prospects did not deter her, and after only a few months he was hopelessly in love with her. They became engaged to be married.

Nelly came from a comfortable middle-class family. She had an uncle with financial interests and a brother who emigrated to New Zealand. She also had a small settlement from her parents, who were both dead, but Kirk knew what bringing up a family without any income meant. He had experienced it as a child. Fear of penury always made him anxious, and when the position of medical officer at the British consulate in Zanzibar came up, he could not afford to say no. He needed a job. He had made every effort to find something more suitable but without success, so with a sense of desperation he accepted the offer. The post was nominally deputy to the agent and consul, he wrote, as though he were attempting to justify his decision, so there was a possibility of promotion. And if it failed to work out, they could just chuck it in, and go somewhere else, he told her with unconvincing optimism.

Kirk loved Nelly with a passion that surprised him almost as much as he was amazed by her agreeing to accompany him to such a terrible part of the world. Under normal circumstances, European women did not go to live in tropical Africa. Zanzibar already had a reputation as a place where men did not last long, but for European women it was regarded as a death sentence. Kirk thought constantly about what Nelly was letting herself in for, and he was beset with doubt. 'If I should be mistaken after all will you ever forgive me? I never knew responsibility before now . . .'[1] He had few illusions, and he knew what Africa was like. The slaving ports of the east coast were filthy and disease ridden, the climate intolerable. He knew that he could take the hardship, even though he might miss the company of other scientists and people of his own kind, but for Nelly the difficulties would be appalling. Zanzibar was a Muslim town with only a tiny western society. It lay outside the main postal routes, at the end of the world. It was known for its slave trading, its corruption and its violence. The European men kept concubines, they drank and they lived short lives. The comparison with her ordinary but respectable life in England was almost grotesque. Yet he had no other option.

As your ship approached 'the mysterious island of Zanzibar', wrote the explorer Richard Burton, you could smell the sweet, heavy perfume of cloves for which the island was famous. From a distance, the buildings of the ruler's palace, the harem and the houses of the grander families all gleamed brilliant white in the sun. The minarets of mosques studded a pale blue skyline on either side of the ancient fort. The harbour was crowded with shipping – ocean-going dhows from the Persian Gulf, as well as schooners from Europe and America. It was not until evening, as the wind changed, that different odours became evident – smells of decay, faeces and rotting flesh. The beaches of the town and its harbour were a fetid mass of decomposing matter and refuse.

'Corpses float at times upon the heavy water; the shore is a cess pool,' Burton wrote,[2] and at low tide it was necessary to pick one's way through this mess of offal, decaying carcases and other filth in order to reach the town. So foul was it that at night gases would rise from the mud and hang like a miasma over the ground, at times catching fire and flaring along the waterside in the darkness.

Zanzibar was a city of contrasts. 'A clean show concealing uncleaness', was Burton's contemptuous opinion. Behind the seafront, the narrow streets were chaotic, like 'the threads of a tangled skein'.[3] They were also filthy and disease ridden. Alleys were populated with abandoned slaves crawling on all fours in the gutter, maimed criminals, gaunt and rotting from disease, and untended corpses. Cattle roamed aimlessly in the streets, and gangs of slaves pushed their way from the harbour to the warehouses without respect or warning. Visitors from Europe in the mid-nineteenth century disliked the place, for they were treated with little courtesy or regard. The labyrinth of streets and the filth and squalor of its markets oppressed them. Some, like Burton, thought the entire place crude and ugly. The sea captains who called for provisions and water despised the Swahili people who populated the island, finding them deceitful and idle. Christian missionaries loathed their promiscuity and moral laxity.

But it was the slaves that western visitors found most upsetting, and they were everywhere – at the docks, carrying goods along the narrow alleys, standing in lines in the filthy water unloading the dhows; carried in by boat for sale, counted through the Customs House and herded to market. In the mid-1860s, Zanzibar remained a city based upon slaves and slavery, but it was also bursting with vitality, the crucial commercial hub linking the seaways of the Indian Ocean with a vast inland territory stretching from the Congo to the Zambesi river. The city occupied a triangular piece of land, almost cut off from the rest of the island by a creek, and faced across the narrow straits that separated it from the mainland of Africa. The population fluctuated between 70,000 and 100,000 people,[4] depending on the time of year.

Shangani, the western 'nose' of the city, caught the sea breeze, and this was where many of the grandest houses and trading firms were located. A few hundred yards north along the seafront was the Customs House and behind it the fort. Farther to the north stood the sultan's town palace. This was Zanzibar's fine exterior overlooking the harbour, but behind it, stretching all the way to the creek that ran along to the east, lay a different town. A maze of intricate alleys, a warren of dark warehouses and shop entrances, soon degenerated into the poor shanty of Melinde, where large numbers of transient Arabs, poor immigrants from the Gulf, lived together with their slaves.

The creek was where the dhows upon which the city depended were maintained. Along the water's edge, they were drawn up in rows for careening, and the high-decked sea craft perched on the wet mudflats looked like giant insects preparing for flight. The air at this end of town was unhealthy and foul. Fighting at night between rival slave gangs was common. There were riots, fires broke out without reason, and just south of Melinde, not far from the creek, was the slave market.

Bounded almost on all sides by either creek or sea, Zanzibar was an enclosed, claustrophobic city, a place of intense darkness and light. The buildings of the main town were flat roofed and covered with white plaster, so that during the day they reflected the fierce sunlight, creating a brilliant glare that hurt the eyes. By contrast, the streets, alleys and doorways were deep caves of darkness. From the open roofs, the town was like a chequerboard stretching out to the sea, but it was a secretive place. Its interlocking alleys and courtyards seemed to muffle and swallow sound, so that the voices of men arguing, and the screams of women and children, came and went as if disembodied in the air. The chants of processions rose up from the alleys, died and rose up again from another direction. The patter of feet, the banging of doors, distant conversations, shrieks of laughter and the rustle of clothes vanished like ghosts in the intense heat.

Kirk arrived in June, between monsoons and just as the great rains were ending, the season the Zanzibaris called the *Tanga Mbili*, or the time of two sails. From the beginning, he was fascinated by this city, which lived according to the movement of the ocean winds, where every trade and every account was regulated by the season, the dhows coming down from the Gulf to meet the caravans from the mainland, and then each returning as the monsoon changed. He made notes on the expeditions that departed for the interior, who led them, where they went and what they carried. There was something compelling about this interlocking rhythm of monsoon and trade – the flapping sails, the accounts settled on the waterfront and the files of men trekking into the interior.

The dhows came south at the beginning of every year, large ocean-going craft with high-pitched sterns and enormous ballooning triangular sails. Driven by the north-east monsoon, they reached the African coast between October and April. As the season changed, men began to look north for the first ships, and their arrival was a moment of great rejoicing. Crowds of people lined the shore, clapping and singing as the boats surged in towards land, and on the decks men danced and sang to the beat of drums. The dhows carried dates, shark meat and dried fish, and they waited for the small boats to come in from the mainland with slaves, ivory and hides, which they would take back north.

Just as the trade winds brought the dhows south, so the rhythm of dry and wet seasons governed the caravans, which moved from the coast inland and then returned with produce to sell. This, too, was a cause for celebration. Their arrival at the mainland ports of Mombasa, Kilwa and Bagamoyo was attended by rituals of singing and dancing that lasted deep into the night. Then the merchants of the town went out to meet the men from the interior, and days of bartering, feasting and argument followed as the elephant tusks and the slaves were sold and bought. Afterwards, the ivory and people were collected and held in enclosures at the sides of creeks, ready for the small coastal ships to take them to the Zanzibar market. By the late nineteenth century, over 200 tons of ivory and up to 25,000 slaves each year left the shores of East Africa in this way.

There was an extraordinary inevitability and timelessness about all the coming and going – the caravans journeying to the coast; the dhows with their huge triangular sails, driven south by the monsoon, and then, as if commanded by God, taken back again by the winds. For just as men said that the seasons had been ordained by providence, so they believed that the collecting of slaves had divine sanction. This was a pattern that had gone on forever. It was unchangeable. Religion and trade went in harmony. The seasons for the settling of accounts were also the seasons of the monsoon, and nothing could ever affect this immutable order.

Zanzibar was at the apex of this trade because of its geographical position. It was situated at the farthest point of the monsoon's reach, and the larger ocean vessels were forced to gather there and wait, while small coastal craft shipped men and goods up and down from the mainland. The country to the north was covered by thorn bush, and difficult to penetrate, so the great land routes into the interior mainly started on the southern coast. Zanzibar was therefore the point at which the trade routes of sea and land came together. It was as though the place had been designed to act as a funnel for the traffic of the interior to reach the outside world, and because of this the merchants of Zanzibar were rich.

They controlled the commerce of an enormous swathe of land that stretched from the great lakes of today's Uganda, across into the forests of the Congo and down to the borders of the Zambesi in the south. The city's Arab rulers informally claimed this great region as their own, and there were Zanzibari traders established across the length and breadth of East and Central Africa. They had a significant settlement at Kazeh[5] on the highlands of modern Tanzania, and many smaller outposts situated elsewhere. In the courts of the more important African chiefs and kings it was not unusual to find a Zanzibari established as a trusted adviser, an intermediary and trader.

This was not an empire in the European sense; it was a vast zone of influence. Zanzibaris and their followers wielded commercial power due to their connections with the city. Due to its trade monopoly with the interior, only in the city could imports of cloth and guns be obtained, and only there could the ivory and slaves ultimately be sold. But in the interior the traders worked closely together. They communicated across vast areas, sending information on which roads were open and where the the best ivory was to be found, on prices and politics, on wars and the deaths of kings, and all this gave them enormous advantage. In their settlements they hoarded their knowledge almost as jealously as they hoarded their ivory. Sometimes they fought their own wars, and they were often powerful – but they were powerful because of the city to which they belonged. A saying of the time summed it up. When a flute was played in Zanzibar, people on the lakes in the distant centre of the continent would start to dance.

In 1859, the British consul noted with astonishment that Zanzibar's trade was more substantial and extensive than that of Karachi, one of the largest ports in India. It had become a major economic force in the Indian Ocean, sucking away business from Mozambique to the south. Its traders were more vigorous and its commercial network more efficient, and that year its annual business amounted to between one and two million pounds. Zanzibar was the world's principle source of ivory, gum copal and cloves. Its imports also had grown substantially – particularly Indian and American cotton, beads and brass wire, all suitable for exchange on the mainland. It imported large quantities of gold bullion. Ominously, it also brought in large numbers of guns. During the year 1859, a total of 22,780 muskets were imported into the island, plus nearly 12,000 barrels of gunpowder.[6] For, while business in Zanzibar was dominated by ivory, that was a dangerous trade, never transacted easily, and seldom without conflict.

Ivory provided the motivation for the caravans setting out each season. It led to the biggest profits, created trade in other goods, and its evidence was everywhere. The Arabs and Swahili who ran the operations into the interior, the Indians who funded them, and the shippers who purchased the tusks for export, all talked about it with an obsessive fascination. On the waterfront 'gangs of serviles . . . wash and scrape ivory, which suggested to a young traveller the idea that the precious bone, here so plentiful, is swept up by the sea,' Richard Burton wrote.[7] The long, curved tusks, unloaded and stacked at the Customs House pier, were indeed manifestation of great wealth. Yet 'the precious bone' was never acquired that easily.

Zanzibar's ivory trade was not new. The earliest trading had been with India, where the constant demand for marriage bangles could not be satisfied by coarse-grained Indian bone. Then, early in the nineteenth century, ivory products started to become fashionable among the English middle classes, and demand increased. Billiard balls, piano keys and knife handles all required enormous quantities, and imports rose from around 250 tons per annum in the 1830s to over twice that thirty years later. A British importer complained in 1856 that demand for billiard balls had caused prices to double in five years. The cutlers of Sheffield alone took 170 tons.[8]

The Victorian love of ornament and inlay work continued to push prices even higher. Ivory was used for an endless assortment of luxury items. Umbrella handles, picture frames, snuff boxes, ladies' fans, statuettes, crucifixes, combs, chess sets, cribbage pegs, doorhandles, napkin rings, furniture inlay and even dildoes were all made from the fine bone. After the end of the Franco Prussian War, demand in continental Europe also rose, and prices per large tusk almost doubled from around £40 to £72. But for all this carving, the bone had to be soft as well as flawless. Such quality came only from the centre of the African continent, and that meant through Zanzibar, 'the principal mart for perhaps the finest and largest ivory in the world' according to Burton.[9] Well over 200 tons were brought in from the mainland each year, and half the country's exports were ivory, most of which went to London. Manufacturers couldn't get enough, and in Zanzibar everyone knew it.

However, ivory trading and slave trading went together. Of the porters who carried the tusks to the coast, some were slaves and some were free men, and often it was hard to tell them apart. But the idea common in England that slaves were recruited specifically to carry the ivory was generally untrue. Slaves, together with guns, copper, beads and cloth, were one of the commodities for barter, and each had its value depending on scarcity and need. Yet because it was ivory that drove the exploration of the interior, the search for tusks fuelled the trade in human beings.

Slaves had a value over and above their tradeable worth. The Zanzibaris of the interior travelled with large retinues of retainers, servants and fighting men. The more successful leaders had their harems and small armies, while their key supporters also had their women and their followers. For all these, slaves were needed – to provide the warriors, the porters and the concubines. As the traders pressed farther into the interior in their search for ivory, they acquired more and more slaves, for their own needs and to exchange for other wealth.

Ivory and slaves, the two were inseparable.

Kirk knew that Nelly was tough – she once removed one of her own teeth – and that she was not unaware of human suffering. In England, she visited the poor during outbreaks of cholera. Yet none of that could fully prepare her for Africa, and Kirk flinched from the task. So although he wrote to her about the cockroaches and the heat, he did not write about the corpses. He mentioned the slave ships leaving port, but he did not describe the sight of boats arriving from Kilwa packed with starving *bagham* from the interior. Perhaps he was afraid to tell her the full truth, for he must have known how her family would plead with her not to follow him to Africa. So instead, in his letters he described his new life in an upbeat and lively manner, almost as though he had gone to a small English provincial town.

The British consulate was sited on the point at Shangani with a clear view across the beach – 'a large solid pile, coloured like a twelfth cake, and shaped like a claret chest, which lay on its side, comfortably splashed by the sea'.[10] At ground level, behind an enormous room, there were offices and an arched courtyard. A carved wooden stair led to the consul's personal quarters, and from there a short bridge over an alley led to the medical officer's rooms. Kirk described his quarters to Nelly in detail. There were no glass panes to the windows, he wrote, and the rooms were cramped, but they would do for the first years of their married life.

His medical expertise was badly needed, moreover, and he was building up a small private practice. 'In the morning I have my practice and see any patients that may wish it. The forenoon and until 4 pm is quiet in house or in some neighbouring house such as the Consulate or Mr. Witt's or the mission.'[11] He described

Seward, the acting consul, and his wife in amusing terms. Captain Pasley, who commanded one of the naval squadrons, and whom Kirk got to know well, was a good man but drank too much. Kirk depicted Zanzibar almost as if it were an English seaside town with its visiting naval officers, its gossip, its clubbiness and its evening social life. His tone was reassuring, comforting, flippant. It was an illusion, one meant to reassure himself as much as her. Nevertheless, if they could believe it, life in East Africa might not be unbearable.

Beneath the amusing banter, though, Kirk knew what kind of place he had come to. He had arrived at the height of the slave-trading season, and at that time of year, the dhows laden with human cargo would have been passing the point at Shangani almost daily. The town was full of northern Arabs down from the Gulf – '[they] despise us – they are slavers all',[12] he commented – and the slave smuggling on fake passes up the coast was an open secret. But Kirk was not shocked. He recognized the kind of society this was, for he had seen it before on the Zambesi and the Mozambique coast, where everyone was complicit one way or another in what made the economy work. In Zanzibar, all the leading merchants, Europeans, Americans and Indians, supported the slave trade. It was in their interests to do so, their businesses depended on it, and Kirk was hardly surprised. They were traders, there to make money and leave before they fell seriously ill or died.

Otherwise, the people bored him. They could talk about nothing but 'cowries, copal and elephants' teeth',[13] he wrote to Hooker. So he resorted to his old saviour, botany. He was also interested in Islam, and had begun to read the Koran. With time on his hands, he took a boat down to Kilwa where he explored the ruined mosques of an older Muslim civilization standing in the bush above the shore. He collected a number of rare grasses, which he sent back to Kew. He did not even mention the other side of Kilwa, this trading port at the end of the slave routes from the interior, where pens filled every season with tens of thousands of men, women and children, where in a bad year, the beaches were littered with corpses.[14] It was as if he did not care.

His indifference is almost shocking, but Kirk knew there was nothing he could do, and his experiences farther south had hardened him. Trading in human beings was just another aspect of life on the African coast, along with the appalling incidence of disease, the mortality and the violence. He was realistic, detached. During his years on the Zambesi he had frequently seen the untold misery caused by slave trading, but he had also seen the disastrous consequences of clumsy intervention by well-meaning Europeans. The missionaries on the upper Shire had done nothing to bring trafficking to an end, and they may have even exacerbated the situation. They had been foolish and unprepared and had little idea of what they were dealing with. As a result, many of them had died. Kirk's attitude was that of a man who gets involved only when he can do good.

He made this position clear when he wrote to Nelly after he heard she had been visiting cholera patients in England. He did not worry on her behalf, he wrote, although he did not know why, and he asked her not to think him cold. Nevertheless, she should not endanger herself needlessly:

> We have our life to live on this earth and a work to do and it is not for us to gret and vex because sometimes danger faces us, but I pray of you not to run any risk. You have nothing to do visiting every poor house with disease. You have no right unless you are of real and great service to go among infectious disease. Many go from a pleasure in seeing distress which all the while they cannot relieve. Where you are of no use you have no right to expose yourself . . .[15]

Kirk could have been writing of his own attitude towards slave trading. If you cannot do anything useful, don't interfere. He did not excuse it, but nor did he condemn it, for both attitudes seemed to be irrelevant to him. He abhorred westerners who came to visit the slave market in Zanzibar from 'a pleasure in seeing distress'. Trading in people was cruel, but unless you could mitigate it, it was better to say nothing.

Kirk was not indifferent but he had become cynical. As he waited for Nelly to arrive, he attended diligently to his medical duties, and he pursued his botany, yet he had no intention of staying long in Africa. He wrote to Hooker in October, 'With all this you are lucky fellows at home after all and I suppose when I can afford it you may expect me to join you . . .'[16] He had quickly discovered that his medical position was a dead end, and there was no chance of making a career for himself in Zanzibar. Any promotion depended on the authorities in Bombay, who preferred those who had done time in the Indian service. Kirk was not one of them.

He was interested in everything he saw, but the scribblings in his notebooks are those of a man not fully engaged, yet whose mind could not rest or stay still. Copal, the fossilized resin dug up on the coast, then sold to Europeans for high-quality coach varnish, intrigued Kirk, because preserved in the clear resin were insects that he thought would be of scientific note. He wrote to Hooker with long lists of plants. He visited one of the outlying coral islands and wrote: 'I am glad to say that during my very short stay on shore I picked several fine additions to the East African Flora . . .'[17] He was still first and foremost the scientist, detached and objective. His time in Africa was valuable for the contribution he could make to the enterprise at Kew, and that was all.

Majid bin Said al Busaidi had never expected to be ruler of Zanzibar. Three of Seyyid Said's other sons were older than he was, although two of them died before their father. Weak and epileptic from childhood, Majid had lived a protected existence, and his family always feared for his life. There is an affecting anecdote of how Said, hearing one day of the severity of his son's fits, in desperation took a small boat from his country palace and rushed to the boy's side, where he wept and prayed in anguish for his life to be saved.[18]

Profound superstition was attached to the affliction – seizures were thought to be the visitations of malign spirits, and in a society where courage and warriorship were admired, the fits humiliated the young man. Fair skinned – his mother was a Circassian concubine – he was possessed of great charm, but was forever afraid. The photographs taken of him early in his reign show a slim young man with thin, regular features and large, clear eyes. Later images show him with a fuller beard, carefully clipped, but his face is gaunt and taut, with dark sunken eyes and a complexion marked by smallpox. It is the face of an unhappy man, and his eyes are haunted by worry and fear. Majid had many anxieties beyond the immediate terrors of his health. His brothers and sisters despised him, and viewed his weakness with contempt. In Zanzibar, his younger brother, Barghash, had twice plotted to take away his throne. His elder brother, who had inherited Said's territories in Oman, also menaced, and on several occasions had threatened to invade from the north. Only British intervention had prevented Majid's overthrow.

Majid was a complex as well as a tormented man. He feared his family in Oman, but he was equally afraid of the Arab traders and pirates who came south every season to plunder his coast in their search for slaves. He knew these northern Arabs despised Zanzibaris, looking on their impure religious practices and degenerate luxury with contempt. Majid's years of illness had eroded his self-confidence. He felt himself inferior to the northern visitors, intimidated by them, and when they arrived each year, he was terrified and locked himself away. Yet at the same time he also craved their respect, and so he resorted to bribes, paying their sheikhs enormous sums to keep them happy. He secretly admired their warlike, violent ways, and he was reluctant to enforce the law against their slave raiding.

As with the northern Arabs, so it was with the French and the British. The French he feared for having designs on his lands, but with the British he had a more complex relationship. English force had the power either to protect or remove him, but Majid also knew it was in the British interest for him to remain secure on his throne for as long as possible. They might harangue him on the evils of slave trading, but what the Indian government wanted above all was stability. With the British, Majid learnt to promise but not deliver. He pretended to comply with their requirements while doing the barest minimum. While the British superpower might bluster and threaten, ultimately Zanzibar was a long way from both India and London, and he knew that, as long as it was quiet, they would do little to interfere. The British colossus always had something more important to concern itself with, and he had to do only so much to keep it happy.

Meanwhile, the young sultan retreated and hid from danger. The old British consul, Hamerton, had saved him from a rebellion on his accession, but Hamerton died shortly afterwards, and when another consul finally arrived in 1858, he found Majid living offshore on a ship, he was so frightened. As he got older, he was seldom seen outside his palace, and was embarrassed to be viewed in public because of the scars on his face. Afraid of the dangers of the city, he began construction of a palace on the mainland, where he believed he was safer. He called it Dar es Salaam, or Haven of Peace.

Majid attempted to accommodate and compromise, playing off his enemies against each other, undertaking what he could not deliver, bribing and appeasing on all sides, but under his rule Zanzibar decayed. Its bridges and roads were never repaired, and the administration became corrupt and venal. Law and order broke down for months at a time. Kilwa, the slave trade's coastal port, was ungovernable, and outsiders were afraid of travelling there. Along the coast there were intermittent rebellions, and the sultan's word was seldom obeyed. Many of the wealthier Arabs retreated to their country estates while younger men went to the mainland, to the frontier, where there were fortunes to be made. Yet even there, they needed credit for trade goods. They needed the financial infrastructure the city provided, and its access to the outside world, and this was ultimately controlled by one man. In Zanzibar, power was increasingly wielded by the Customs Master, Ludda Dhamji.

'An unobtrusive and dignified native of Bombay', Ludda was so rich he was sometimes referred to by westerners as the Rothschild of East Africa. A photograph taken of him seated on the steps before the fine carved door of his house shows a man in simple white robes and ceremonial hat. He looks away from the camera with shrewd, confident eyes and a firm expression. He has a straight nose and a white tidy moustache. His face gives away nothing.[19]

Ludda not only controlled the Zanzibar economy, he was also the sultan's banker, and Majid had borrowed huge sums from him over the years. Ludda farmed out the Zanzibar customs duties, having bought the rights from the sultan for a fixed sum, and because of that he controlled all trade with the mainland and all the privileges that went with it. The Indian traders in every port up and down the coast lived in fear of him, and when foreign visitors attended the sultan's durbars, the Customs Master was there, quietly listening. The sultan's soldiers were partly financed by him. He knew everything of importance that happened in Zanzibar, and much of it he profited from.

Ludda used his power quietly and without ostentation. The pact between the Indian traders and the ruling Zanzibar families was a complicated one. Omanis had increasingly interbred with Swahili and other Africans, and gave political legitimacy to the state. Their forebears had come down with Seyyid Said from Oman, and had helped him claim the coast as part of his ancestral empire. Some of them continued their old freebooting ways, leading long expeditions to the mainland, but they needed the Indian merchants to finance their caravans. So each depended on the other, and holding the balance was the ruler.

The sultan was guarded and watched at all times, as though living his life in a prison. He spent long hours in his harem, and one European referred to him contemptuously as 'an effete voluptuary given up to pleasure'.[20] He attempted to neutralize his brothers, either by exiling them or driving them to financial servitude, confiscating their inheritance and reducing them to impotent fury. One of them insulted him in his durbar. When Majid struck him, the young man drew his sword. He was overpowered by guards, taken away and incarcerated. Majid's sister, the energetic and tempestuous Salme, was treated no better.

Seyyida Salme, or Bibi Salimah as she was known, had been Majid's favourite sister since their childhood. As one of Seyyid Said's daughters, she had enjoyed a life of luxury, travelling the country with retinues of slaves, yet living the closeted life of an Arab princess. Even as a girl she had chafed at the limitations of this claustrophobic life, and when she was sixteen, she had taken part in a conspiracy to replace Majid with his younger brother, Barghash. During the fighting, she had helped to smuggle Barghash out of the city, disguising him as a woman, and Majid never forgave her.

As she got older, Salme found her life more and more restricted. It was said she was prevented from acquiring a husband, the sultan considered her so dangerous. Life for rich women in Zanzibar had always been a mixture of indolence and intrigue. There were scandalous accounts of ladies who maintained secret liaisons with young slaves while their husbands were away, but Salme was more ambitious. At night in the hot weather, social life for the women took place on the roofs of the houses, where people could communicate from building to building across the narrow streets. In 1866, the house next to Salme's was occupied by a young German businessman, Heinrich Ruete, and the two became acquainted. Either he was smuggled into her house, or she gained entrance to his, but Salme became pregnant.

To save her from scandal, Ruete attempted to have her taken secretly out of the country aboard a German ship, but at the last minute the plan was given away by one of her slaves. Majid by now had heard the rumours and sent round a female relative to examine his sister and report on her condition. Knowing what the result would be, the woman hid the truth, but the sultan was not satisfied. Finally, he sent a letter to Salme allowing her to leave Zanzibar on a pilgrimage to Mecca in a *bugala*[21] belonging to his chief eunuch. It was a death sentence. Other young women had left the city this way and never reached their destination. Distracted, Salme went to see the British consul's wife to ask for help.

Mrs Seward was a tough woman whose role in life consisted of protecting her kind but ingenuous husband from stumbling into danger. Seward was only acting consul, and she realized that if he took up Salme's cause, it would inevitably provoke problems with the sultan. Mishandled, it could damage his career. Determined to keep him innocent of any involvement, she consulted Kirk instead.

Kirk had arrived in Zanzibar on board HMS *Highflyer*, a Royal Navy cruiser. The commanding officer was Captain Pasley – 'a shy funny man with a stoop and awkward manner,' Kirk wrote. 'Yet he is in fact a kind man, and full of fire when the ice is broken and to this the best plan is to give him a moderate amount of wine. Then he jokes and converses most agreeably.'[22] The *Highflyer* was in harbour at the time, and perhaps Kirk gave him enough wine to make him agreeable.

The first day of the Muslim year was known in Zanzibar as *Nauruzi* or *Siku ya Mwaka*, and on that night it was customary for the women to bathe in the sea and pray for good health in the coming year. In 1866, *Nauruzi* fell on 24 August, and that was the night planned for Seyyida Salme to leave Zanzibar. Although Omani, she had spent all her life in Zanzibar, and it was natural for her to take part in the local ceremony with the crowd. After dark, she and two of her slaves went down to the beach, and no one paid much attention as they walked into the shallow water. During the festival there was much fooling around, laughter and high spirits, so when one of the slave girls was heard running from the beach shrieking loudly, no one took any notice. But next day the *Highflyer* had left her anchorage, sailing during the night without the usual notification, and Seyyida Salme had not returned to her house.

In a letter to Nelly, Kirk described how he had enjoyed pretending innocence of any involvement:

> Only those here [i.e. in the British consulate] knew what was going on, of course I knew nothing of it, I never get information till very late. I heard nothing of it until next day, and did I not look astonished? I am told she got into the cutter, taking down all her boxes of dollars safely, springing into the boat although it was manned by infidels. Her two servants who knew nothing of the whole affair, screamed, howled and roared as women will, but a blue-jacket covered the mouth of one with his hand and lifted her in, *nolens volens*, to follow her mistress. The other unluckily got off clear away, bellowing up the street. Some blame the English Consulate, as if the ships of war were under us, and I am sure no man is more innocent than poor Dr. Seward.[23]

In Zanzibar, there was uproar. The sultan had been made to look a fool. Not only had his sister been defiled by an infidel, but one of their ships had taken her off from under his nose. Humiliated, he was unsure what to do, and it was Kirk who went to the palace to discuss the matter with him, pointing out that he had been freed from a far greater difficulty. This may have been the first time he met Majid – 'the Sultan has no power and is a weak and timid man,'[24] he wrote – and he realized that Majid's treatment of his sister had been inspired only by fear. Ruete, lucky to escape without harm, went to join his lover in Aden some months later, where they were married.[25]

For Kirk, the incident had been an adventure, enlivening the boring routine of his life. He hated to be sitting on the sidelines, and needed the stimulation this kind of action provided. Even though he had treated it as a kind of game, he had managed to save a woman's life, and a difficult crisis had been avoided.

However the British agency and consulate in Zanzibar had always been involved in crises, and Kirk knew that. Its short history was intricately connected with that of the city itself, and had been almost from the beginning. By now he would have read the bound volumes of letters that stood on the shelves at the back of the office. He must have known the story of the building and its inhabitants, and been aware of how Zanzibar had become a curse for every man who had taken the post.

4: AZRAEL, ANGEL OF DEATH

Je ne suis qu'un negociant, aimait-il a dire de lui meme, avec un
sourire dont la modestie ressemblait a la fierte du succes.

A. DE GOBINEAU ON SEYYID SAID

The consulate records went back to the arrival of the first British
agent in Zanzibar. His letters and reports had been carefully
collated and bound in leather, and placed on a shelf in the office.
They told a tortuous and difficult story. In the first half of the
nineteenth century, Zanzibar and its trade in human flesh had
become a source of bitter conflict between the two great poles of
the British Empire: London and the Company in India. Mainly
conducted discreetly, by letter and behind closed doors, the
argument was never entirely resolved.

Zanzibar, in the very early years of the century, had been
virtually unknown to the outside world. The last remnant of an
earlier Omani empire in Africa, its slave market was run by an
avaricious eunuch who sold labour to French slavers, and no one
cared. But after the 1830s, once Seyyid Said had reconquered the
African coast and moved his capital from Muscat to Zanzibar, the
island began to attract British attention. Said had long been an
important client of Britain's empire in the East. In Muscat, he
controlled a crucial port on the long sea route to India, and to the
Bombay government, he was a vital ally, so they were prepared to

overlook his bad habits. In London, however, the growing trade in human beings from his African capital had become a deep concern, and difficult to ignore.

By the 1840s, tensions rose to a new level as both sides attempted to control this distant island state. Zanzibar had exposed a fault line dividing Britain's global power, and for the men appointed as agents to the island state, the conflict proved crippling. They came to East Africa determined to use the might of the British Empire to root out this scandal but were thwarted, each of them in turn, by the indifference of their superiors, the complexity of the law and their own inevitable ill health, while the Zanzibaris continued their trade unconcerned. Their trade was an ancient one, they believed it was protected by the laws of providence and nothing could stop it.

Kirk was aware of this history, he would have read the letters and reports, and knew how impotent the British agents had been. They had often acted 'with a high hand', he wrote to Nelly shortly after his arrival, 'but their power was doubtful . . .'[1] It was a reason for never wanting the job.

Captain Atkins Hamerton of the 15th Regiment Bombay Native Infantry arrived on the island on 4 May 1841, having sailed down the African coast from Oman, where he was based. The monsoon winds at that time of year were turbulent and dangerous, and the two-thousand mile voyage from Muscat had taken him forty-eight days. Just north of Zanzibar his brig had been blown off course and badly damaged. The crew were afraid to continue, so Hamerton was forced to trek overland on foot, and in torrential rain.

> For all my people were sick and knocked up . . . I walked across to the western coast at Chuck Chuck, where I procured . . . a boat in which I proceeded to Zanzibar, and on the 4th instant anchored opposite to the Imam's (i.e. Said's) house . . . and immediately went ashore and had an interview with His Highness . . .[2]

He must have presented a ragged and desperate appearance that day, but Hamerton was tough and resourceful, and the circumstances of his arrival troubled him little. Tall and powerfully built, with a ruddy complexion and dark hair, he had originally come from Dublin, joining the East India Company as a boy. In 1841, he was thirty-seven years old and at the peak of his career. His loyalty to his company was uncompromising and total. As a member of its elite political department, he had served for several years in Muscat, where he was known for his blunt, outspoken character. He responded directly to situations, and was fearless in the face of danger, but he was not a reflective man. He had a quick temper.

Said and Hamerton already knew each other well. There was even a suggestion that during Hamerton's residence in Oman, following a disagreement, the ruler had attempted to have him put away. But twenty years in the East had hardened Hamerton. He spoke Arabic as though the language was his own, and he was not easily intimidated. Life in Oman was unpredictable and often violent – Said himself had come to power when he was just sixteen by assassinating his own uncle. There was little that could shock the new agent, but that year in Africa he saw things that he had not expected.

Hamerton had come south to Zanzibar out of duty. The Company had been upset when Said, at the height of his power, suddenly announced he was moving the capital of his empire to Africa, leaving one of his sons as regent in Oman. For years they had depended on him as a linchpin in their strategies to keep peace in the Gulf. Even in Africa he was still too important to be left alone, so Hamerton was detailed to follow him. His interests in Zanzibar were therefore strictly political and commercial, yet from the moment of his arrival, the human trafficking disturbed him.

Slave trading in Oman was not unusual, but in Africa it was different. The sight of dead and dying people fought over by dogs on the African shoreline shocked him, and the Zanzibar slave market he found detestable. Unlike in the Arab world, there seemed to be no morality governing the way slaves were treated. In Zanzibar, they were cheap to buy, and women and children were frequently sold merely to gratify the casual sexual appetites of any purchaser.

The meanest ruffian frequently buys a number of young girls in the slave market, with an understanding between him and the broker ... on their being resold within a given time (when he has satisfied himself) that should there be a deficiency on the girls being resold, ... the buyer is to sustain the loss.[3]

But slavery was not Hamerton's business; he had other matters to occupy him.

In 1841 Seyyid Said was fifty years old. For almost two decades this subtle and ambitious man had dominated the politics of the Persian Gulf. In the Arab world he was famous, and when he had visited the holy places of Mecca and Medina, crowds had gathered to watch him pass. But his cultivation of the British had most contributed to his fortune. Over the decades he had received frequent military and naval support from the East India Company as they fought common enemies, but Said was more than just an ally. He had studied the British closely, and uniquely for an Arab seemed to appreciate the concerns and values of the English in the East. He understood their naval protocol, and he shared their interests in trade, ships and horses. He was also exceptionally loyal. In 1820, while fighting alongside British troops in Oman, he had been badly wounded in a dramatic attempt to rescue an English officer 'cut down' in the heat of battle. Said had saved the man's life, and earned himself lasting fame among the officers of the Company.[4]

Said had moved south because of Africa's wealth, and although he depended on the British, he still preferred to keep them at a distance. In Zanzibar he lived in a luxury unattainable in Oman, owning fine buildings and extensive estates. Visitors remarked on the splendour of his palace at Mtoni, where from lush gardens of fruit trees they could look out across a beautiful bay. From a *bendjle*, or watch tower, Said liked to examine far-off islands through a telescope.[5] He was still a compelling presence, by turns charming and enigmatic, but he was visibly ageing. He limped permanently from a battle wound, and had grown stout.

Said had not expected his visitor that season, and Hamerton

found him perplexed and suspicious. The British were not popular in Zanzibar, and during his first weeks Hamerton was surprised and annoyed to hear men in the court speaking openly with contempt of the East India Company. American and French interests were strong, and paintings showing British naval defeats were openly on display. Hamerton soon discovered the reasons. The French had long supported the slave trade, and shippers from Massachusetts dominated much of the ivory business, receiving particular privileges in their commercial arrangements. The Customs Master was in their pocket, and Hamerton took immediate exception to the situation. This was against a treaty signed by the Seyyid himself, and it also offended his deepest loyalties.

Within months of his arrival, he was able to demonstrate evidence of the corruption before Said in open court. The result was uproar. Turning on the Britisher, the assembled advisers shouted loudly, attempting to prevent him being heard. The matter should be referred to the *kadis* or religious judges, they claimed, but Hamerton refused. Countering his adversaries, in fluent Arabic, with detailed knowledge of their dealings, he told them this was a commercial matter concerning signed treaties. Reluctantly, Said had to give way, but Hamerton had offended powerful interests. He was breaking down a system from which his enemies took 'considerable pecuniary advantages', he wrote, and from that day the new Company agent was hated.

Said's advisers told him it was obvious now where the agent's attentions would eventually be turned. It was the trade in slaves he was really after. Deeply concerned, Said raised the matter when he and Hamerton were out riding together one day, alone and free from the spies of the durbar room. He was constantly troubled, he said, by people asking if the agent had come 'to emancipate the slaves and stop the trade'. But Hamerton avoided the issue, replying cooly that he 'was astonished to observe how little people here regarded His Highness's authority'.[6]

Nevertheless, the situation remained volatile, and Hamerton's own actions continued to arouse fear and suspicion. In late 1841, a British merchant vessel visiting Zanzibar, the *Joshua Carroll*, was discovered by Hamerton to be fitted out for taking slaves on board. Since the ship was British, he had it overhauled, and its captain arrested and sent to Cape Town. But he was able to do so only because of the timely presence of a British cruiser. Once the cruiser had left, taking away the unfortunate *Joshua Carroll*, he was on his own again, without support or friends. His full appointment as British consul had not been confirmed, and the Customs Master had warned the Indian community against having any dealings with him. He was living on the waterfront in poor quarters that were continually flooded, and attempts to have them repaired were mysteriously delayed. Without medical assistance, he was repeatedly laid low by illness, and he had been threatened with violence. Only the Seyyid's regard for an officer of the Company stood between him and an accident, or worse.

The inevitable confrontation came in June 1841, with Palmerston's letter instructing his representative in Zanzibar to tell its ruler that slave trading would no longer be tolerated. The day it arrived, Hamerton went directly to the palace, and delivered the ultimatum personally to Said. Infuriated by the agent's presumption, Said lost his temper. Contemptuously, he accused Hamerton of acting beyond his brief – of being merely a Company man and not the British consul he claimed to be. Hamerton, insulted, responded in kind.

> I told him I was sorry to see that he was even yet under the influence of foolish and bad advice, and . . . if he further believed in it, he might have cause to believe the East India Company and the Governor General possessed power different to what his advisers wished him to believe.

Only then did Said realize how dangerous the situation had become. Quickly he attempted to conciliate the enraged agent. Hamerton had misunderstood him, he replied smoothly. From then on he would naturally agree to any request the British might make. 'This letter and the orders of Azrael, the angel of death, are to the Arabs one and the same thing, nothing but to submit,' he said. He then suggested he should send an envoy to London to make his peace and, mollified, Hamerton agreed.[7]

For Hamerton, the months of prevarication were at an end, for he did not distinguish between Company policy and his instructions from London. Perhaps naively, in his mind the two were the same, and he considered his orders were now clear and unambiguous. He had been confirmed as British consul as well as Company agent, and slave trading had to cease. He immediately set about achieving this with every means at his disposal. He began to put pressure on members of the Indian community, many of whom had families in Bombay, and set up a network of informers. He was uncompromising and made it clear that he intended to win.

The Zanzibaris were passionate gamblers, and at the weekly races held outside town on an open stretch of shore called *Nazemodya*, thousands gathered to bet on the horses. In early 1842, Hamerton, in a very public gesture, ran a horse against one of the Seyyid's own animals. Before a massive crowd of seven thousand people, Said watched silently while his animal was beaten by that of the Britisher. His horses were dear to Said, he prized and loved them almost like his children, and this was a clear challenge.[8]

Yet the agent was vulnerable, although the threat came from a quarter he could never have guessed at. Another Englishman was living in Zanzibar to whom Said now turned, and it was in London, not in Africa, that Said had decided to counterattack.

Robert Cogan was older than Hamerton by several years. Better educated, less principled, he was a renegade East India Company naval officer with a mixed past. Throughout his career he could never resist playing political games, and during the 1830s, had repeatedly infuriated the Company by advancing his own interests wherever he could. In 1834, while in Muscat, Said had offered his largest warship, the *Liverpool*, a vessel carrying 74 guns and weighing 1,800 tons, as a gift to the British government in London. Bombay, jealous of a deeper relationship between their client and the home authorities, attempted to frustrate the idea. Cogan, who was British commissioner at Muscat at the time, insinuated himself into the argument. Disingenuously, he sugges-ted he might assist by captaining the ship personally to Britain, which is exactly what he did, to his own advantage and his colleagues' intense annoyance.[9]

A few years later, he was discovered to have committed an even more heinous crime. In the early 1830s a conflict had developed between Bombay and the small Indian state of Satara, where the ruler resented Company attempts to govern him. The youthful rajah had escalated his cause first to Calcutta and then to London, and the case became notorious. The governor of Bombay and his staff were criticized and lampooned in the press both in Britain and in India, but it was not until 1839 they discovered that behind the scenes one of the rajah's unofficial advisers was a man from their own service – Robert Cogan.[10]

Cogan was never forgiven for this treachery, but by then he had moved on. His motive had been the same in each instance, to profit from the largesse of a rich oriental ruler by playing the Company off against the London authorities. It was a risky game, but by taking the *Liverpool* to London in 1836 he appeared to have struck gold. His arrival with this splendid gift from an obscure Eastern potentate was a triumph. It was reported in the press, and he secured an audience with the Queen, even staying at Windsor. He also met Lord Palmerston, the foreign secretary, who was known as a zealous fighter against the slave trade. Cogan, who personally did not care either way about the issue, dangled before Palmerston vague details of slave trafficking in the Indian Ocean, and returned to the East with an expense account and a brief to find out more.

Conceited, obsessed with his own dignity, and a consummate flatterer, Cogan began to take himself seriously. In Muscat, he boasted of his high connections, but in the Indian service he was now despised. When he visited Bombay in 1839, he was snubbed as only a prestige-conscious imperial establishment knew how. At a grand and formal dinner he was relegated to the distant ranks of the governor's table, and then further insulted on leaving Bombay harbour, when the guns were instructed to give the lowest possible salute. It was public humiliation, and Cogan was determined to get his own back. In Zanzibar, he found his opportunity.[11]

Cogan preyed easily on Said's paranoia. He spoke knowledge-ably of the Satara affair; he convinced Said that distrust of the Company in London could only help his cause; and the Seyyid trusted him. So when in early 1842, Said sent his envoy, Ali bin Nassir, to England, Cogan went along to assist. He already had useful friends. He took up residence with an influential retired Indian merchant in London's Fitzroy Square, and he was on familiar terms with men at the Foreign Office. A member of parliament was primed to ask embarrassing questions about the government's Zanzibar representative. Slowly, Cogan began to blacken Hamerton's name.

Cogan's ambitions were clear. If he could only finesse the issue of the slave trade, and persuade the government that this was too sensitive a matter to be left to the unreliable attentions of the Company, his own future was assured. With Hamerton gone, Cogan's influence in Zanzibar as representative of the home power would be supreme. The Seyyid would depend on him. Great fortunes in the East had been built on less.

Hamerton was an easy target. He had left Dublin as a boy, and his entire adult life had been spent in the rough and tumble world of the East. He was not well educated and had no experience of dealing with the urbane politics of Whitehall, where he had now to send his reports. His dispatches were repetitive, awkwardly written and dashed off in haste. Sometimes the detail was perfunctory, and the grammar poor. He was used to reporting to pragmatic people who understood the nature of his work, but to the refined gentlemen of the Foreign Office, Africa was a remote place, and they demanded reports presented with formality and style. Cogan, helping officials interpret what they could not understand, easily exploited their prejudice against this 'Indian' consul.

The foreign secretary, Lord Aberdeen, also became involved, for during his stay in London, Said's envoy insistently presented his master's cause. He, too, spoke bitterly of the agent in Zanzibar. He described how Said had been needlessly insulted, suggesting darkly that this might even lead to a resurgence of French influence on the African coast. Questions were asked in the House of Commons, for members were concerned about the slave trade. Letters were judiciously leaked, in which Cogan disparagingly referred to Hamerton as a man whose 'services and acquirements could, in my opinion, be better employed elsewhere . . .'[12]

Soon Hamerton got a name for representing everything that was crude and irresponsible about British rule in the East, and in Zanzibar during the next two years events continued to embarrass his cause. His temper was easily aroused, and his enemies set out deliberately to provoke him. He was insulted by a workman in his own home, and his employees were harrassed in the street. One morning a slave was sent to defecate openly in front of his house, and after a scuffle, Hamerton complained to Said at the indignity after which the slave was beaten. The story was too good to waste and, much embellished, some months later Cogan personally relayed it to the foreign secretary with unctuous relish.

> An inhabitant of the town, in furtherance of the calls of nature, squatted himself on the beach, which is the usual place of resort for latrines, not far from the British Consul's house, where he was seized and severely beaten by a servant of the Consul's . . .[13]

Lord Aberdeen, sitting in his office in Whitehall, read the account with civilized distaste. There were unfortunate echoes of brutalities meted out to slaves by British officials in the West Indies. The situation had become embarrassing.

Then, early in 1845, Said abruptly banished his eldest son and heir, the Prince Hilal, ordering him to leave Zanzibar. To Aberdeen's dismay, and without consultation, Hamerton offered the young man asylum in England, and in October that year, the prince arrived at Southampton without funds, expecting to be maintained at the British government's expense. A house had to be hastily provided for him and his retinue in Brooke Street, where he lived for several months, spending the government's money freely on clothes and entertainment. Showing little desire to return to Africa, he sought an audience with the Queen.[14]

The foreign secretary, furious at such a breach of protocol, had

had enough. He had censured his consul twice already, and in December 1845 his patience snapped, and he finally instructed the East India Company to sack their awkward representative in Africa. Reluctantly, the men in Bombay were forced to agree. For a loyal Company servant to be humiliated in this way was virtually unprecedented. Nevertheless, letters for Hamerton's dismissal were drafted and approved, and Cogan in London, ready with an alternative candidate, planned his triumphant return. As trusted and influential intermediary between Britain and Zanzibar, his future seemed secure.

Cogan had apparently been successful, but in his efforts to destroy Hamerton, he had made a big mistake. He had ensured that the East African slave trade remained firmly in the British government's view, and politically slave trading was a very sensitive issue, still capable of arousing strong opinions among the British electorate. The Seyyid's envoy to London, visiting the foreign secretary and declaiming on slavery's long and honoured history under Islam, therefore found that his pleas for tolerance were received with surprising coolness. On the contrary, the Foreign Office responded with long letters to Said exhorting him to discard his 'inhuman practices' and take up a 'more legitimate commerce' in its stead.[15] This was not what Said had expected, but even Cogan could provide no resolution to the argument. His enemies in India, however, were more astute. They knew that to avoid further meddling from London they needed a different answer, and cynically they had instructed Hamerton to find it. They became committed anti-slavetraders, at least for the time being.

While Cogan intrigued in London, Hamerton was instructed to put pressure on Said relentlessly. He had been well trained, and his tactics were effective. The wealthy Indian community in Zanzibar was predominantly from British India and, under the law, not permitted to own slaves. Hamerton threatened to enforce the law, causing consternation on the island. This would ruin business, disrupting the trade in every commodity, and Said complained bitterly. Meanwhile, throughout 1844, there were conflicting rumours along the waterfront in Zanzibar. Merchants returning from India reported that the East India Company's forces had been defeated in Afghanistan, while from London came reports that representatives of the Satara rajah had met with great success. It was said the Company was finished and that its charter would not be renewed. A new consul was reported to be coming out to Zanzibar from Britain, and Robert Cogan's name was mentioned. Yet nothing happened, and it was then that the crisis erupted within Said's own family.

Of all Said's many sons, Hilal was the most popular, and his exile had split the court. 'The most shrewd and energetic of all His Highness's sons, [he] has the goodwill of all the Arab subjects,' Hamerton wrote. 'The people in speaking of him always say he is a model of what the Imam [i.e. Said] was.'[16] There was much speculation on the reasons for the terrible rupture, for Said himself was in poor health, and there was talk of a fight for the succession, were he to die. Hamerton thought the ruler's decline was self-inflicted. In 1844 he wrote:

> The Imam at present is 56 years old; and within the last three years he has become much broken and altered in every way from the effects of stimulating condiments which he is constantly taking in order to qualify him for the joys of the harem.[17]

Said's desire for the pleasures of his concubines was destroying his health, but Hamerton also believed it was the reason for his rupture with his son. In March 1846, he informed his colleagues in India that it was even said of the young prince 'that he debauched some young girls whom His Highness intended for his own use'.[18] It seemed the son had infringed his father's rights within the royal harem.

The affair seemed to break Said. He was deeply attached to the young man, and the betrayal provoked in him a profound emotional crisis. He could never talk about the reason for the rupture, and he could not bear to have the young man near him. When Hilal left Zanzibar in late 1845, the family trouble spread out into the city.

When the Prince Seyyid Hilal went to take a final farewell of his father, the Imam was greatly distressed, his women rushed out the house, and wanted to give their ornaments and what little property [they] possessed to the exiled prince, and for some time a state of melancholy was observable through the town . . .[19]

Hilal's exile shattered the already fragile balance among Said's advisers, who argued among themselves. Weakened by his son's treachery, Said himself seemed incapable of dealing with the crisis, and Hamerton reported that he was now 'in great distress of mind and frequently says, "I have no friends, in the hour of need they come not around me." '[20] His daughter gave a more personal account, writing how her father went alone to his chamber and prayed and wept and called out aloud to his estranged son. Only Hamerton proved consistent and incorruptible in his advice. Growing weaker, perhaps Said now realized he needed to compromise with this man and the interests he represented, and that time was no longer on his side. He needed help. He needed the support of the one man he had tried so hard to dislodge.

At some point in 1845, the two men came to a compromise. Said agreed with Hamerton that henceforth trading in slaves should take place only within his African territories, along the coast as far north as the little island of Lamu, the point at which his control of the *mrima*, the African coastal belt, ceased. Shipping slaves by sea for export to Arabia and the Gulf would henceforth be forbidden. The treaty signed late that year was a triumph for Hamerton, and it drew the sting from the conflict between the two men. For from then on, Said began to rely on Hamerton more and more; he was the only man who never lied to him, he once said. In January 1846, Hamerton was ill yet again, and for several weeks he was confined to his bed, at times unconscious, and close to death. He wrote that he had been in agonizing pain with an attack of the 'gravel',[21] and had not known where to turn. Only the Seyyid's support had sustained him.

Hamerton had been ill every year since 1843, on each occasion more seriously. Zanzibar was a punishing place for Europeans.

Malaria, cholera, smallpox and many other diseases were endemic. So when he recovered in February that year, it would not have been a surprise had he left. He had secured the vital agreement his employers required, and he could have gone with honour and dignity. Yet he stayed on, for he was now indispensable, to both sides.

In February 1846, Hilal returned to Zanzibar, forgiven by his father, and there was celebration in the town. Hamerton wrote that the schooners in the harbour were . . .

> . . . all saluting with twenty one guns . . . the Imam's flag at the fore, the excitement . . . was extraordinary, all hands on the beach, and before the boat touched the shore, the people ran into the water to see and put their hands on the prince; almost all were weeping. His Highness the Imam came out to secure his son, and took him by both hands without saying one word, he could not speak, he appeared greatly affected, and when he entered the palace, [he] made the sign for everyone to leave for a while, and gave vent to his feelings . . . And after the Arab fashion, he embraced his son; and wept from his very soul . . . When he retired to the private apartments, and on my intimating to the Imam that I wished leave to retire, he said, 'Now Hilal shall live in the same house with me.'[22]

Hamerton, deeply moved by the scene, wrote as someone now very close to the ageing ruler. The crisis seems to have been the event that brought them together, and the relationship became closer and more affectionate with every year.

Hamerton's own position had been transformed, and he now became an increasingly powerful man in Zanzibar. The mainland trade, so valuable to the city yet vulnerable to outside interests, became his personal concern, and he used his authority to protect it rigorously. Perhaps this had even been the hidden bargain he had made with Said in securing the treaty, for during the next decade the consul ruthlessly used the threat of British power to keep access to the interior closed to all but Zanzibaris. Western merchants attempting to trade with the mainland were prevented from doing so.[23] Explorers were seldom allowed to venture inland, and those who did, met fatal ends. The few missionaries remained there at his discretion. It was said that 'a veil of secrecy' hung over the East African mainland, for few knew what went on there.[24] The coastal people did not like intruders, they were jealous of their grip on the inland trade and they did not want anyone interfering.

In Bombay, the Company was pleased with this outcome. Cogan had been seen off, and the government in London was satisfied and unlikely to interfere further. Hamerton had achieved what the Company had always sought at the fringe of its empire – influence and power without responsibility. The new treaty had defused concern in England over slave trading in Zanzibar. The papers for the consul's dismissal were quietly allowed to gather dust. No one in London complained.

In Zanzibar, Hamerton moved to secure his triumph. He employed a 'writer', and his correspondence became more polished. He enjoyed his unseen power, and there was even a slight swagger to his manner. In the evening, his house was the centre of social activity among the island's cross-cultural elite. The Seyyid honoured him, and everyone knew of his influence. He was referred to in Zanzibar as 'the Baleaze', meaning consul, as if there were no other.

In 1846, the Frenchman Charles Guillain visited Zanzibar and, when he met Hamerton, found him to be courteous, confident and full of charm. Nevertheless . . .

. . . beneath an exterior of bonhomie and frankness, the amusing Captain Hamerton hides a cunning mind as well as a profound knowledge of political matters . . . He has seen and experienced all the intrigues and tortuous paths which characterize the Machiavellian and ruthless politics of the Indian Government. But in serving his masters with such devotion and astuteness, he has in a way made himself into their image . . . He gives himself up, body and soul, to their requirements. His zeal and his energy combine with a finesse and savoir faire to give him in Zanzibar an influence which is not always moderate or even discreet. He is up to date with anything he is concerned to know about. His ears are everywhere from the highest points to the most local issues . . .[25]

Guillain was right, for Hamerton had given himself up in ways he could not have foreseen. There was a bitter twist to the agreement crafted between Said and the British, which only became apparent over time.

Traffic in slaves outside Africa was forbidden, but slaves could still be shipped legally along the coast within Zanzibari territory as far north as the Somali coast. Lamu, the little port at the northern most reach of Said's 'dominions', until then not especially notable for its labour demands, suddenly became the destination for thousands of slaves every year. Dhows, obtaining papers for Lamu, sailed there legally, and then freshly provisioned, chose their time, before making the last illegal leg of their journey up the Somali coast, and across to the Gulf, just as they had before. The smuggling trade boomed. For the treaty to ban slave trading to the Gulf was in truth a dead letter, and existed only on paper. In securing this loophole, Said had, in fact, ensured that nothing would change.

Perhaps Said could have enforced the treaty, but he never tried. He may even have gambled on such an outcome, for everyone in Zanzibar knew what was happening, and it was impossible that the ruler did not. The licences were granted by his men, and at least once, a vessel found trading slaves in Muscat belonged to him. But he stayed aloof. If smugglers were caught, he never excused them, but nor did he act against them except when forced to. A slave trafficker who appealed to him for help was dismissed as a fool for not managing his business better. When confronted, he told Hamerton he had not the force to impose the law, which may also have been true.

The Indian navy could perhaps have stopped the smuggling, had it committed resources to enforce the treaty but, as ever, the East African coast was of little concern. In London, parliament believed all was now well, for slaves were no longer to be exported from the East African coast. So Bombay had what it wanted, and it actively discouraged its ships from getting involved in chasing slavers, penalizing captains who let themselves be distracted by such a worthless pursuit.[26] And the boatloads of slaves, emaciated from disease and hunger, continued to pass along the shore, as before, rounding Shangani Point where the consulate looked out to sea, to be unloaded before the Customs House, and then fattened for sale like beasts to market. Nothing had changed. Nor would things ever change, said Zanzibaris, for that was the nature of the world.

Hamerton's victory was a hollow one, and he knew it. He had indeed given up body and soul in the interests of his employers, and the price had been high. During the mid-years of the century, the slave trade flourished, and in his wholehearted support for Zanzibar and its ruler, Hamerton became complicit in supporting what he had tried most to destroy. His health continued to suffer, as every season during the south-west monsoon his illness returned, an insistent reminder. He was promoted to the rank of lieutenant colonel, but beneath his easy conversation he became a disillusioned and sometimes bitter man. His closest friends and companions on the island died, one by one, and he recorded their passing sorrowfully but with stoicism.

Zanzibar had become his fate. He was tied to it because of his relationship with its ruler. As their interests had become entwined, the rapport between them had become a deeply personal one. When in April 1854, Said was summoned back to Muscat to deal with a crisis fomented by his sons, it was Hamerton he nominated as governor in his absence.

It was the last Said was to see of Zanzibar. About to set out from Muscat a year later, he had a premonition he would never reach Africa alive, and as he embarked he ordered a carpenter to bring on board materials to build a coffin. While at sea he became seriously ill and, as he slid into a coma, it was said that, in his delirium, he repeatedly called out to Hamerton for help. The consul did not fail him.

Said died at sea in October 1855, but when the fleet came back to Zanzibar, the death was concealed so his body could be taken ashore quietly. The oldest surviving son, Majid, was an epileptic, and another son, Barghash, who had been travelling with his father, had his own ideas on the inheritance. Slipping ashore before the death was known, he raised troops, intending to seize power.

There was great mourning in Zanzibar when Said's death was announced. As the line of concubines from his harem filed down to the seashore in the evening to begin the ritual of purification, one of the leaders of the coup approached the consulate, and asked Hamerton whether he would support the attempt. The old consul did not hesitate. He told the man he would personally blow his brains out if the Seyyid's wishes for his eldest son to inherit were not followed. So Majid, his father's favourite son and a young man of just nineteen years old, became the new ruler of Zanzibar.

Hamerton did not believe Europeans could survive in the interior, and he acted accordingly, but in December 1856 Richard Burton, another Indian Army officer, came to Zanzibar to mount a search for the source of the River Nile. Burton was already a well-known explorer. He spoke Arabic fluently, even travelling under an Arab name,[27] and perhaps that was what persuaded Hamerton to support the expedition.

During the year and a half Burton stayed in Zanzibar preparing for his expedition, the two men became close friends. The picture Burton painted of Hamerton was of a gaunt man, his health shattered, who 'lived only for the evening'. Some years later, Burton wrote:

> I can even now distinctly see my poor friend sitting before me, a tall, broad shouldered, and powerful figure, with square features, dark fixed eyes, hair and beard prematurely snow-white, and a complexion once fair and ruddy, but long ago bleached ghastly pale by ennui and sickness. Such had been the effect of the burning heats of Maskat and 'the Gulf', and the deadly damp of Zanzibar . . .

But Hamerton's disease was more than physical.

The worst symptom in his case – one which I have rarely found other than fatal – was his unwillingness to quit the place which was slowly killing him. At night he would chat merrily about a remove, about a return to Ireland; he loathed the subject in the morning. To escape seemed a physical impossibility, when he had only to order a few boxes to be packed, and to board the first home-returning ship.[28]

The consul secured from the new ruler Burton's free passage to the mainland; he arranged an introduction to Ludda Dhamji, the Customs Master, and he advised Burton on the safest route inland. Despite being near the end of his tether, he even escorted the expedition to the mainland in his own boat, and waited for several days as the caravan moved inland, letting off a canon every few hours as a threat to potential raiders tempted by the goods they carried. It was to be almost the last thing he did.

Burton was away nearly two years, travelling as far as Ujiji on Lake Tanganyika, and although he did not find the Nile's source, he became the first westerner to reveal the complex trading empire of which Zanzibar was the outlet and control point. Arriving at Kazeh in the highlands, he was astonished at the sophistication of the Zanzibari establishment there. A number of wealthy Omani traders now lived inland semi-permanently and in considerable luxury, with farms, harems and retinues of slaves providing necessary military support. From there, they sent trading expeditions farther into the interior, as far as Uganda in the north, and down to the state of the Kazembe on the Congo borders. Kazeh was the centre of operations across a vast area, where information was exchanged on the location of slaves, and the prices and sources of ivory; on which markets were open for business and which rulers were favourable to trade; on the safety of routes, and the politics of kingdoms. Kazeh was the refuelling centre for the caravans, it was where the ivory was stored and it was where necessary provisions were sent from the coast. There, notes of credit could be drawn on the merchants in Zanzibar, and used as money. Coming and going every season, its caravans filed in every direction, reaching other traders attached to tribes and monarchs in the remotest parts of the continent.

The Zanzibaris had set up this infrastructure over a matter of decades. They had faced and overcome the extraordinary risks and dangers because of the huge profits to be made. The caravans brought up cloth, beads, copper wire and guns, and they took down slaves and elephant tusks. Ultimately, ivory was what every trader sought. It was what made their fortunes. One successful expedition could transform a man for life; an unsuccessful one could destroy him.

Yet it was the slave trade that sustained the whole operation. Slaves were a currency and a commodity. They staffed the caravans, they were the fighters when battle was necessary, and the women slaves provided concubines for travellers. Burton noted they were for sale everywhere, and he described cryptically the practices of the tribes he met along the way. Some sold their own people; others even their own families. A number of tribes buried slaves alive with their chief when he died, to cradle and attend him in the next world. Women taken in adultery were sold by their husbands, children borne disfigured were disposed of likewise. The Arabs, he noted, liked to purchase those being sold because of witchcraft, since they were least likely to desert for fear of being killed. Slaves were bartered for ivory and sold for a few pieces of cloth. Human beings were expendable. They were collected in ones and twos, or bought in numbers from a chief. They were taken to a market – Ujiji was one of the most famous – and slowly arrived on the long road to the coast, or went farther into the interior.

Burton did not return to Zanzibar until March 1859, and he found it much changed. Hamerton had died immediately after the caravan's departure, his health fast deteriorating as he had waited at the coast. His final words to Burton were that he quitted the world without regret, and he had left little behind. The list of his effects sent on by ship to Bombay consisted of uniforms and wearing apparel, some plate, a new dinner set, a few watches, pistols, telescopes and saddlery. For fourteen years he had been close to great wealth, and his patron would have given him anything he wished, but the only recorded present from the Seyyid was an ostrich, which later was returned to Majid, the new ruler.

* * *

Hamerton's compromise had failed, and in a way it had killed him. To his successors, it proved just as poisonous. The first man to follow him, Christopher Rigby, was a passionate opponent of the slave trade. Shortly after his arrival, Rigby, a highly educated and courageous soldier, deliberately intervened in another rebellion by Majid's half brother, Barghash, and saved the young sultan from disaster. Rigby assumed that, from that moment, the ruler would be in his debt. He was also convinced that he could destroy slave trading out of East Africa, and he told the Zanzibaris so, informing them that Divine Providence had chosen Britain as its instrument to crush human trafficking forever. The Zanzibaris loathed him for his preaching.

Then Rigby's health began to suffer. As he repeatedly went down with jaundice and malaria, he was treated with ill-concealed contempt by the court and the ruling families. He kept a journal and it shows how, as the years passed, he succumbed to overwhelming depression. His employers in India did not share his concern. The cruisers he relied on to police the illegal trade were frequently taken elsewhere. The superstition, corruption and his own ill health began to erode his spirit as month after month he lost ground.

He knew he was failing. He could see the slave ships from the consulate, and he knew his enemies were merely waiting for him to die. Shortly before he finally left the island, Rigby had a last audience with one of the sultan's advisers, who told the Englishman what he thought. The consul had misjudged things, he explained patiently. The slave trade had gone on since the time of Noah, it was God's will and it was useless to attempt to change it. The practice would continue long after they were both dead, a part of the natural order of the universe.

Throughout the middle years of the century, consul after consul was sent to the island. Some were more passionate than others in their opposition to the trafficking, but all found there was little they could do as long at it was legal and while India remained indifferent, reluctant to intervene. None of them remained long, as the illnesses endemic in the island struck them down.

Disease was the Zanzibaris' secret weapon in their conflict with the West. They lived with the island's maladies, and even seemed to understand their causes – the wealthier families insisted on water being brought at great expense from unpolluted wells in the centre of the island, and were obsessive about cleanliness. Others living in the city were less particular and paid a price. Westerners, convinced the notorious local fevers came from a miasma rising from the ground at night, took care to avoid the evening air, but still many of them suffered. And everyone, whether foreigner or Zanzibari, regarded the high incidence of illness as inevitable. That, too, for the Zanzibaris was part of the order of things, and it seemed right that foreigners should be particularly vulnerable. It was evidence of how little the outside world could affect the island's most vital interests.

Hamerton had died before his time, following long bouts of sickness. His successor, Rigby, had to be taken out before the same happened. His successor, Playfair, was stricken down by disease within two years of taking up his post. His deputy, Seward, who stood in for him, in turn became dangerously ill and was forced to leave.

For officers of the Indian service, Zanzibar had become an accursed place. Each agent and consul arrived unaware of how appalling the conditions of the slave trade at this, its nexus, really were; and equally, within a short time, discovered just how difficult change would be. Zanzibar itself seemed impervious to reform. India would always protect Zanzibar to keep out the French, but would never exercise itself sufficiently to root out the slave trade. The patrol by British cruisers mustered only a few ships at any one time, since for the British it was not worth the effort or the money to provide more. The Zanzibar agency had become a posting to fear. Anyone who was sent there was expendable, and knew it.

A month after Kirk arrived, in July 1866, Acting Consul Seward sent an urgent appeal to his employers in India and London. He acknowledged that the Zanzibar economy was growing strongly, something to be encouraged by all supporters of free trade. Yet this growth, he wrote, was inextricably tied up with the continuation of the traffic in slaves. Within the previous five years alone, he estimated some 72,000 slaves had passed through the

Zanzibar Customs House. In words that jump out from the dry, emotionless documents, he begged his superiors to consider . . .

> . . . the death rate, the murder, the rapine inseparable from the slave hunters' pursuit; . . . the social chaos, the disorganisation, the absolute destruction of those conditions which help the multiplication of mankind, and ever advancing degradation of the persecuted race; the kidnapping of the thousands for other countries to which our toleration of the slave traffic at Zanzibar opens the way . . .

Surely, he wrote, no growth in the trade of other commodities could ever justify such a practice.[29]

The British government's response was dry and to the point. Slave trading was legal within the Zanzibar state and should not be interfered with. It was none of their business.

5: DATES FOR SLAVES

*These Northern Arabs are a turbulent race, ready to resist our own
sailors when their slave trading is meddled with . . . The Northern
slave trade is far from being suppressed and . . . the means now
adopted are far quite insufficient to check it effectually. Every year
Arabs of Oman . . . come to Zanzibar with a few dates, clothes, and
other trifling articles, which they exchange for slaves. During the
three months of their stay in Zanzibar they are a constant menace . . .
and should Syed Majid attempt severe measures to stop their slaving,
they would set his power openly at defiance.*

JOHN KIRK TO THE SECRETARY OF THE GOVERNMENT OF BOMBAY,
22 APRIL 1869

Nelly Cooke arrived in Zanzibar at three o'clock on 13 March
1867. She was twenty-three years old, and had not seen her fiancé
for eleven months. When they met again on board the *Highflyer*,
she found herself completely unable to talk. 'John soon came on
board, and came down to me in Captain Pasley's cabin and I felt
rather inclined to lock myself up somewhere or run away. One
always feels so strange at first with anyone you care very much for
that you have not seen for some time.'[1]

She cared so much for him that she had followed him halfway
across the globe, but at first sight Zanzibar was even worse than
she had expected, and on going ashore, crossing through the deep
stench and filth of the beach, she became quite hysterical, and had
to return to the ship to recover. Nevertheless, they were married

the next day on the ship's deck, Captain Pasley gave her away, and she immediately moved into the tiny doctor's quarters behind the British consulate to live with her husband. The rooms were reasonably spacious for two people, but they faced inwards towards the city, and away from the shore breezes. They were intensely hot, the windows looked down on to the busy street behind the consulate, and the noise from people passing below throughout the day and until late at night was constant – the shouting of women, the patter of feet, the wail of beggars, the drums of processions. Early in the morning, the incessant call of muezzins came from across the town, and the evening gun was fired at sunset. Here Nelly began her new life, which was to last almost uninterrupted for twenty years.

A few years later, Kirk took a panoramic 360 degree photograph of the town from the consulate roof. The picture shows an endless jumble of white plaster walls and flat roofs over thin narrow streets and alleys, stretching out to the horizon beneath a leaden sky. There is a mosque, and farther over, the seafront with the fort and the sultan's palace is just visible; between the far buildings, flat water and lines of ships can be seen. One can almost feel the heat and claustrophobia of this intense and introverted town, which so shocked the young Englishwoman.

She arrived when the north-east monsoon was near its end, and the long rains, the *Masika Mku*, about to begin. This was the season prior to the departure of the northern dhows, when the high-sterned ships riding in the choppy waters of the harbour were taking on cargo, and long lines of semi-naked porters stood chest deep in the sea, chanting and passing out goods from the shore. Slaves, shuffling through the Customs House, were tied and manacled in small groups, as they were got ready for shipment up the coast. The streets were packed with a cosmopolitan crowd of extraordinary variety. Cutchees, resplendent in white muslin, with scarlet and gold turban, rubbed shoulders with Persian mercenaries, armed and in embroidered jackets, rough northern Arabs from the Gulf, and Gallas from the African horn. Omani women masked in gilt filigree passed attended by their slaves. On the shore Swahili women caught fish using their under garments as nets.

The rains changed the city. The town's familiar glare became dulled by a heavy grey sky. Great cloud towers built up on the horizon, and crows cawed repeatedly as they flapped away like black rags peeling off the roof tops. Sudden gusts of wind tossed rubbish in the air, played with the veils on the women's faces, rattled the palm fronds and endlessly banged the doors of the houses. When it arrived, the rain was abrupt and violent, falling first in drops like bullets and fast turning into a roaring onslaught of water. In the harbour, the dhows bent like supplicants before the force of the wind, then rose again. The filth in the alleyways was endless, the rubbish and detritus of months streaming in stinking torrents across the ground.

The storms were short, and afterwards in the sun naked children laughed and played in the puddles, maimed beggars returned to mutter and catch at passersby, and the long call to prayer echoed again from mosques across the town. Men and animals crowded once more into the streets. Merchants, *hamalis* carrying sacks, cattle and donkeys, personal slaves and semi-naked Africans from the mainland, all screamed, pushed and thrust their way through the alleys. Women, dark robed and veiled, their finery visible from under the cloth, hurried silently by in small groups through the standing water and the mud. Latrines were emptied into the street, to be swept away by the water. The stench, briefly doused by the falling rain, was overpowering.

It was a world utterly alien to a young woman fresh from mid-Victorian provincial England. Kirk, struggling with propriety, had written suggesting her dresses were a little too fine for the 'rough easy ways in Zanzibar'. Rather than lace or muslin, he had recommended black silk. 'All say [it] is the best by far. It looks well and is not hot and can be kept nice. All the ladies praise it above other things.'[2] So Nelly wore silk, and did everything she could to make her new home as 'normal' and as amenable as possible.

There were between fifty and sixty Europeans and Americans living in Zanzibar at the time, mainly trading people together with a small group of missionaries. A tiny number of them were women. Nevertheless, Nelly immediately threw herself into a constant round of domestic and social activity. She was industrious, and within the tiny western community there was continual contact. She had a house to establish. She acquired linen, she made puddings and she ironed clothes. There was a fierce energy about her as she tried to impose some kind of order and familiarity on her small corner of this profoundly different world, as though she had to create a recognizable life in a place that was utterly unrecognizable. For there was to be no going back. She kept a regular diary, and its clear, neat, strong handwriting is evidence that she was holding her own.

On Sunday, 24 March, she recorded that a Mr Northcote came by for tea, and a few days later, a Mr Ramsbottom. On Tuesday, 2 April, she and John had a beautiful ride through the plantations. They went to church, they took a boat out sailing, and in the evening sang duets with friends; on their own, they played chess. Their relationship was very close – as they rode, sailed and walked about the island, they collected butterflies and plants. Nelly's comments have the innocent simplicity of a woman delighted to rediscover a deep affection for the man for whom she had come so far. After three months, she touchingly recorded her surprise that she had already been married that long.

Her diary tells a story of careful regularity. The external life of Zanzibar is portrayed as exotic and sometimes interesting, but it is only allowed to intrude when entertaining enough to warrant mention. It was never allowed to threaten the rigour of her ordered routine. After that initial moment of shock on the *Highflyer*, Nelly confronted Zanzibar with a will that was unrelenting. John had described to her a way of life that was possible if their marriage was to be a success, and she was determined to demonstrate this was achievable. It was as if together they conspired to make it real, and her journal would be proof that it was working.

On 13 May, a number of Arabs came to see John and they amused her very much. One of them had a squint and used opera glasses to cure it. The following day they went to the palace, and the sultan took her upstairs and introduced her to his sisters and his daughter, entering the royal harem by a special door. They went to an auction where the bidding was all in Arabic, which Nelly found very entertaining. 'The auctioneer got very heated every now and then and screamed at people when they would not bid high.'[3] Nelly's routine and enterprise were indomitable. She darned stockings, she sorted out the storeroom, she arranged the linen, and she went to the mission on Sundays. She walked or rode round the island on a donkey, from which she fell frequently, knocking her head. She visited the sultan's stables. She tried to make ice with an ice machine, but it was a failure. When their spirits were low, she and John picked themselves up with a bottle of champagne, and sometimes Nelly made marmalade.

But of the slave market or the trade in slaves, or the dhows bringing their human cargo up the coast beneath the consulate, there is no mention. They are excluded from her record. She must have seen them, she must have known – in Zanzibar it was impossible to avoid the sight of the tied and manacled people, taken every season from the hinterland and delivered, destitute and in a terrible state, to the warehouses in the town. And Nelly was religious – in England she had been moved to visit the poor who were afflicted by disease – but her husband had told her that unless you can do good, you should not involve yourself, and for his sake she complied. By an act of will, she refused to see what would otherwise have destroyed her peace of mind, what might have made her life in Zanzibar intolerable.

Despite this conventional life, the Kirks entertained unconventional visitors. Some of them were officers on British ships that were employed on the slave smuggling patrol, while at other times, their visitors were men who supported and profited from the trade. Sheikh Suliman, adviser to the old Seyyid and a friend of the British, came for sherbert and coffee, and Nelly liked the old man. It was as if some tacit agreement existed not to mention or acknowledge the brutal traffic. Relationships with the palace were cordial, and all courtesies were maintained, while out at sea the cruisers chased, captured and burnt any ship they caught suspected of trafficking people.

Nelly was resilient and tough, which was just as well since with the middle of the year came the south-west monsoon. The tone in her diary begins to change. She became unwell, suffering from giddiness and fevers, and repeatedly experiencing dreadful pain and bleeding. Then one day there is the bald entry, 'I suffered a miscarriage last night.'[4] She was not alone in her suffering, for in October that year one of her friends gave birth to a baby who died almost at once, soon followed by the mother. In November, another friend, Mrs Drayton, died of disease, to be followed not long after by her husband, leaving a small baby. The orphaned baby then also died. On 10 November, Nelly went to the mission for the sale of the Drayton effects, buying a chest of drawers, a travelling mattress, an epergne, jugs, basins, dusters and lavender water. She had been married eight months.

Other friends left, retreating from the climate. In the hot weather the Kirks slept on the roof, despite the stench of refuse and decay from the beach being almost unbearable. This was the Zanzibar of which every westerner was afraid, a city that destroyed lives with a dreadful inevitability. The ill health it bred was one of its inhabitants' most potent weapons against the incursions of the West. Yet late that year, Nelly wrote that she was definitely staying on in Zanzibar – an entry suggesting she had, if only briefly, considered leaving. The ache of watching friends either depart or die was becoming part of her life.

Nelly kept up the attempt at an appearance of normality for one more year, but as her journal goes on, it becomes evident how increasingly fragile this was, and how, in the end, it could not work. The life of the city around her, which she deliberately tried to exclude because it did not fit into the life she desired, would not be kept out. Bit by bit her routines were being eroded until little of them remained. That was when she stopped writing.

Throughout 1868, she continued her account of an increasingly precarious social existence, although with every month she seems to be more aware of how vulnerable it was. So she played dominoes with Mme Jablonski, the French consul's wife, she took communion on Sundays, she went on a picnic, she walked on the roof, talking Swahili with Sheikh Suliman's wife; and she recorded it all. She adapted; she made friends with Zanzibari women. The violent, dangerous city occasionally intruded, like something just out of earshot, only to withdraw again. In April, she recorded that two of the northern Arab tribes were fighting in the Melinde quarter, and fifteen people were wounded. Later in the year a large fire broke out in the town, and they were worried lest their own house might burn. On 23 May, she defiantly notes that she kept the Queen's birthday, and was 'busy in the morning turning out and arranging my drawers'. In the evening there was a formal dinner at the consulate and Nelly wore 'foulard trimmed with blue loose jacket'.[5]

In June the previous year, the new consul, Henry Churchill, had arrived with his wife, a Moldovian who spoke no English, two children and a maid. Churchill, until recently serving in Algeria, had arranged to swap posts with Playfair, the current consul, who had been desperate to leave Zanzibar for the sake of his health, and for some reason Churchill had agreed. It did not take him long to realize his mistake. By October, Nelly had already written in her journal that the new consul was very sick, and the following May she recorded that he had become seriously ill again.

Churchill's ill health continued, and by September 1868, he was suffering severely, and Kirk advised him to go to Bombay on sick leave, 'it being the cool season there, and not to return until his health had been reestablished'. But within a month the consul was back in Zanzibar 'therefore exposing himself to the hottest and most tiring portion of the year'.[6] His improvement did not last. Soon he was again showing symptoms of illness, and within three months he was prostrate. Kirk commented, 'from that time he has not been able to enter into business or even to pass over the work in a regular manner.'[7]

Henry Churchill's brief year and a half as consul had been wracked not only by fever. Like each of his predecessors, the endemic slave trafficking in Zanzibar had shocked him. He was determined to make an effort to restrict it wherever he could, and the obvious targets were the large numbers of slaves owned and traded by Indian merchants, in particular Kutchees, who were nominally citizens of British India.[8] In early 1869, after establishing with his superiors in Bombay that he had the Governor General's support, he decided to act. Following the end of the festival of Ramadam, he officially informed the sultan that as far as the Kutchees were concerned . . .

. . . although domestic slavery may for a time be tolerated, to a certain extent, amongst those already possessing slaves, all attempts purchasing, selling, or trafficking in slaves shall be summarily put down.[9]

A public notice to this effect was posted at the Customs House. All Kutchees were required to present themselves to the British consulate with a list of slaves in their possession so that Churchill might establish those held for legitimate domestic reasons, as opposed to those who were held for trading.

Shortly afterwards, he was presented with his first case. Late in January . . .

> . . . a native of Kutch was reported to me as having put up one of his slaves for sale in the marketplace . . . He did not deny the fact but laughingly declared that he ignored my power to punish him. I sentenced him to a fine of $500 and to imprisonment . . .[10]

The sultan was furious and immediately sent a letter in protest, and Churchill, already weak in health, prepared to defend his position. But before he could do so, on 13 February, a letter arrived from Bombay. To his surprise, he was informed that he had gone too far, that in fact he 'had misinterpreted the sense of the Governor General's letter . . .'[11] The consul was bluntly instructed to back off, and leave the Kutchees and their slaves alone. The Indian government had no interest in disturbing matters any further.

Churchill was forced to contact the sultan's secretary, visit the palace and make a humiliating climbdown. His mumbled attempts to explain his conduct were transparent excuses, and his authority never recovered. In March that year, while justifying his action, he wrote bitterly to his employers:

> I am afraid . . . that so long as domestic slavery is allowed to flourish the slave trade will exist . . . Until then our endeavours, however active and energetic, will no more keep this trade down than grass will be stopped from growing by being trampled upon. Like rice of every kind it will crop up wherever it has not been thoroughly eradicated.[12]

But it was clear that, as far as India was concerned, the rice and the grass could grow without interference.

Churchill's health continued to fail, and at the end of March 1869 Kirk told him frankly that if he wanted to save his life, his removal from Zanzibar was imperative. On 8 April, Nelly recorded in her diary that the Churchills had finally left Zanzibar for the Cape of Good Hope. On the 19th, 'the sale of the Churchills' things began. A good many people were there. We bought two couches and [an] ottoman.'[13] She was now surrounded by furniture that had belonged to those who had left Zanzibar or had died. That month, she and Kirk moved into the consul's rooms above the offices, because in January, Nelly had given birth to a baby girl. They were desperate for the space, and for the fresh air on the seafront of the building. As Churchill was not expected to return, Kirk had been asked to manage as acting consul and agent until a successor could be found.

Nelly wrote little in her diary after that. Her baby girl was constantly ill with fever, and she was frightened the child might not survive. On 12 August 1869, she made a final brief entry, and then nothing more. For later that year, Zanzibar changed dramatically, and it was no longer possible for any of the small European community to ignore what it meant to live in this turbulent African city.

Following Churchill's departure, Kirk was placed on the front line in dealing with the slave trade, and he could no longer assume this was not his business. April was close to the height of the season. Within three days of the consul's leaving, he was sent a confidential message from the sultan's chief minister.

At about half past one, on the morning of the 11th instant I received private information from Sheikh Suliman bin Ali, Wazeer to the Sultan whose name for obvious reasons it is particularly desirable should not appear, that Northern Arabs [were] now engaged in embarking slaves at a point within rifle shot of the consulate.[14]

The activity was evidently illegal and so conspicuous as to be an open provocation; it was as if an immediate test had been set for him.

Kirk did not hesitate. Immediately contacting the commander of HMS *Nymphe*, a British cruiser that was in harbour, he requested boats to establish whether the information was true. An hour later, two cutters sent along the coast south of the consulate spotted a dhow lying twenty paces off the beach, where a large group of Arabs were guarding a crowd of slaves. The dhow was boarded and found to be already half occupied with slaves. The few Arabs on the ship leapt off into the sea and swam to shore, and a gun fight broke out between the British sailors and the men on the beach. One seaman was killed, and one of the lieutenants commanding the cutters was seriously wounded in the head. Nevertheless, 'under a murderous fire, crept up from the beach the boats' crews, behaving with the greatest coolness and gallantry, [and] succeeded in towing off the prize.'[15] Kirk himself took part in the action, and once the dhow was secure, he began to question the slaves, asking them how they had been taken and by whom. He discovered more than he had expected.

> I also seized thirty private letters the greater part of which proved to be invoices and advices of shipments of slaves with ... charges on them. The consignment was meant for Ras el Had and Jailan, the country of the Beni bin Ali and Beni bin Hassan, subjects to the Sultan of Muscat.[16]

Many of the letters contained lists and prices of slaves shipped in that particular dhow, as well as individuals to whom they were consigned. Some referred to shipments that had already taken place, and many of them complained at the current high price of slaves. One man wrote of the difficulty of being able to execute an order at the present time because of Majid's unwillingness to cooperate with the northern Arab freebooters. The correspondence not only identified the ultimate purchasers of the slaves in Oman, it also incriminated 'several influential men in town'. Once the letters were presented to the authorities, the men were immediately arrested.

Kirk was pleased at this first success. The culprits were smugglers, and had been caught openly breaking the law, while information on their activity had been provided directly from the sultan's own palace. The dhow had been captured *in flagrante*, and the slaves released. It had been a direct and unambiguous challenge, and Kirk had dealt with it decisively, throwing himself personally into the operation. On 12 April he wrote to Gonne, the governor's secretary in Bombay, giving him a full account.[17] He had no doubt that he had been successful, and that he had dealt effectively with this provocation. He seemed exhilarated at the prospect of meeting the challenge, but he did not send to his masters in either India or London an account of the aftermath, for he must have been bitter at what happened.

The northern Arab smugglers actively engaged in the fight had been easily identified – their 'tribe and place of residence in the town were perfectly well known,' wrote Dr James Christie, another European on the island.[18] Yet during the following month, they were permitted to walk about Zanzibar openly without interference, and some weeks later they left the island unpunished. The sultan was either not prepared or too afraid to act against them. The incident must have been a painful lesson for Kirk. He had discovered that combatting the slave trade was not as direct or as simple as he had thought and as acting consul his own authority had proved to be weak. One British life had been lost and an officer seriously wounded, but for what end? Christie later wrote that the operation had demonstrated only how feeble the powers of the British representative really were.

The slave trade was violent, chaotic and totally out of control. The sultan, beyond a few ineffectual bribes, barely attempted to restrict the incursions of the northern Arabs who came south each season in growing numbers, increasing the town's population by more than a third, and behaving with total impunity. The reasons for their annual migration were clear from a letter received by Majid from Sheikh Ibrahim bin Sultan, Chief of the Beni Yaas tribe of Abu Dhabee earlier that year. It referred to the sultan's desperate request to a fellow ruler to control his kinsmen and neighbours, and prevent them coming south, kidnapping and raiding with such terrible violence. Sheikh Ibrahim's reply was not encouraging:

> We did warn them my brother [he wrote] and sent people to tell them and made public your letter, but it will I am afraid have but little effect in keeping them back. The gains are so enormous that it is hopeless to think of stopping them. With ten baskets' worth of dates that a man now gets on credit he can get 20 slaves at Zanzibar worth $1000. God is great. You may punish them condignly if you like by burning their dhows or by putting them in irons but if you do not punish them you had better let them alone for we cannot do it.[19]

It seemed that no one could punish the slavers, and no one could prevent them. The sultan was afraid of them, and they had no consideration for him, but in any case they were only part of the problem. Reputable Zanzibaris might pretend that trafficking was beneath them, but the profits were too high for them to ignore it.[20] Even Majid's own family and many of the court hardly concealed their own participation in the business.

At 11 p.m. on the night of 18 September, Kirk received a message that a ship had been wrecked on the Latham sandbank forty-five miles to the south of Zanzibar.

> The news reached Zanzibar by a small boat which the survivors had managed to save and launch through the surf, and in which five of them made their escape. Their tale was that on the island there remained upwards of fifty men, women and children who for seven days had not tasted water, but found abundance of sea fowl and eggs.[21]

Several had been drowned at the time of the wreck, others had died of thirst. Among the survivors was the daughter of Seyyid Suliman bin Hamed, one of the most senior men in Zanzibar, a relative of the sultan, who had served as ambassador both to London and Bombay. The lady had recently made a pilgrimage to

Mecca with a large number of retainers, and returning to Zanzibar she had chartered a British ship, the *Hyderabad*, which had been caught in the winds of the south-west monsoon. Driven on to Latham's shoals, it had been wrecked, then smashed to pieces in the surf, leaving the survivors desperate.

The sultan was absent on the mainland, but Kirk at once got hold of his wazir, Suliman bin Ali, and together they took a steam yacht out in the dark to search for the wreck.

Having safely passed by moonlight through the reefs and sand banks near Zanzibar we reached Latham Shoal at one pm of the following day. A more dangerous or desolate spot I have never seen ... It is a solitary remote atoll about 300 yards in length rising about 10 feet above the sea level at high water and out of sight of land. No tree or blade of grass is to be seen on it. This barren islet is covered with sand and coarse guano from the sea fowl that are seen to rise in dark clouds from time to time.[22]

The currents were very strong and they anchored with difficulty three-quarters of a mile from the breakers while they attempted to take off the sixty-three survivors who remained, carrying them one by one through the surf. It was slow work, and not until eight o'clock that evening did they have everyone on board. Four people died during the night, and only fifty-five people in all returned to Zanzibar.

While Kirk was assisting the survivors to come on board he came across two people completely unlike all others on the ship.

Two lads of fair European complexion and about 12 years of age at once excited my suspicion, but being observed by arab attendants it was impossible to put any questions to them with a fair chance of being answered, until I discovered that one of them spoke Turkish ...

Kirk, who knew the language, was able to talk to the boy without risk of being overheard.

This lad's story was that after being carried away from Trebizond he was taken to Mecca and there sold to his present mistress, the lady of Seyd Hamed bin Suliman along with several others males and females that she had purchased during her stay in the holy city. As far as I could ascertain all the females (Georgians) were drowned at the time of the wreck.[23]

This was the first time Kirk had encountered the slave trade going the other way – the importation of luxuries, white Turkish slaves from the Caucasus, for use by the Zanzibari elite. The purchases did not come cheaply. Several thousand dollars had been spent on 'this fine collection of Georgians', and individually they had cost between $500 and $1,000 each, infinitely more than any purchase in the Zanzibar market. Kirk was no more shocked at what he had discovered than at anything else he saw in Zanzibar. However, these slaves had been imported on a British ship, and by a relative of the sultan, and Kirk decided it was worth exploiting the incident to embarrass both Majid and the lady's father. Once again, he was to be disappointed.

One of the boys died that night, but on his way back to Zanzibar Kirk called in at Dar es Salaam to report the incident to the sultan, making it clear that to import slaves from outside the country in a British ship was particularly insulting. It was not until 23 September that Sheikh Suliman himself came to the consulate to see Kirk and to express heartfelt thanks for saving his daughter's life. When the matter of bringing in slaves was raised, however, the old man attempted to portray the matter lightly. As a matter of fact, he told Kirk, the Georgians had been freed on purchase, prior to boarding ship in Turkey, which would therefore exonerate his daughter from any blame. Technically, they were not really slaves any longer, he explained, although as they did not understand Arabic they may not have been aware of this rather important fact. In any case, the boy about whom Kirk was so concerned had now been released, so there was no further cause to be worried.

Everyone parted on cordial terms, and Kirk kept his views mainly to himself, but he had discovered yet again that to the men who ran Zanzibar, any agreements on controlling slave trading were of no importance whatsoever. Such discussions were treated with polite disdain, for the law would never be enforced, and no one would compel them to observe it. They knew that.

By now, Kirk had realized how pointless it would be to expostulate, or harangue the sultan and his advisers, on the immorality of their dealings. Others had exposed themselves in this way, and been humiliated. He also knew from his own experience how entrenched in Africa the selling and buying of slaves was, and how difficult it was to prevent. Yet he had still been drawn in – by the temptation of action, having to deal with an emergency, and simply doing his job. Now he was faced with the moral complexities of a situation he had warned himself against. He knew how little support consuls in Zanzibar could expect from their superiors in Bombay. He had seen at first hand how helpless both Seward and Churchill had been, caught between a negligent Indian government and a debilitating, corrupt environment. It was a kind of trap, yet he could not walk away.

However, Kirk's action in going out to Latham's Shoal and rescuing Sheikh Suliman's daughter and her retinue that night must have impressed the Zanzibaris. He had been under no obligation to do it, but had risked his own life for one of their people. They may have considered that this was merely something a doctor did, but they began to see Kirk as different from other British officials who had come to their country. He did not declaim to them on the superior morality of English and Christian ways, or harangue them on the evil of their people trading. He was even interested in Islam. But more significantly, unlike all the others, he did not fall ill.

In late 1869, more people than usual in Zanzibar succumbed to disease. Towards the end of the year, ominous reports had been received of people dying in large numbers from an outbreak of cholera on the mainland. Caravans had even been abandoned by their porters. Several weeks later, the first cases of the sickness were reported in Zanzibar itself.

6: THE TRACKS OF COMMERCE

The epidemic at Kilwa was so severe that slaves were a drug in the market; they were dying at the rate of two hundred a day, and human beings were offered for sale at fifty shillings a dozen, without finding a purchaser. Lots of this kind were purchased at a lower figure by speculators, and sent to the Zanzibar market in the expectation that a sufficient number might survive and leave a margin of profit.

JAMES CHRISTIE, *CHOLERA EPIDEMICS IN EAST AFRICA*

The tentacles of the East African slave trade penetrated deep into the Asian continent, reaching Muscat and the Gulf ports of Ras al Khymah, Dubai, Bandar Abbas, Bushire and Basra. The slaves were bought and then sold down long chains of brokers, dealers and merchants, into the heart of Persia and present-day Iraq. Bussorah and Baghdad were said to be significant centres, where slaves could always be purchased, but the business was largely informal, even secretive, with sales mainly taking place at caravanserai or through private dealers. The trading dhows went up into the Red Sea to Jidda, from where slaves were taken overland to the holy cities of Mecca and Medina, and even farther into northern Arabia. Slavery was ancient, and throughout the nineteenth century it continued to be widely practised across the whole land mass covering Arabia, Turkey and Persia – and wherever there were slaves, significant numbers often came from Zanzibar and the Swahili coast.

Young boys were in particularly high demand because of the constant desire for eunuchs. Due to their lack of family ties, castrated males were regarded as unusually trustworthy, and were employed not only to guard harems, but also as administrators and family stewards. In the holy cities of the Hejaz, they formed a special elite to guard mosques and other religious sites. They were given and received as valuable gifts among the wealthy. However, even among recognized slave dealers, the traffic in *castrati* was a furtive business, and the operation centres on the Upper Nile and in southern Arabia where boys were 'treated' were not widely known even within the trade. For the mortality rate was terrible – scarcely one in ten survived the terrible maiming surgery – but as a result, demand was high, and prices were at least ten times that of an uncastrated boy.[1]

The network to supply the slaves had evolved over centuries. It was enormous, far-reaching and complex, consisting of hundreds, even thousands, of intermediaries across two continents. Beginning perhaps with a Yao trader in a village near Lake Nyasa, the chain might end with a broker in a town in Persia several thousand miles away. Its persistence was due to its very informality, its involvement with the trading of other goods, and a widespread and constant demand from households, markets, small farms, businesses and craftsmen across a vast area. Prices changed constantly, depending on a wide variety of factors, but at the end of the chain local circumstances often determined what the slave fetched. 'The price of slaves seems to be as capricious as that of horses,' remarked one observer.[2] It was a clandestine business and few people really knew how it worked.

It was resilient, perhaps because it was so hidden, and British consuls posted throughout the Middle East were often astonished at how the traffic reappeared in the most unlikely places. But as the trading routes entered into the mainstream of the Muslim world, they coincided with paths used by another, equally old and respected practice – the annual migration of pilgrims to the holy places of Islam.

Mecca especially, where the clerical establishment had resisted every attempt to change ancient ways, by the mid-nineteenth century had become an enormous centre for the buying and selling of slaves. During the holy months, when thousands of pilgrims gathered there, great numbers of slaves were imported through the port of Jidda, and exchanged or sold in the holy centres of the Hejaz. Inevitably, where huge concentrations of people lived in transient camps with little sanitation or hygiene, there was also disease. Cholera, in particular, took hold, following the incessant movement of people. It accompanied the streams of pilgrims as they returned to their places of origin, and it was carried by the slaves themselves.[3]

In Zanzibar, the first warnings came in mid-October 1869 when a caravan recently arrived at the port of Pangani on the mainland reported that thousands of people were dying in the Masai country of northern Kenya. The disease was apparently heading towards the coast. Cholera had come to Zanzibar in the past, but never from the mainland, so the warnings were discounted. 'It is nothing; cholera never came to us in this direction before,' people said.[4] At the end of October, it was reported that the disease had reached Pangani itself, and people were dying there in great numbers, yet still no precautions were taken. When Kirk and others questioned the Zanzibar authorities, they were told that, in any case, an epidemic could never be averted by human means. If it should come, so be it, for that would be God's will. For a month the city had time to prepare, but nothing was done.

It appears that the epidemic had started years before in Mecca itself, accompanying returning pilgrims back across the Red Sea into Sudan and Ethiopia. From there it had spread south down the Nile valley as people migrated, following the elephant and buffalo into Central Africa. Travellers had reported the disease at the great annual slave market of Berbera on the Somali coast, and by 1868 it had reached the Masai country of East Africa, where it met the caravan routes to the coast. Once established on the trade routes of the interior, its arrival in Zanzibar was inevitable, and refugees fleeing the disease only helped to bring it nearer. The city, filthy with sewage, its wells polluted with faeces and its streets blocked with domestic refuse, was already very vulnerable.

In late October 1869, a dhow from Pangani landed on the Zanzibar coast, and the first deaths immediately followed. But the 'Blessed Month' of Ramadam was approaching, and people continued to ignore the threat.

That year, the season was one of the hottest on record. On 6 December, with the appearance of the crescent moon, the festival was announced as normal, and cannons and muskets were fired all over town. The housetops were crowded, and the beaches lined with people celebrating. All night long there were constant explosions from firearms, and from the front of the palace rockets were fired. Families got ready to dress in their festival clothing. They prepared great trays of sweetmeats for the evening feast, and purchased presents for their friends. It was a period of great rejoicing. After dark, people gathered in the streets and on the roof tops to celebrate and indulge after the day's abstinence. Wild dances and great displays of swordsmanship were held in public. Within a few months, many of these same people would be dead.

Another doctor on the island, James Christie, aware of the first cholera cases, was concerned that the fasting could increase the danger to people's health. He approached leading Muslims in the city and attempted to persuade them to suspend the rules due to the unusual circumstances. They replied that all regulations must be maintained, for only by doing so could the people intercede with God to prevent the threatened pestilence.

By January, the disease had become entrenched in the crowded district of Melinde where large numbers of Hadramauti Arabs lived together, sometimes in the same houses as their slaves. Soon the whole area was affected, and every day men and women were dropping unconscious in the streets. Almost every dwelling was touched by the disease, and the mortality levels became dreadfully obvious, as every small neighbourhood cast out its dead. Early each morning and in the late afternoon, Africans were seen hurrying along to the burial grounds on the outskirts of the town, carrying corpses bound up in matting and lashed to the centre of a pole.

Zanzibar became a beleaguered city, as if under attack from a vicious enemy. Daily, its inhabitants were falling in their hundreds, and yet they did not flee or attempt to leave. The city had regarded its right to plunder a continent as God given, and now accepted that it should receive whatever the interior chose to send it. There was no panic. The living tended the sick and dying, even though this in itself was dangerous. The heat was intense, and during the day the city was silent in the burning sun.

The epidemic had now spread to the Khojahs, Muslim traders from India, and many of their shops remained closed. Business at the Customs House was suspended, and men no longer met and talked in the streets. Trade on the mainland had also virtually ceased. In January, it was reported that a large and valuable ivory caravan from Ujiji had been overtaken by the disease, and so many deaths had occurred among the porters that the survivors had scattered, leaving the tusks strewn on the ground.

Slaves covered themselves with white ash, a symbol of death. Funerals, plain and simple, went on every day from morning to night. Small groups followed the biers, reciting passages from the Koran, and when the ceremony was over, waited patiently and silently in the street outside the house of the deceased. Groups of praying parties toured the town at night, chanting and invoking God's help to stay the pestilence and save the living. As they passed down the empty streets, ghostly voices could be heard from inside the houses, praying in response, like an echo. In the graveyards at Nazemodya on the town's outskirts, the sight was grim. The ground was broken up with constant grave digging, and it resembled a newly ploughed field. Thousands had been buried there. The cemeteries were full, and slaves had begun throwing bodies on to the beaches and into the sea. Fresh bones and skulls were scattered across the ground, and decomposing bodies lay at the water's edge, giving off dreadful smells. Packs of wild dogs fought over the corpses.

In December 1869, Kirk had written to Hooker that the outbreak had killed seven thousand people in thirty days. He calculated this was nearly 10 per cent of the town, and the sight of the dead had reminded him of sacks of potatoes lying on a field in Scotland, 'and the disease although diminishing still carries off about 100 per day. There was one day we lost nearly 500 in town, no one knows the state of the plantations . . .'[5] His baby daughter had contracted the disease, but by then had recovered. In late January 1870, the number of deaths seemed to have abated a little, and people believed the worst was over, despite the awful evidence in Melinde. Yet that was the very time when the north-east monsoon brought down the greatest influx of traders and visitors from the Gulf. Zanzibar Harbour was soon packed with dhows arriving for the start of the season, and they became a fresh centre for spreading the contagion.

As May approached, the epidemic took off once more, and so did the season for the shipping of the new slaves. Early that month Kirk informed Bombay that the total number of deaths in the town could not have been less than thirteen or fourteen thousand – that is a fifth of the whole population. On the island as a whole, between two and three times that number had died. He added that 'the upper classes as usual have suffered less, but entire establishments of slaves have been carried off.'[6] The cholera was making it difficult for vessels to put into Zanzibar, and slaving operations, like every other trade, were beginning to suffer. Kirk wrote to Wylde at the Foreign Office:

It has been a dreadful 6 months . . . There can be no doubt that every fifth person in town has perished, but statistics are impossible when we do not know the population. This we do know, that for some time there were five hundred dead bodies taken out of town daily.

Slave prices were depressed, because, Kirk thought, people were too 'afraid to invest in such property while the disease lingers . . .'[7] The scale of trafficking would probably suffer. He wrote too soon.

Two weeks later, the Customs Master, Ludda Dhamji, came to Kirk with an unusual request for help. He was concerned at the condition of slaves being imported from Kilwa on the south coast for re-export. A dhow had recently reached the Customs House after three days' voyage carrying 277 slaves who had been loaded in Kilwa under the usual warrant. No supply of food or water had been provided. Nevertheless, cholera had broken out on board, and by the time the dhow had reached Zanzibar, ninety of the slaves had died. Ludda believed a dying slave woman found on a beach outside town had been thrown from this vessel, ejected to avoid customs duty on entering the port. She was not expected to survive.

The epidemic had reached Kilwa. It was the height of the slave-running season, the pens were full and the slaves were dying in large numbers. Ludda urged Kirk to support him in trying to convince Majid to restrict imports to Zanzibar; otherwise the epidemic would start all over again. Majid refused to heed them. Perhaps he did not wish to countermand his advisers, who had no faith in human efforts to prevent the disease's progress. Many of them, in any case, were involved in the trade, and did not wish to bear the losses. So the slaves continued to arrive. Christie, who witnessed the shipments, described the arrivals at the Zanzibar Customs House that season:

> The dhows were literally packed with slaves as close as they could possibly stand, some of them suffering from cholera, many of them in a dying state, and all of them in a condition of extreme emaciation.[8]

The shippers knew how little the slaves were worth, and during the passage the dead and dying were indiscriminately cast overboard. There was no food or water for the remaining slaves, and on arrival at Zanzibar, the boat's *nakhoda* did a final cull before entering the harbour. Those so emaciated as not to be worth the two dollars duty were summarily disposed of.

> Gangs of living skeletons were landed, with death imprinted on every feature; full grown men and women as naked as at the hour of their birth. On the 4th of May a large cargo was landed from a dhow, and amongst them I observed a woman quite naked. She was carrying in her arms a child of about four years of age; but it was quite dead, and she was apparently not aware of the fact. The upper half of the body was hanging over her shoulder, the arms flapping about, and

the tongue protruding. It had evidently died in that position
a few minutes before . . .[9]

Thousands of Africans were rushed up the coast to Zanzibar that
month under the most appalling conditions, in order to get them
there before they might die. 'The most pitiable sights ever
witnessed by human eye were daily to be seen on the streets in
open daylight,' wrote Christie.[10] But once in the market, few
would take the wretched creatures, and prices plummetted. Slaves
were being offered in job lots of fifty shillings a dozen without
finding a buyer. Speculators finally cleared the market at
negligible prices in the hope of gaining a few living people among
the many soon to become corpses. And still the slaves came.

The epidemic continued into August 1870, when thirty or forty
people were still dying daily, although by then the worst was
indeed over. Kirk never described what he and his family went
through during the conflagration that overwhelmed the city in
those ten months. His own journal is almost silent. As a doctor
his services were required continuously during the period, and his
exposure to the dead and the dying would have been frequent. He
still had his duties at the consulate to maintain, and the strain
must have been intolerable, while the temptation to send his
family away and out of harm, constant. But they survived. Kirk
himself was sure that a major cause of the contagion came from
drinking water contaminated by cess pits in the soil, and so, like
the wealthier Zanzibaris, he made sure his family used only water
brought from unpolluted sources.[11]

Nothing could have prepared either him or Nelly for the
horrors of that year. The devastating numbers perishing every day
all around them, the sheer scale of the suffering, the eerie silence
of the city streets, and the constant fear for his family gave life an
unremitting nightmarish quality during those months – and to a
modern doctor and scientist, such as Kirk, this had been a
nightmare both gratuitous and unnecessary. The reasons causing
the epidemic had not been simply medical. 'Slave dhows have
been the chief means in propagating the disease . . .' Kirk wrote.[12]
Slave trading itself had caused the contagion to spread, putting

the city at risk, and almost destroying it. The links between human trafficking and disease had always been present in Zanzibar, but now they were clear for everyone to see – yet still no one would admit it.

The epidemic altered Kirk, and after it was over he was a different man, more serious and determined. Working in Zanzibar was no longer an adventure for him, or even merely a way to earn his living while he considered alternative options. For nearly a year it had been an ordeal, but now it had become part of his mission in life. He had once written to Nelly that if matters did not work out, they could always chuck it in and look elsewhere. She had known the risk she took in following him to Africa, although not the scale of it; now she found that when confronted with difficulty, and even disaster, he would not turn back. It was as though the situation had been sent specifically to test him. It had become central to what he was.

By mid-1870, the tone of Kirk's letters and of his journal had changed. They seem to have been written by a much older person. In 1869 he had not kept a detailed notebook, and it was not until early 1870 that he resumed making regular entries. No longer the curious scribblings of a passing visitor, his notes were now focused and purposeful. Nearly every day he collected data and information with a relentless intensity. In particular, he was interested in everything connected with the island's trading activities, as if convinced that some secret lay in the patterns and detail of its commerce. Conversations with merchants, the destinations and origins of the dhows, who owned them and the duties they paid, the products they carried, the shipments of ivory from the interior, the motives of those who were involved and what drove them – all this was noted down, clinically and without emotion, then put away for future reference.

Kirk was a good listener, and one senses he rarely expressed an opinion or comment to the merchants and traders he talked to. Standing inside the dark musty shops amid the heaps of marked ivory tusks, some of immense size and often stored for years, the mounds of uncleaned copal stacked against the walls, and a smell of putrid shark, decayed vegetables and sour ghee everywhere, the constant pad of porters' feet in the background, patiently he learnt how this extraordinary city functioned. Sometimes it is possible to catch him reflecting to himself for an instant on what he has discovered, as he stood in the shop or street, scribbling in his tiny notebook. The governors in the mainland ports provided no service for their huge 'subsidies', but the tribes on the mainland charged '*hongo*' or bribes to let the caravans pass – so 'this is another thing', he commented dryly to himself. He was gradually discovering that although the system may have been sanctioned by the protective rituals of Islam, and justified by an almost mystical belief in the Zanzibaris' special destiny, its roots were fundamentally economic. The country was driven by greed and gain at every point.

The person who knew most on the island was Ludda Dhamji, the Customs Master, and from early 1870, Kirk was in constant contact with him. They met often, sometimes several times a week, and Ludda gave Kirk much information as the relationship developed throughout the year. The state of the sultan's treasury, the size and details of his fleet, the revenues of his state, the economics of slave trading – all were passed on in extraordinary detail. Ludda was the country's financier, he controlled its external commerce and he bankrolled many of the caravans to the interior. Nearly every merchant depended on him for permission to trade. He was very rich, and he knew everything.

It is difficult to be sure what the Customs Master wanted from the relationship. However, he had much invested in the Zanzibar economy. The parlous state of the mainland, and its disorderly system of bribes and tribute, concerned him. At the same time, Majid was sick and clearly would not last, and the succession was uncertain. Ludda's trading house of Jariam Sewji had held the contract for managing the harbour and customs for two generations. Every five years he paid an upfront sum to the sultan for the privilege of 'farming' the customs, but the profit to be made from the contract grew even faster than the fee. Between 1840 and 1869, Ludda told Kirk that the customs dues had doubled from $140,000 to $300,000,[13] but these figures were probably understated, since they would not have included the profit from slave imports.

Ludda therefore took both the risk and the profit, but he also had the more dubious privilege of being the sultan's personal banker, and over the years he had lent huge sums to Majid, which might not be recoverable after the sultan's death. So perhaps his growing friendship with Kirk was only a means to hedge his bets. Churchill had left, no one knew if he would return and, in the meantime, Kirk was in charge. He was considerate and discreet, and did nothing in a hurry, and no doubt Ludda, the secretive cautious merchant, appreciated that. The two men seemed to understand one another. When Kirk discovered certain anomalies that seemed to disadvantage British shippers, he informed Ludda he would 'act with the greatest caution, not rashly', and take no decision until he had talked to all the merchants. For Ludda, who had been used to consuls who blustered and threatened and spoke darkly of the power of their masters in India, this was a refreshing change. He quickly agreed to put the situation right.

Kirk knew that, in any case, he could make few threats. The Zanzibar appointment was first and foremost as agent for the Indian government, and he was acting British consul only as a consequence of that. Kirk had little connection with India. He had never been there and was not one of the Indian establishment. If Churchill did not return, Bombay would appoint one of its own. Kirk realized that he had no chance of ever getting the job permanently, but still he persisted, and the Customs Master must have been intrigued at the extraordinary tenacity of this temporary man who was always anxious to know so much.

Throughout 1870, Kirk worked hard at understanding the intricacies of the Zanzibar trade. The Byzantine complexity of tariffs and products, the attempts by merchants to manipulate the system, the constant complaints, the negotiations he was called upon to settle, attempts by northern Arabs to obtain the British flag to conceal their activities, the dodging and weaving and dissembling that so infuriated previous British consuls – all of it fascinated him. He made copious notes on the various weights traders used in the market, and how they manipulated them to cheat in deals. He had an exhaustive mastery of detail and, in passing, he also learnt much about the trade in slaves.

He talked to Ludda and to other merchants about ivory and copal, and almost as a matter of course he talked to them about slaves, too. He did not discriminate, for slaves were merely a commodity like the rest. He made himself think the way they thought; he put himself in their position in order to understand the economics of the business. The merchants knew what the British felt about slave trafficking, but as this non-committal doctor did not preach to them, they were as willing to talk about slaves as anything else. So they told him quantities, numbers, prices, shipping times and seasons, and gradually Kirk built up a picture. He even learnt about the sultan's family, how they were free from paying tax to the Customs Master on slaves ostensibly imported for their own requirements, but how they also traded these without qualms, and were therefore major supporters of the illicit traffic.

Kirk also learnt about the trade from other, more direct sources. In 1867, a Vice Admiralty court had been set up in Zanzibar to examine cases brought by the Royal Navy patrol against dhows captured smuggling slaves to the Persian Gulf and Arabia. As acting consul, Kirk presided over the court, which was held in the front office of the consulate, a large dark room with views out to the sea. The court sessions were informal and held without ceremony, for Kirk knew many of the witnesses personally. He spoke both Swahili and Arabic fluently, and would chat easily to the dhow captains, the interpreters and the naval officers alike. He appeared to have no bias towards one side or another.

The days when the Indian navy had turned a blind eye to slave smugglers on the East African coast had long gone. The Royal Naval patrol now watching the Indian Ocean was initially based in Cape Town, and regarded as an extension of the West African blockade that had been established to prevent slave shipments to the Americas. But the East African trade was very different. Shippers coming south to Zanzibar, and then returning to Arabia and the Gulf, were traders in many products, and they did not always take slaves on a substantial scale. They might carry them in small numbers together with coconuts, hides and shark meat, and anything else they had picked up on the coast. Moreover, the transport of domestically owned slaves was permitted, and so it was often impossible to distinguish between a ship that was a slaver and one that was an authentic legal trader with domestic slaves on board. Slaves were terrified into masquerading as crew, or as domestics belonging to the *nakhoda*, the captain.

In response, evidence of guilt was easily found or even fabricated by the cruiser captains, who were not necessarily scrupulous about the process. Tanks of extra water, bamboo decking or other details were often accepted as sufficient evidence of slaving activity.[14] But the number of ships in the naval patrol were few – seldom more than half a dozen in any one year. Detailed to cover some four thousand miles of coastline, they were easily avoided. Sometimes a major shipment was caught, and the slaves taken on board for landing at Aden or Bombay. On other occasions, commercial slavers would drive their dhows into the mangroves along the shore, beyond reach of the cruisers. Others threw the slaves overboard to drown, to destroy the incriminating evidence. But usually the big shipments got clear. Along the Zanzibar waterfront, information was easily obtained on the location and direction of the patrol ships, and the interpreters on whom the cruisers depended were frequently bribed to lead them astray. Other interpreters were bribed by the cruiser captains to manufacture proof to make captures easier. A cat and mouse game developed with desperate consequences, for in the end it was often the small shipper, perhaps carrying an occasional slave, who was caught and found guilty on the spot, and his dhow destroyed.

For British sailors, bored after months at sea, chasing dhows along the east coast had become a sport. They were fascinated by the strange sea craft, so apparently ungainly and yet so swift and agile. One captain wrote: 'before the wind they sail like witches',[15] and the cruisers competed to catch them. The dhows were game to be hunted, and when a bulging white sail was spotted out to sea 'sweeping down on the wings of a slashing fair wind – joy of joys. Already she is looked upon as ... [a] capture.'[16] Dhow hunting was not only fun, it was also lucrative – a bounty was paid on every ship that was taken. One captain wrote bluntly: 'It is a money question. There are bounties on the tonnage of vessels condemned, and there is head money on slaves rescued.'[17]

Booty was also there for the taking, and once a dhow was overhauled, the British sailors were difficult to restrain.

> The blue jackets clambered pell-mell over their sides, and with drawn cutlasses and bayonets, their ugly revolvers capped and cocked, pointing . . . they are soon in the very bowels of the dhows, rummaging, ransacking, finding, stealing, pilfering, breaking, destroying, and enjoying themselves mightily, regardless of all results . . .

Passengers were violently divested of their finery as the sailors gathered up trinkets, wrenched silver from swords and pistols and looted indiscriminately.

> Silver chains, watches, rings, antique earings and nose suspendors, weighty anklets and bracelets, scimitars, daggers, dangerous flint guns and Birmingham pistols, necklaces and charms, silks and cottons, articles of arab costume from the concubine's silver spangled skullcap to her chemis, and from her lord's turban to his primitive sandals – all taken.[18]

After months at sea, this was seen as every sailor's right. It was all part of a war against the infamous practice of slave trading, and every Arab was considered a slave trader at heart.

A dhow judged in no condition to be towed to the nearest Admiralty court could be burnt on the spot. Unsurprisingly, dhows were usually burnt at sea, and the bounty claimed on 'evidence' presented by the captain. Few questions were ever asked. One officer later wrote with shame:

> The system of indiscriminate and careless destruction of these dhows cannot be defended. From my experience on the coast, I am sure that many a legal trader is unjustly captured.

It was, he wrote, no less than piracy.

I believe many a man has been hanged for doing far less on the high seas than the boats' crews of our ships have been guilty of . . . Along the coast from north to south, we are looked upon as robbers.[19]

In Zanzibar, the sailors were hated, and went ashore in groups to avoid being attacked. The French and American consuls regarded the British patrols with complete cynicism, and it was widely believed the English merely used the rhetoric of fighting the slave trade to plunder shipping for their own gain. There were rumours in Zanzibar that they even freed slaves to take them for use elsewhere. Dhows were increasingly seen sailing under the protection of the French flag, using it to camouflage their trade.

On 26 March 1869, Hamed bin Sahel, a fisherman captaining a dhow belonging to a man of Soor from the Yenabi tribe, was achored off Keonga on the East African coast, when he had the misfortune to meet sailors from HMS *Nymphe*. Earlier that year, Hamed had come down from Arabia to Zanzibar, and then had returned to the island of Socotra off the Arabian coast. His trade was to exchange fish from one place with corn from the other, and that was how he earned his living. Later that season he remained in Zanzibar, and then went down the coast towards Kilwa, catching fish. 'We are fishermen,' he said. 'We had been cruising about, fishing about between Takamungi and Keonga – we were about to return to Zanzibar when we were taken by the ship's boats.'

That day he had been lying off the mouth of a creek. In his boat were a crew of fourteen together with some passengers. 'Then we went to fish,' he repeated again and again, as he stood in the court in Zanzibar, as though this was his crime, the terrible mistake that had caused the loss of all he owned, that moment of stopping on the coast when he was caught and struck down. 'I had no intention of going to Soor, in Arabia that year . . . Last year I sent a hundred dollars to the owner, the profit of our fishing . . .' He had also made $80 freighting corn. It was how he made his money, he said.

He was at anchor, his sail being mended on shore, when he was suddenly boarded by two English boats. He gave his pass to the officer. He remembered them, both the ship and the officer – he had met them earlier in the year off Socotra. The native interpreter, too, was the same. Hamed pleaded not to be put ashore at Keonga – he knew no one there. But when his brother refused to leave the dhow in a canoe, the sailors threw him into the sea, so Hamed reluctantly left his ship. He asked why they were doing this to him, and he was told his papers were not valid. He pleaded he was about to return to Zanzibar to get them renewed. It was too late, they said. His pass was not over a year old, but still they destroyed his dhow.

Sitting in the consulate in Zanzibar before witnesses, on 1 May 1869, Kirk heard all this and took it down. The room was low ceilinged and dark, contrasting with the brilliant light of the seashore outside. The wind was tapping in the trees, and the fisherman was afraid, desperate, having lost everything he owned.

In late August, Kirk heard the testimony of Mr Clarke, the officer from the *Nymphe* who had carried out the capture that day. Mr Clarke told the court that a Portuguese sea captain had informed him that a dhow on the day previous to the event had left full of slaves, and that another dhow was in the creek about to ship slaves, but that it was pretending to be a fishing vessel. They were sure Hamed's vessel was the one, and on examining his papers, the interpeter had informed him they were out of date. On the dhow, there were two water tanks and a large cooking place on the upper deck, which seemed too big for a fishing vessel. They also recognized the dhow as one they had already accosted off the coast of Socotra. 'She had some ballast, a good deal of shark, and pots full of ghee besides dates and arms,' Mr Clarke said.

He told the crew that he was sure the dhow was a slaver, but he would not act on his own suspicions. He would take the interpreter's opinion rather than his own. The interpreter then said she was a slaver. There was some discussion, for the dhow could not be brought alongside the cruiser without her sail. The only option was to destroy her, and Mr Clarke said once again he would take the interpreter's opinion. 'He [the interpreter] then said, "I consider her a slaver, and you may burn her as soon as you like."' So Mr Clarke ordered Mr James Allen, the cox, to set fire to the vessel. It was burning when they threw the man overboard, said Mr Clarke. They did it for his own safety.

However, the interpreter, Ali Saeed, had already been summoned to the court, and questioned on 5 May. He had told the court that the dhow had nets and stone ballast, one water tank and one empty cask, two or three bags of dates, earthern pots, cooking pots and shark flesh. The captain of the dhow swore he was not carrying slaves. He 'said that he would give all he had, dates and fishing nets, but prayed us not to burn the dhow. Mr Clarke said that because the Captain had given a false account of the time he had been at Zanzibar he must be a slaver and that having bought no cargo shewed that he was doing nothing else.' He was no fisherman, said Saeed, 'for fishing dhows are small and this was a large one.' And, anyway, the pass was out of date, so the dhow was burnt.

Then Kirk, who had the pass, showed it to the interpreter, and asked him if he would read it. Ali Saeed refused to do so, and Kirk asked him again. The man still would not and Kirk asked why. Ali Saeed then confessed he could not, for it was written in Arabic. 'On being pressed to read the pass,' wrote Kirk, 'the witness cannot.' Yet it had been because of Saeed's advice on reading the pass that Clarke had burnt the ship. The case for destroying the dhow was shown to be worthless, for Kirk considered the other 'evidence' was trivial. He did not write whether he thought the interpreter might have been bribed to say what he had, but his judgement was unambiguous. He immediately awarded against the Royal Navy, declaring that compensation for damages should be paid to the shipowner, with interest chargeable at 9 per cent per annum.[20]

Some British naval officers were not happy with the verdicts coming from the Zanzibar Admiralty court, and complained bitterly about them. One captain would not abide by Kirk's decision, refusing to return goods his ship had confiscated, and swearing he would take up the matter with the British courts. Kirk was unmoved, and eventually the Navy supported him.[21] However, for the Zanzibaris it was slowly becoming apparent that in this court at least they could expect a judgement to be given fairly.

7: A DISCONTENTED MAN

My brother Majid's wish is to give the country to the English . . . We
however will not give our country either to the English or to the
French or to the Americans or to anyone else; but, if we sell it, we
shall do so only at the cost of our blood . . .

BARGHASH IN A LETTER CITED BY THE ZANZIBAR–MUSCAT
DISPUTES COMMISSION, 1860

In 1869, to worldwide acclaim, the Suez Canal was declared open,
and for the first time the Indian Ocean became directly connected
to the mainstream of European shipping and commerce. The
world was becoming smaller. The average time for mail to travel
between London and Bombay was reduced to just twenty-four
days. Busy shipping lanes crossed the globe with increasing
regularity. The telegraph had begun to link far-flung spots in
almost instant correspondence, and by 1865 the line from Europe
to Persia had already been extended by submarine cable to
Karachi in India. Zanzibar, however, midway between Cape Town
and the Persian Gulf, lay outside the new dynamic of global
communications. It was a distant backwater, hardly part of the
known world, almost beyond regular contact. Correspondence
was sent via ships to the Seychelles, Madagascar or even St Helena,
from where letters were sent on to Aden, and thence to either
India or Britain. Interminable months passed before any reply
might be expected. Sometimes letters were even returned, for

Indian postal arrangements were not always respected, or their stamps acknowledged.

The sense of isolation from the rest of the world was overpowering. In the heavy torpor of the African coast, time seemed to have been suspended, and the only measure of its passing were the changing monsoons. One missionary commented, 'In such a climate, one can understand how people come to lose count of time, and forget how old they are.'[1] Kirk, writing in 1868, was more prosaic: 'We have no mails for four months – a more out of the world place never existed.'[2] Zanzibar seemed to be almost independent of the modern era, with which it had only the most tenuous connections. Its commercial success might have been created in and of itself. Yet in reality the city was far from immune to external influences. The constant growth in ivory trading was primarily driven by appetite from Europe and America. British commercial dominance of the oceans forced shippers from the Gulf to turn more and more to slave trading; and economic growth in distant Persia increased the demand for African slaves. But the indifferent, almost careless protection of the island by the British and Indian governments between them, still meant there was little obvious interference on the East African coast, and so the ancient traditional trading routes of the Indian Ocean appeared to function much as they had always done. Men exchanged dates and cloth for slaves and ivory, as they had done for centuries – only now more so.

There was no obvious reason why Zanzibar could not have continued like this for decades to come. Western travellers came and went in tiny numbers with little apparent effect. Many if not most came to difficult ends, which may have been one reason why the traders of the interior set such little importance by these pallid wanderers. The German explorers Roscher and von der Decken were both murdered, one near Lake Nyasa and the other in Somalia during the early 1860s. The British explorers Grant and Speke were more successful, reaching the great lakes and then returning safely to Europe via the Sudan. Farther east, on the Juba river, following the wreck of the British ship, the *St Abbs*, there had been reports that some of the passengers, male and female, had been enslaved by Somalis. Books and billiard balls from the wreck, together with strange tales, turned up from time to time in the Zanzibar market, fuelling rumours of the horrors faced by white people in the interior of Africa.

Livingstone, most famous of all the explorers, had returned to Africa in early 1866, arriving in Zanzibar in January and leaving for the mainland two months later. But after that he had simply disappeared, and was even feared dead.

He and Kirk had remained on good terms, corresponding in England on Livingstone's return from the Zambesi. Kirk's preferment for the job in Zanzibar had even come directly as a result of Livingstone's recommendation to the authorities in India. But, as ever, the Doctor had borne his own needs in mind. Thinking of his next trip into the interior, he had written to Kirk, 'It would be a great benefit to me to have you on the coast . . .',[3] as if he were imposing a deliberate obligation, one that he would at some time call upon.

Kirk was conscious of the charge. In his journal and his letters to Nelly, he speculated on whether Livingstone were still alive, and shortly after his arrival in Zanzibar, he even went to Bagamoyo on the mainland to follow up rumours about a white man seen in the interior. After interviewing the man who brought the reports, Kirk was persuaded that the white stranger seen inland was indeed Livingstone, but some months later, one of the explorer's original porters returned to Zanzibar to claim back pay for his labour, and reported that the Doctor was in fact dead.[4]

The interior was a dark void, criss-crossed by Zanzibari caravans and traders, a place from where information leaked out irregularly and often after periods of long silence. Rumours, reports of wars, tales of great deeds and of great wealth, much of it contradictory, reached the coast intermittently. The city fed on the stories and the wealth, but otherwise continued in its indolent, exploitative ways. The desultory attentions of Europe it treated almost with contempt. The constant depradations of the Royal Navy infuriated and insulted the people of the island. They sometimes fought back in petty skirmishes with the cruisers when they were caught, but otherwise they avoided them with a skill and aplomb that the British seamen could never quite understand. On shore, British sailors and officers were regarded with sullen hostility, and trading in slaves had become almost a matter of faith.

In Zanzibar itself, there was a conviction that nothing would ever change. The world was thus and always would be, and the continuing trade in human beings, despite every effort by the most powerful nation in history, seemed sufficient proof of this. The inertia, the entrenched respect for the way things had always been done, and the venality of the place, all seemed to be embodied in its ruler. But Sultan Majid was a sick man. His epilepsy, which had left him for three years, had returned, and other illnesses also plagued him. He was repeatedly unwell from malaria, and visitors reported that he seemed prematurely aged. He refused to consider western medical prescriptions, and by late 1869, his health was deteriorating fast. 'He is always weakly, sometimes at death's door, but comes round.' wrote Kirk. 'Still he has the confirmed, worn, anxious face of an old debauchee . . .'[5]

Majid himself professed opposition to the slave trade, but was unable to impose effective controls. His immediate family were active in the business – one slave-carrying dhow caught and destroyed by a British cruiser turned out to belong to his sister. Humiliated by the British navy, tormented by the contempt of his family, and plagued by his own desperate health, Majid spent much of his life out of sight, leaving the daily management of his affairs to his wazir, Suliman bin Ali, a pragmatic man who dealt with the tiresome British as best he could, trying to protect his master, and minimizing the damage.

Most of all, Majid's sense of inadequacy centred around his family in Oman. Ever since Seyyid Said's transfer of his court to Africa, native Omanis had maintained an aloofness, and even contempt, towards their Zanzibari kinsmen. When they visited the island, they ostentatiously held cloth to their faces to avoid the polluting smells and disease. They despised the racial degeneration as Arabs, Swahili and mainland Africans mixed in Zanzibar's growing population, and they disliked the African influence on the country's religious practice. But Zanzibar still had one thing that drew Gulf Arabs south – wealth. Majid himself, longing to be treated with respect by his cousins in Arabia, even toyed with absurd ideas of using his wealth to become ruler one day in Muscat also. When his elder brother, Turkee, was supplanted in Oman by Muslim fundamentalists, Majid helped fund his campaign to regain his throne. Oman, from where his family came, exercised a hold on him. He wanted to be taken seriously there, but in the meantime he neglected his own country.

Moreover, the cholera epidemic of 1869–70 had been a disaster of unimaginable proportions, for a time crippling the city's economy. Yet Zanzibar was resilient. The city and its ruler had accepted the plague as part of the natural order. Trade on the mainland recovered slowly. Slave trafficking, too, recovered, as demand for labour in the north picked up. Things went on as before.

The epidemic had exhausted Kirk, and by 1870 the isolated, introverted culture of the city, together with the relentless pressure of work, were beginning to tell on him. The effort of living through the cholera and the demands of running the agency combined to erode his energies. He had been supported by a European clerk, Roberts, but Roberts had left, and Kirk was forced to shoulder the full burden of the consulate on his own, with only one Arabic speaking 'writer' and eight 'peons' to assist. He was underpaid, since the agency still carried the cost of Churchill's salary, although no one knew if he would ever come back,[6] and the work had increased due to the additional demands of the Admiralty court. Kirk was forced to abandon his medical work.

In April, he wrote to Hooker gloomily that after 'three heavy days as judge in the admiralty court' and a fight with the northern Arabs, he had had not one moment to spare. He depended on Nelly, who assisted him on clerical matters, and 'who is as good as anyone's clerk'. But he was becoming desperate. There had been no time to look at plants, although once the 'slaving season was over' he would do what he could. The exchange of information and letters with Europe had now become a lifeline for him, a guarantee of his sanity, but it was one that was all too fragile. When Kirk heard of a rumour that he had been ill and was coming back to Britain, he responded in a letter to Hooker with hollow sarcasm. 'No such luck that I know of and no prospect either. Of course if anyone in a . . . fit of generosity goes out of his way to make me rich . . . I shall be delighted.' But Kirk was not rich – 'if I had a fortune I would not stay here' – and if he came back to England, he did not know how he would make his living. He had a family to support, and without an income, he knew how hard that was. So he had to remain in Zanzibar. There was no alternative.[7]

His sense of purpose began to alternate with periods of deep pessimism. His work remained unrecognized, and Zanzibar itself seemed immune to improvement. Following the epidemic, he had proposed a system of piped water supply to improve the city's public health, but there was little enthusiasm for the idea, and from India he received minimal interest. Yet despite everything, he continued to acquire plants, sending them back to England. It had become his means of fighting back, of not giving in. He wrote to Hooker in September: 'I enclose two things new to this island's flora I think just to let you know that I have the will,' and during late 1869 and 1870, his need to collect became obsessive.[8] He dispatched samples and specimens with a near religious zeal, sending them off with a regular, desperate commitment.

Even though he knew the timing, and perhaps the certainty, of their arrival was in doubt, between December 1867 and May 1870 Kirk sent back a total of nine consignments, often with long pages of detailed notes, scribbled and written late at night when he was tired and 'dead beat'. 'You can have no notion of the difficulty in getting botanical specimens when unable to select them in person,' he wrote to Hooker. 'I am busy here in town and seldom get out of it any distance. The neighbouring islands and mainland are rich . . . Still I do the little that I can.'[9]

His letters to Kew and the plants he sent back had now become almost a personal justification for his existence. Replies were infrequent, but when they came, they brought snippets of London gossip, comments on the doings of the Royal Society, details of Hooker's reforms at Kew, as well as the arguments in which he was frequently involved. They were like rare bulletins from an alternative universe, and Kirk craved them.

His botany helped him to organize his mind, and it provided him with recourse from his work; it gave him purpose and structure, and a sense of self-worth. It was his way of demonstrating to himself he had not been overcome by the desperate situation in which he found himself, of proving he still had the will. He was still a scientist, engaged in a great project, the classification of the world's plant life. If here, on the edge of Africa, the modern world of scientific endeavour seemed to have abandoned him, he had not abandoned it. And he would not, because if he were not a scientist, at times it seemed to him he was effectively nothing – a mere stand-in for an absentee consul in an African slave port, overworked, underpaid, his reports ignored, destined to remain there forever. In botany, in pure knowledge, lay his only salvation. He clung to it desperately.

It also led to intense frustration. Out there in the hinterland, mountains and habitats might yield riches of which he could barely dream. He asked a missionary friend who was planning to climb the peaks of Kilimanjaro to bring back what he could, and the results, carried to the coast carefully preserved in the leaves of a newspaper, exhilarated Kirk. He wanted to go into the interior himself, to climb those hills and mountains and find out more, but he could not. Instead, he was tied to this Admiralty court, and to these interminably bickering Arabs and Swahili, forced to be passive, to watch and wait, noting and collecting a different kind of data, which might never be used.

After almost nine years in Africa, Kirk realized he had little chance of making an alternative career in Britain; he was trapped. Zanzibar was where he was; it was the work he had been given, and if that was dealing with the slave trade, he had to do it. In early 1870, therefore, he sent back his first major report on the island's trafficking, and into it he fed much of the data he had been accumulating during the past eighteen months. He had obtained from the Customs Master the unofficial records of all slaves imported into the island during the previous season, each shipment scrupulously itemized, vessel by vessel. He also had the numbers, again by vessel, for those slaves who had been exported from Zanzibar and sent north during the same period. All this he put into his report, and he was as precise as he could be, at pains to exclude any possibility of exaggeration.

> These statistics have not been prepared expressly for me by the Arab authorities, but I have had access to the original books of the Customs House and of the Sultan's Secretary. [He added] The Customs Master assures me that few slaves are smuggled into the island without his knowledge and that I may place full confidence in the statistics.[10]

After calculating in detail the numbers of slaves who were taken into Zanzibar and held for local requirements, as well as those shipped directly from coastal ports without entering the island, Kirk concluded that the total number of slaves sent north that season was 13,215. Of these, over 60 per cent, he reckoned, were shipped 'legally' up the coast to Lamu before making the final dash across the Gulf and on to Persia and Arabia. 'The largest exports occur just when it is possible for dhows to pursue the voyage to Arabia and the Persian Gulf,' he wrote – that was at the beginning and end of the south-west monsoon, or from March to April, as well as later in the year during September. He added dryly that bad weather was a far greater deterrent to the shippers than the attentions of Her Majesty's cruisers.

Kirk was characteristically unemotional in his rendering of this dreadful trade. He quoted facts, statistics, data, and he made no reference to the evils of the business or to the suffering of the victims. However, never before had such detail on slave dealings from the East African coast been made available,[11] and the report should have made explosive reading when it arrived back in London. But Kirk could have been under few illusions about the practical impact it would have. Although the East African slave trade was of concern to the British government, there was little appetite for action to prevent it.

There was, however, a great appetite for discussion. The foreign secretary, Lord Clarendon, was a keen admirer of Livingstone's, and in 1869 he had appointed a commission to advise him what should be done. Its recommendations were inevitably muddled.

There was concern that outright prohibition of slave trading in East Africa might ruin Zanzibar's economy, and that the sultan's revenues, power and even throne could be at risk, leading to instability in the region. In considering the matter, the civil servants and other advisers had become confused in their recommendations. Britain, torn between its hatred of slave trading and its desire for commercial stability, chose the latter.

Kirk was aware of most of this. He was in regular correspondence with Henry Wylde, the senior official at the Foreign Office responsible for matters concerning the slave trade.[12] He knew how little London would exert itself, and that from India he could expect nothing. He foresaw endless years of drift, and yet now he had become committed. He had done too much work and come too far with no way back. He had to go on whether he wished to or not, so perhaps it was unsurprising that he began to consider alternative solutions.

Shortly after Kirk's arrival in Zanzibar in June 1866, he had been asked to treat an unusual patient, the Prince Barghash's sister. The prince had twice attempted to take Zanzibar by force, and he now lived, distrusted by his half brother, in semi isolation on the island. Kirk knew and liked Barghash, even though the sultan disapproved of any contact, and had already discussed his sister's illness with him. The lady had wished to try traditional doctors but when their remedies proved ineffective, and 'after suffering at their hands the application of a hot iron very freely', Kirk was finally asked to examine her. Reluctant to take on the case at such a late stage, he agreed because he wanted to help the prince. 'I would willingly do what I can for his sake,' he wrote to Nelly.

That morning Kirk rode out early to see the woman at her country villa, which stood on a hill above the city, surrounded by clove plantations. He crossed the creek into the open country, and passed through village streets before many people were about. The road continued through groves of mango trees, and the early sun picked up the dew on the grass and the undergrowth. A servant sent by the prince ran in front of his horse, clearing the path in advance, pushing people aside 'in a most unceremonious manner, so that I might ride at a trot without anyone standing in the way.'

The woman's house was built of stone, surrounded by a courtyard where the cloves were brought in baskets and laid out to dry. It looked out over the plantations down to the port and the sea in the far distance. On arrival, Kirk was met by the prince himself, who had gone ahead at dawn to be there to meet him, and he was then conducted inside to meet his patient. Kirk was allowed to examine the lady, without seeing her face, but he found he could do little for her since . . .

. . . unfortunately the disease proved to be of a very serious nature and of five years' standing. When small and limited, they had not called in anyone . . . It would be dangerous to promise a complete recovery and in the meantime we must heal the sores caused by native practice and then decide on a further course.

After he had finished with his patient, Barghash asked Kirk to eat with him, and the two men spent a short while together. 'The Prince, you must know, is a great cook,' wrote Kirk. 'He in person superintends the cuisine and I had an ample and elaborate breakfast spread in the upper room.' Barghash had clearly made an effort on behalf of his visitor. A huge dish of rice covering roasts of fowl and joints of meat was followed by a stew of mutton in a raisin sauce. Then came 'a large dish of vermicelli done up in something sweet and oily and a dish of blanc mange made of ground rice'. Finally, the morning was rounded off with 'thick cakes sweetened and cooked in oil, with sesame seed on the top . . . Two huge spongecakes, nearly two feet in diameter, completed the feast and made one drink the sherbet and tea which followed.'[13]

Kirk did not yet speak Arabic well, and conversation between the two men was limited, but over the meal they built on their relationship. Barghash had been grateful for Kirk's attention to his sister, and was lavish in his hospitality. He was different from other Zanzibaris, Kirk wrote – 'a man of energy, determination and intelligence, much more intelligent than Majid' – and Kirk enjoyed his company. He was charming, but also interesting and clever, and during the next three years he and Barghash continued their friendship. After Nelly arrived, Kirk made a point of introducing her to the prince, and Barghash presented her with a Muslim 'rosary' and a beautifully carved Chinese puzzle.

Barghash was certainly clever, but he had learnt his political skills the hard way. As a young man he had tried twice to wrest leadership of the country from his brother, and both times had failed because of British intervention. His subsequent exile in India had left him bitter and humiliated, with a dislike for the overweening manners of the English, yet fully aware of their power. Consul Rigby, who had helped defeat Barghash's second attempt, thought him 'a sullen and discontented character . . . [who] detests all Europeans . . .'[14]

However, by 1866, Barghash had been back in Zanzibar for five years. He was isolated, resentful of his brother's ineffective rule and still extremely ambitious. Nevertheless, he had been forced to bide his time. His position was a difficult one. He knew he could not risk conspiracy again, so when another brother, Abdul Azziz, made a clumsy attempt to supplant the sultan, Barghash stayed aloof from the intrigue, and even under torture, the conspirators could reveal nothing to incriminate him.[15] Barghash knew Majid would not last long, and he had become more disciplined with age. He was pragmatic, and was prepared to build relations with people who could help him in the future. He did nothing to endanger himself.

The British had proved a great difficulty for Barghash in the past, and he knew they continued to distrust him, not only because of his propensity for rebellion. He also had a tendency to keep bad company. He had been influenced by the French when he was young, and had connections with the Mutawas, a Muslim fundamentalist sect with anti-western views who had recently taken over the government in Oman. Previous consuls in Zanzibar had deeply distrusted him. Only Kirk, less conventional than other British officers, did not feel constrained. 'The Sultan resents my intimacy with Burghash, whom he has never forgiven,' he wrote. 'He has prohibited all persons going near his house even saluting him, and even the European Consuls . . . have found it convenient to keep away.'[16] So Barghash encouraged their relationship, responding to Kirk's friendliness with charm and generosity. Kirk continued to find him 'a very intelligent liberal man, outspoken and quick, but a man of energy, and very well disposed to us . . .'[17] He considered the official view of the prince misplaced, and their friendship grew.

Barghash had nothing to lose, and he may have even considered that one day the British doctor could prove useful to him. By early 1870, the two men, although from different worlds, had more in common than might have been supposed. Each felt uncomfortable with the position he found himself in. Barghash, brother of the ruler and apparently living a quiet country existence, was regarded with suspicion by the commercial and social élite of the island. Kirk, acting consul yet officially only a medical officer, occupied an equally uncertain position. Like Barghash, he had to contend with suspicion and ambiguity, and was frustrated at the limitations placed on his ability to act. Reporting to an Indian imperial service that was distrustful of anyone untrained in its own traditions, he felt equally disconnected. Perhaps it was not surprising the two men got on well, and that each may have seen in the other an opportunity for the future.

This was now part of the ambiguity of Kirk's life. He knew there was no chance he would be appointed Churchill's successor if the sick consul failed to return. That gave him a kind of freedom, and he deliberately exploited it. He certainly did things his predecessors would not have done. He had taken a tough stand with the officers on the patrol, which would have brought him credit among Zanzibaris. He had a relationship with the Customs Master that skirted round the evils of slave trafficking. He had a friendship with a prince who had been a traitor, and whose associates were anti-western religious fanatics. He was difficult to place.

Kirk continued to chafe against the uncertainty of his situation. He was informal and unconventional, but he was also becoming cynical, even disillusioned with Zanzibar and the service he worked for. He could make practical recommendations on clean water and public health, but any ideas on larger questions would never be taken seriously, certainly not by his masters in India. At the end of the day, he was only a medical man; he was not one of them.

Barghash, on the other hand, knew that time was on his side. A few years earlier, Majid's eldest son had died, leaving the succession wide open. The young man had been popular in Zanzibar, but had been notably anti-European. Shops were closed, and there was general concern at what his death would mean. In Oman, the Busaidi family had been displaced by fanatics who had clamped down on indulgence of any kind. The Indian traders, who had no liking for the Mutawas, were worried. The succession in Omani culture was never certain – the saying was that power went to him who wielded the longest sword. Barghash, enigmatic and non-committal, was beginning to look the likeliest to take over. At the same time, there were rumours that Consul Churchill might return, although no one, least of all Kirk, was sure. The future was suddenly unpredictable.

Henry Churchill had been spending part of his sick leave in Britain, where the government had asked him to attend the discussions on the slave trade. While there, he had been reflecting on the terrible mistake he'd made on transferring to Zanzibar. His health was fragile, and he knew he could not spend much longer in the tropics, but he was short of money, and concerned about his career. Then early in 1870, Lord Clarendon, the foreign secretary, offered him an opportunity to redeem his fortunes. The Foreign Office was keen on a more robust attitude towards the sultan of Zanzibar on the irritating matter of slave trading, and Churchill was summoned to a personal meeting with the Minister. Once the consul was well, Clarendon said, he wanted him to return to Zanzibar specifically to obtain a treaty from Majid forbidding further slave trafficking out of Africa. Churchill, knowing what this might mean for his health, was reluctant. He had taken only nine of the twelve months due to him for medical furlough, and he complained that the government still owed him expenses for attending their conference. Nevertheless, in February he eventually agreed to go back.

In reality, he had little choice. He knew this was his only chance of obtaining a less demanding post, or even retirement. So later that year, he finally set out for Africa again. By June he was in Cape Town, although his health was still weak and Kirk was unsure whether he would make it to Zanzibar. But make it he did, arriving once more on the island in August that year. 'Churchill has come back staggering on his last legs and uncertain in his temper, poor fellow he has come to a bad place and I wish him safe . . .' Kirk wrote. 'He looks now so ill that I should be almost afraid to go home for any time . . .'[18] The consul was desperate to do what was needed. If he was in poor health, so was Majid, and he was determined to drag a treaty out of the sultan before it was too late for either, or both, of them.

8: ZEALOUS SERVICE

... the mtawas are supposed to be the exponents of the Abathee faith
... the concentrate essence of fanaticism.

HENRY CHURCHILL

Lord Clarendon had been forthright about his policy in East Africa, and Churchill may have been more than a little intimidated by what was expected of him once he returned to Zanzibar. Not only did he have to bring back a full and effective treaty, but there was also the question of the disappearance of Livingstone, whom Clarendon greatly admired. The explorer had not been heard of for many months, and his whereabouts were the subject of constant debate in learned and geographical circles. Rumours from Zanzibar suggested that he was already dead, and the sum of £1,000, authorized by the British government, was to be made available to the explorer, if he were ever located. Churchill was instructed to draw upon the money as soon as he returned; Clarendon wanted an urgent update on the Doctor's progress – a matter 'which is of the deepest interest to HM's Government'.

However, the slave trade was really the issue. 'You are well aware of the anxiety of HM's Government to drive this horrible trade from its last stronghold on the east coast,' the foreign secretary wrote, and then proceeded to dictate to Churchill just what he expected. He was to tell the sultan that all slave exports from the

159

coast of Africa should henceforth be limited to one port so that shipments could be carefully regulated and monitored. Numbers were also to be restricted specifically to the existing needs of the inhabitants of Zanzibar and the other offshore islands. In this curious way, the Foreign Office believed it had finally devised an elegant solution to the problem, one that would reconcile fairness to an old ally with humanity, and commerce with principle. Gradually, in time, the traffic would thus be eradicated, and everyone would be satisfied. In the process, Clarendon insisted, it was important that the sovereign and people of Zanzibar were treated 'with all the consideration due to an independent and friendly state'.[1]

How this was to be achieved was left to Churchill to decide. In the most unlikely event that His Highness were to resist such a sensible solution, Clarendon went on, 'you must remind him that he is now the only sovereign who openly permits the traffic in slaves by sea, with all its attendant horrors, to be carried on . . .'[2] Zanzibar, one of the last places in the world where slave trading was legal, had become an affront and an embarrassment, but Clarendon still hoped to achieve by moral admonition what the naval patrol had failed to deliver by force.

Churchill was under no illusions about the problems he would face, but this was a last opportunity for him to get his career back on track. Having decided to return to Africa, he wrote plaintively to Clarendon that he hoped he would not have to spend long there. He was returning solely in order to persuade the sultan to agree to the suppression of slave trading. Once that object was accomplished, he trusted the foreign secretary would take his past services into account, and find him a more congenial posting. He had, after all, held successive positions in Bosnia, Moldavia, Beirut and, finally, in Algiers, where it seems matters had not worked out too well, inducing him to make his disastrous swap with Playfair. 'My exchange with Colonel Playfair was a mistake, but it was done with no other motive than that of placing myself in a position to render services of some value to Her Majesty's Government . . .'[3] But the mistake had been made, and the government now wanted more service.

Churchill set to work as soon as he arrived back in Africa, immediately presenting his suggestions for a new treaty to Majid. During late 1870, he did all he could to persuade the sultan to consider his proposals, and the sultan did everything he could to evade them. When the consul pressed for an answer, Majid dodged the question by bringing up the tangled politics of Oman, where his family had been displaced by usurpers. Would the British government turn a blind eye if he mounted an invasion to restore his family, he asked? Churchill, frustrated, tried to deal with this tactfully. Naturally, the British did not wish to see a Zanzibari expedition into the Gulf, he replied, when their whole policy was to reduce conflict there. But, responded Majid coyly, what if the expedition were raised secretly, without the British knowing.

The subsidy that Majid paid annually to the ruler of Oman as compensation for inheriting Zanzibar was also brought up. Why should he continue to pay this now that the country had been forcibly taken over by people of whom he disapproved, he inquired, causing further delay to the discussions. Majid was spending more of his time at Dar es Salaam on the mainland, where he was difficult to contact, and there was also the question of his poor health, which frequently prevented him from responding. When Majid did return to Zanzibar that September, he once more succumbed to a bout of fever, and was weakened by further epileptic attacks. Shortly afterwards, he almost died.

Churchill began to worry; his own health was worsening, and he was forced now to consider alternatives. The most likely contender to the succession, Barghash, he neither knew nor trusted. A few weeks after his return, he had noted to India that the prince had been giving 'evident signs of increasing fanaticism' due to his association with the same fundamentalist sect that had taken over in Muscat.[4] Bombay had no love for the Mutawas and Churchill had purposely kept away from the prince since his return, yet it was clear Barghash was preparing for a change in circumstance. He had recently made an advantageous marriage, putting significant sums of money at his disposal in the event of a struggle, and he 'seemed to enjoy the prospect of coming to the throne', Churchill wrote.[5] Desperately hoping to avoid such a disaster, he watched impotently as the sultan gradually declined in health.

Then, on 6 October, Kirk was asked to go to the palace together with the French doctor who had been treating Majid. They found the sultan exhausted, refusing to take quinine, and Kirk thought him unlikely to survive a renewed bout of fever. Early on the morning of 7 October, it was reported that Majid was 'in his last agony' and not expected to last long.

This was not a crisis for which Churchill had prepared. He thought of the other claimants to the throne, but they were too young. He discussed the matter with Kirk, and reluctantly agreed to invite Barghash to come to a secret meeting to discover what his intentions were. Kirk went to contact the prince, and at the same time Churchill requested Commander Blomfield of a visiting British ship, HMS *Teazer*, to remain in port, and even come closer to shore. It was a feeble attempt to keep up pretences, and to maintain the initiative.

Barghash came round at once to the consulate, and he, Kirk and Churchill talked together.

> I spoke very plainly to the Prince [wrote Churchill] and told him that I required to be assured before I pledged myself to back his candidature that he would be friendly towards England and would not revert to bigotry or to mutawa principles with which HM Government could have no sympathy.[6]

Barghash readily agreed, promising that once he was in power he would do nothing without first consulting the British. He would naturally respect all debts to British traders and, most important-ly, he promised to assist the British in the suppression of the slave trade. 'All these he promised,' Kirk noted in his journal. 'He then retired and in an hour, on the death of Majid, went to the palace as chief mourner.'[7] Yet Churchill was still worried, and drawing up an account of the crucial conversation, he got Kirk to countersign it. It was as though he wanted a record to excuse himself in case events should not go to plan.[8]

Majid died later that day, on 7 October. Churchill immediately met Barghash, accompanied by Blomfield as though to emphasize the reality of British power, and formally congratulated the prince on his succession. The wazir, Sheikh Suliman, went to inform the troops of the change in the head of government, and the town was quiet. Churchill, relieved, wrote to Bombay and London:

The decided attitude of this Agency with regards to the succession of Seyid Burghash has closed the mouths of many who were inclined to reject his candidature.

He allowed a note of self-congratulation to enter his tone.

In reality there was not a single man in Zanzibar who could have opposed him with success, while the Prince was made to understand that he himself had no chance if Her Majesty's government were against him.

Two other circumstances helped to seal the arrangements, Churchill thought. The presence in port of a Royal Navy cruiser projected overwhelming British authority, while the astounding news' of the French military defeat at Sedan reached Zanzibar at the same time.[9] He was pleased at his success.

Churchill also paid tribute to Sheikh Suliman. Without his timely information on Majid's failing health, Churchill wrote, he would not have been able to take such decisive action. 'As it is, a peaceful succession has been secured and the new sultan has pledged himself to do everything in his power to be agreeable to the British . . .'[10] He had also pressed ahead with the first steps in tutoring this inexperienced new ruler. He sent Barghash a message that he considered it appropriate for him to write immediately to the Queen, and to the Governor General of India. He was convinced he had done everything necessary.

He was soon to be disabused, however, because it was not he who had manipulated Barghash, but the other way round. Three days after his letter of quiet self-approval, Churchill was forced to report that 'on the subject of Zanzibar politics, matters have developed themselves unfavourably. Barghash has thrown off the mask . . .' Gloomily, he reported that almost at once the new ruler had revealed where his principle loyalties lay, which were to 'the fanatical party of which the headquarters are in Muscat. A council of priests is to direct the affairs of state, the law of the Koran is to be revived . . .'[11] Moreover, it was clear that all promises regarding the suppression of the slave trade were to be repudiated. Churchill had seriously miscalculated, and he knew that both in Bombay and London, his letter would be read with dismay. Zanzibar falling into the hands of the same fundamentalists who ruled Muscat would be badly received by the authorities in India. From London's point of view, however, the slave trade was the big issue, and Barghash now seemed a worse bet on that score than his brother had ever been. Churchill stood guilty of actively facilitating this desperate turn of affairs.

Aware of how his actions would be regarded, the consul now began to panic. Knowing of Kirk's personal relationship with Barghash, he sent him round to talk to the new sultan, but Barghash the ruler was unyielding. Churchill then sent a formal letter. 'I did not think that it would be my painful duty so soon after your accession to the throne vacated by your brother, to remind you of certain pledges . . .' he wrote.[12] It was 11 October, and Barghash had been in his new job for just a few days, yet this British official was already lecturing him on what he should do, even threatening to report him to his government if he did not behave. Barghash sent a reply the same day. It was courteous, but equivocal.

> Your letter has reached me and your friend has understood what you said namely that I pledged myself to you with reference to what you want, I do not recollect it, for if even the question referred to at the time were in my hands, I could not have promised you its fulfilment before calling together the great men of the state from all parts of the country and taking their advice, and was this possible when my brother Majid was still alive?[13]

Barghash was skilfully evading the question. Surely Churchill understood that in accordance with Omani tradition, a ruler did not wield absolute power, but was dependent on others for his authority? He was also telling the consul, subtly but clearly, that the game had changed. The conversation they had had in the consulate on 7 October did not happen because it could not have happened, since logically he had not been in a position to have such a conversation. This reasoning was beyond Churchill. All he knew was that he had been duped, and he was angry. He began to dash off letters to his superiors in India to show that he was dealing with the situation, sending them almost on a daily basis, for he knew he was running out of time. Clinging to the idea that it was he who had put Barghash in power, he now suddenly proposed ejecting him. The new sultan could not be relied upon, and therefore 'how desirable it would be to unseat him on the first pretext', by force if necessary.[14] His suggested replacement was the senior member of the Busaidi family, Seyyid Turkee, who had never left Oman, and was at the time trying to wrest back control of his family's position there. Churchill decided that he might as well be offered Zanzibar as well, with British assistance.

The idea was not only absurd, it showed how desperate Churchill was. He had been outmanoevred by Barghash and was now frantic to find a solution, no matter how impracticable. Meanwhile, the new ruler began to treat the consul with polite contempt. He was aware that Churchill could not last long, and his tactics were clear. Kirk wrote pessimistically in a letter to Hooker that the consul's deteriorating health was obvious to anyone who met him. 'I fear . . . the Arabs can read [it] in his face.' They had only to maintain pressure on him 'by delay so as to let disease work its way'.[15] Nevertheless, Churchill continued to blunder on, insisting plaintively that the sultan confirm his adherence to previous treaties. Barghash, moving quickly to consolidate his power, ignored him.

Responding to Arab resentment at the way Indian merchants had moved into the lucrative clove business, he issued new orders depriving Indians of their rights to trade and farm cloves in the Zanzibar countryside. Street criers went round the town, beating on a buffalo horn, calling out the new rules so that all might hear. Many of those penalized were British Indians, so Churchill, antagonized further, wrote again to Barghash to complain. Barghash replied urbanely that the traders had been inciting slaves to steal cloves from their Arab masters. Churchill responded that they were British subjects, and therefore subject to British consular authority. Treaties, he demanded, must be maintained. Barghash informed him that this was a domestic matter, a question of satisfying local grievances, with which treaties were not concerned.

Churchill, sick and increasingly desperate, continued to ignore Zanzibari sensitivities. It never occurred to him that Barghash could not allow himself to be bullied like this during the first few weeks of his rule. So throughout late October and early November, sometimes twice a day, messengers went running back and forth along the Zanzibar seafront between the sultan's palace and the consulate half a mile away, carrying letters between the two men. Churchill, hoping to force the sultan to back down, continued to harass him by citing treaties and by threatening force. But Barghash had not studied this particular game for decades without preparing for such a moment. He understood his opponent's weakness, and the rights or wrongs of treaties had nothing to do with it. The British warship had departed, the consul was sick, and Bargash calculated that having backed his succession, it would not be easy for Churchill to reverse the situation. He took his time replying to Churchill's letters. He was busy winding up the estate of his late brother, he wrote. He had other things to occupy him, without spending time on such trivial matters.

Infuriated by these insults, Churchill finally attempted to confront the matter head on, and went to address Barghash directly in his council chamber. Bringing a letter from Lord Clarendon, the sick consul went down to the palace and informed Barghash, in front of his advisers, that 'his independence was in peril' if he did not do what he was told. It was a courageous act, but Churchill's heart was no longer in the struggle. He was fighting for his self-respect and for credibility with his employers. Barghash understood his position far more clearly than he knew. To the consul's surprise, he was given short shrift and the letter dismissed out of hand. But he still hadn't learnt, and so he played his last card, and openly threatened Barghash with force. The might of the governor of Bombay was invoked. Antagonized by such disrespect in his own court, the sultan declared, in front of his council, 'in a towering voice that he was not under his [i.e. the governor's] orders and did not know nor care for the man.'[16]

Churchill was giving his opponent every chance not only to demonstrate his independence but also to enhance his standing in front of his supporters, but the consul continued to blunder. On 10 November, the previous sultan's wazir, Suliman bin Ali, came to ask Churchill for help. His position as secretary and chief adviser had been taken from him, and he was now threatened with seizure. Churchill agreed to accept him into British employment, which would put him beyond arrest. Barghash was furious. He regarded the consul's actions as overt interference in Zanzibari affairs. Suliman bin Ali, he wrote, 'was in the service of our father and our brother and our own after the death of our brother Majid and we have not dismissed him. We do not consequently consent to your taking him in to your service. It was wrong of you to do so . . .' The consulate was surrounded by troops, and officers were sent to arrest the former wazir, cowering within. Churchill sent a letter to the sultan protesting that if the troops were not withdrawn, he would lower the British flag, and Barghash unwillingly pulled back his men.[17]

Inside the consulate, the atmosphere was becoming tense. Each day, senior Zanzibaris were being arrested and sent to the fort for the slightest offences against the Mutawa council. Meanwhile, Churchill, knowing how his conduct would appear in Bombay and London, was rapidly losing confidence. On 12 November, HMS *Teazer* returned and anchored offshore opposite the palace, but she had no instructions to threaten the city and nothing happened. Churchill anxiously discussed with Kirk whether one or other of them should depart for India to obtain instructions, but Kirk was sceptical. If Churchill left, it could be misinterpreted as giving in, and the *Teazer* left again for the Seychelles. Barghash knew then that he had finally called his opponent's bluff. Later that month, he wrote again to Churchill. 'The purpose of this letter is to inquire after your health. We hope that you are well and we have learnt from our mutual friend Ludda that you shortly purpose leaving for Bombay . . .'[18] Outwardly polite, the tone was sarcastic, for Churchill was far from well, and Barghash knew it.

By late November, Kirk had realized that Churchill's tenure in Zanzibar was impossible. The consul's health was deteriorating fast. Physically emaciated, he was sleeping through much of the day, and vomiting continually.

> In the morning he comes down stairs at 8 a.m. and is placed in a bath but can hardly move about from one place to another without help. Commonly after a bath he is prostrate and rests. By and by vomiting or rather nausea which he brings to vomiting by placing his finger in his throat sets in. Then he gets an injection . . . and sleeps.

He was unable to complete any work, and the slightest effort exhausted him. He could not hold down food, and in early December, Kirk wrote, he was 'losing flesh daily'.[19]

The consulate was isolated. The sultan had forbidden anyone to contact them, and relationships within the beleagured building were breaking down. There was 'marked coldness' between Kirk and Mrs Churchill. Perhaps she blamed Kirk for misadvising the consul. Although she was desperate about her husband's failing health, she refused to let Kirk see him alone, even threatening to lock the door against him. Kirk was instructed to communicate with Churchill only by letter, but Churchill, prostrate on the roof of the building, was incapable of taking a decision. Afraid to leave his post lest it seem desertion, and afraid to stay lest he die, he held on day by day, at times barely conscious. Finally, the French doctor, MacCauliff, was called in to confirm Kirk's diagnosis, and he was adamant that Churchill had to leave Zanzibar immediately if he wished to survive. He was taken off by ship a few days later.

Barghash had won through a combination of guile and astutely negotiated alliances, but once again, Zanzibar itself had played its part. Churchill was the fifth agent to fall victim to the diseases endemic to the island. Days before he left, he sent a final valedictory letter to his superiors.[20] Sick and bitter at what had happened, he tried to place blame for the disaster entirely on the new sultan, citing his deep 'spirit of animosity' towards the British. Expressing his conviction that only force would bring Barghash to heel, at the same time he hit out at the two demons who preoccupied politicians in London and India: the rich Arab slave traders and the Muslim Mutawa fanatics who plotted 'the downfall of everything European'. Together they had Barghash completely under their control. The letter, confused and contradictory, never reflected on why Barghash acted as he did, and Churchill never considered for a moment that he may have contributed to the fall-out.

A few days later, Kirk and his family moved from their cramped rooms at the back of the consulate into the official quarters once more, and again he prepared to become the acting consul – a medical officer with partial authority and uncertain status, and a man who would at some stage be replaced. He had already experienced the difficulties of working without official recognition, but he knew that recent events would hardly have endeared him to his superiors in India. In Bombay, officials had been appalled at Churchill's miscalculation, and in December had sent him a strong rebuke. The consul's response to the crisis had been 'precipitate and injudicious', and he should have thought further before supporting Barghash so openly. His conduct was to be referred to the governor general of India.[21]

By then Churchill had gone, but Kirk had no illusions that he would not be regarded with similar disapproval, for they would guess that he had been party to Churchill's decision. He could only hope for support from London, and on 12 December he wrote:

> Having thus again taken charge of the office of agent and consul, I have respectfully to suggest that my having done so may be duly notified, in order to avoid those technical questions that formerly arose as to the solidity of certain acts done by me . . .[22]

But London could give him little reassurance. To them, he was an Indian problem.

* * *

The developments of the previous few weeks had been a shock to Kirk. He had trusted Barghash, and he had been deceived, and even made to look a fool. The new sultan had, ironically, taken Kirk just as he presented himself, a diffident and apolitical doctor, uninterested in policy, and he had exploited their relationship to get what he wanted. Indeed, Barghash did not seem to think his conduct would damage their friendship in any way, for when Kirk called upon him in mid-November at the height of the quarrel, the sultan was quite happy to meet and talk on a purely personal basis. At the same time, Nelly went to see the sultan's wife 'and was well received'.[23]

Barghash clearly thought that Kirk was irrelevant to the conflict, and Kirk was forced to swallow his pride, but from that moment, his attitude towards the sultan changed. He was not going to allow himself to be deceived again, and he no longer considered Barghash a 'jolly fellow', as he had once described him. Outwardly, he remained friendly and conciliatory as though nothing had changed, but in private his comments became cynical and calculating. If Barghash had exploited their relationship, he was capable of doing the same. The guise of unthreatening doctor was still a useful one, and he too could mask his true intentions.

In the weeks after Churchill's departure, Kirk began to study the sultan closely, analysing his political situation, his motives and his weaknesses. He followed in detail the arrests that Barghash was making, noting in his journal how they made the new sultan even more dependant on the Mutawas – 'a somewhat dangerous step', he thought. And he began to plan for the future. In early 1871 he wrote to London:

> Taken as a whole I am not sorry at what has happened as we shall if we play our cards . . . make better terms than we could have done with so available and easy a promise as Seyid Majid.[24]

It was an attempt to reassure his superiors while he reassessed the situation, but he was franker in a letter to Hooker – 'He [Barghash] is a man of very peculiar temper and luckily I knew him well long before he became Sultan.'[25] Nevertheless he thought he could handle the situation, although it would not be easy, for it had become a kind of game. Everything Kirk did now was deliberate. He played on his old relationship with the sultan, using it to rebuild confidence, but outwardly he was pretending, just as Barghash had done with him.

The tactics soon produced results. In December he wrote:

> Since taking over charge subsequent to Mr. Churchill's departure HH Seyed Burghash has shown a marked change in his attitude and bearing towards this Agency.[26]

With Churchill gone, Barghash thought himself free of the British for a while, and Kirk did not disillusion him. No longer under the barrage of constant threats, the sultan was able to relax, and even use Kirk's advice.

> Not only have the arbitrary and unjust acts of himself and fanatic councillors to British subjects been set aside, but these very cases have been placed in my hands for settlement and HH has shown himself peculiarly anxious to do nothing that could be taken as a slight by me.[27]

For Barghash trusted his old friend, and in any case he had other matters to preoccupy him. He had consolidated his power through the influence of a small group of Muslim fanatics, who now had undue leverage. Senior members of the Arab community had been sidelined, and one of the princes had been imprisoned 'with heavy chains on his hands and feet'. The Mutawas were demanding a stiff price for their support, and changes were made to the law to conform to their doctrines. But the more austere religious observances were not to everyone's taste, and Kirk thought he saw fissures beginning to develop among Barghash's friends. Churchill had talked of Barghash throwing off his mask to reveal his true self, but Kirk reckoned the sultan was still dissembling. '[I] have good reason to believe that he is [still] acting a part,' he wrote.[28] He was sure that Barghash's alliance with the Mutawas was opportunistic, and that they would prove unpredictable friends. In the meantime, he was prepared to wait. In early 1871 there was other business to attend to, business that had been left unfinished when Churchill departed so hastily the previous December, and that, during the drama of Majid's death and Barghash's succession, had inevitably received little attention – the not unimportant matter of David Livingstone.

In December 1866, a number of deserting porters from Livingstone's expedition had arrived in Zanzibar claiming the explorer was dead. Kirk had met them and, believing their story, had reported back to the Royal Geographical Society whose president wrote to *The Times* on 7 March confirming the explorer's death. Almost a year later, a slave attached to an Arab trading party, as well as others from the interior, reported that the Doctor was still alive somewhere in the vicinity of Lake Nyasa. This was confirmed when, in August 1868, letters written by Livingstone the previous year arrived in Zanzibar. They were received by Churchill, who sent a consignment of supplies to Ujiji, where the main route into the interior reached Lake Tanganyika. There they were to await the explorer.

A year later, in October 1869, Kirk had received a further request for additional supplies, which were duly sent with a caravan of fifteen men. The cholera epidemic had been raging at the time, and although the caravan was dispatched, Kirk knew that five of the men had died before reaching the inland station of Kutu. The remainder were supposed to have continued but nothing further was heard of them.

Continued cholera on the coast had prevented sending immediate replacements, but in November 1870 Churchill had managed to send more supplies inland. Then on 6 January 1871, not long after Churchill's departure, an American journalist arrived in Zanzibar, and set about making preparations to travel into the interior. He was ambiguous about his reasons for venturing there, but said he represented an American newspaper proprietor, James Gordon Bennett. He was well funded for his purpose, and soon after his arrival he contacted Kirk. The two of them discussed shooting, an interest they had in common. His name was Henry Morton Stanley.

Part Three

BEGGAR ON HORSEBACK

Slavery is a great evil wherever I have seen it. A poor old woman and child are among the captives; the boy, about three years old, seems a mother's pet: his feet are sore from walking in the sun. He was offered for two fathoms, and his mother for one fathom: he understood it all, and cried bitterly, clinging to his mother. She had, of course, no power to help him; they were separated at Karungu afterwards.

DAVID LIVINGSTONE, 28TH JULY 1867,
THE LAST JOURNALS OF DAVID LIVINGSTONE

At Zanzibar the slaves generally change hands. There is a considerable exchange of refractory or idle island slaves for more docile importations, and much money is earned by residents who make it a business, as it were, to break in fresh arrivals, or to feed up cheap slaves and make them more marketable.

BARTLE FRERE IN HIS REPORT TO LONDON

9: THE GATHERERS OF WEALTH

Ivory is like grass – this is great news for Suahili . . .
LIVINGSTONE TO KIRK, 14 MAY 1871

On 14 September 1867, Zanzibari trader Hamees Wodim Tagh waited impatiently in his camp for the peace offering he had been promised following the recent battle. After months of stalling, skirmishing and negotiation, he and his allies had attained a significant victory. They had finally defeated Nsama, the most important ruler in the region to the south west of Lake Tanganyika. Now there was little to stop them moving deep into the forests of Katanga, and opening up valuable new sources of ivory. A European travelling with Hamees wrote:

> The entire population of the country has received a shock from the conquest . . . and their views of the comparitive values of bows and arrows and guns have undergone a great change. Nsama was the Napoleon of these countries; no one could stand before him; hence the defeat . . . has caused a great panic.

Finally, the promised offering arrived, carried on a man's shoulders. One of the great chief's daughters was to be given in marriage to the Arab. She was a 'nice, modest, good looking young woman, her hair rubbed all over with nkola, a red pigment, made from the cam-wood, and much used as an ornament.' Accompanied by a dozen female attendants, she was welcomed by the Zanzibaris and their slaves. Dressed in fantastic clothes and other finery, they yelled, flourished their swords and let off guns as she arrived, and when she was brought to Hamees' hut, she descended and went inside with her maids. Hamees, a dignified man who had been sitting waiting for her, rose then, and as he did so, he muttered quietly to himself, 'Hamees Wodim Tagh! See to what you have brought yourself!'[1]

The European who observed this scene was David Livingstone, and he had been travelling with the Arabs for several months. During the past year, he had frequently been desperately sick and weak, without necessary drugs or medicine, and only the attentive support of various Zanzibari traders along the way had saved him from dying. At times delirious, confused and fatalistic, he had managed slowly to recover under their protection, for the unstable nature of the surrounding country made it unsafe for him to travel on his own. Tied to the Arab caravans, his progress had been slow. They moved in great numbers, often consisting of well over a thousand men and women, including huge parties of slaves. They often stopped for weeks while the leaders debated on the best districts for trading, which chiefs were reliable and where the finest ivory was to be found.

In their remorseless search for the valuable tusks, by the late 1860s the Zanzibaris had reached the centre of the continent, and were poised to cross the watershed into the river valleys flowing west to the Atlantic. But Nsama was not the only ruler who interrupted their progress. Farther north, King Mutesa of Buganda maintained a suspicious independence, restricting Arab penetration of his country, while to the south, the Mwata Cazembe had held one of the leading Arabs in his capital as a kind of hostage for twenty-five years. Such powerful rulers would not be easily displaced, and the traders preferred to reach an accommodation with them if at all possible, for conflict was fraught with risk. They treated the despots as equals, flattering them, and the formalities when they met were elaborate and often went on for months.

The kings and rulers flaunted their power. When Livingstone visited Mwata Cazembe, he sat on a bench covered with leopard and lion skins, and was dressed in fantastic beads and feathers. He was entertained by a lively dwarf, his chief wife travelled in a palanquin, and his courtiers and musicians treated him with studied deference – perhaps because a number of them were notable for their cropped ears and hands, 'his . . . way of making his ministers attentive and honest', Livingstone remarked wryly.[2] Such rulers often had large armies, and traded extensively in both slaves and ivory. So although privately the Zanzibaris may have regarded the people of the interior as *washenzi*, savages and unbelievers, they treated their leaders with caution. The conflict with Nsama had been discussed and debated for months, and the Koran had even been consulted for advice. Life on the frontier was dangerous, and a man could make his fortune or lose his life.

Nevertheless, throughout Central and Eastern Africa the coastal men were powerful, and the extent of their commercial influence was enormous, stretching in a great swathe south to the Zambesi, and north to the edge of Lake Turkana. They had access to external markets and capital, they carried desirable trade goods, and their networks provided them with valuable knowledge about prices and the availability of merchandise. But increasingly it was their guns that counted. During the second half of the nineteenth century, gun running into East Africa became a major business. Already by 1859 nearly 23,000 muskets were imported into Zanzibar annually, virtually all destined for the interior, and this figure continued to grow relentlessly. Arms gave the Zanzibaris an immeasurable advantage, and as local leaders sought to imitate their methods, weapons became a valuable article of trade. In the interior, the coastal men were imitated in their dress, in their religion and in their manners. Petty local chieftains began to wear the white *kanzu* and skull cap, and mixed Islam with their own religious practices. Traders sometimes flew the red flag of Zanzibar as a sign of their cooperation with the caravans from the coast. But on the frontier west of Tanganyika, as new regions were opened up, the interaction between Zanzibaris and the local Africans began to change.

As ever, the reason was ivory. The plains and highlands of eastern Africa had been largely depopulated of elephant herds, and the eastern Congo offered new riches. Not only were there more animals to be killed, but past generations of accumulated ivory, used as door frames or hoarded unused, were there to be taken. Moreover, the ivory from the Congo, because it was soft and easily carved, was in high demand. One of the other leaders in the battle with Nsama, Hamed bin Mohamad, summed up the opportunity succinctly. 'A country into which no freeborn man had penetrated since the Creation must certainly harbour ivory.'[3] He was right. The quantities brought out from the new lands and sent to the coast were enormous.

Hamed was one of the first and the most aggressive traders to exploit this vast area. When Livingstone met him in 1867, he was at the beginning of a career that would take him campaigning and trading in the Congo for another twenty years, until he was ruler of an empire covering much of the region. Energetic and forceful, he impressed all those who met him with his intelligence and the manner by which he dominated his peers. With Europeans he was courteous and considerate, and Livingstone depended on him for many months. The explorer noted how the victory over Nsama had been a key moment in this young trader's career, even giving him a new name by which he was later invariably known. 'When [he] stood over the spoil taken from Nsama, he gathered it closer together, and said, "Now I am Tipo Tipo," that is "the gatherer together of wealth".'[4] But although the name Tippoo Tib became his alone, its significance could equally have been applied to several other trader-warriors who established sway over great areas of Central Africa at the time.

Throughout this region, around Lake Tanganyika and the upper reaches of the Congo, slave trading was widespread, but the slaves captured in these lands rarely reached the coast. In their first major centre inland at Kazeh in Unyanyembe, then later at Ujiji on the lake, and in the late 1860s in Ngwangwe and elsewhere in the Congo, the Zanzibaris settled, building substantial establishments, which grew over time. At Kazeh, they numbered some fifteen hundred people in all, inhabiting large houses with carved doors, lofty rooms comfortably furnished with Persian carpets and fine bedding. Copper and brass services were used for meals, and in front of the finer houses groves of fruit trees had been planted.

These were no temporary settlements. Luxuries such as tea, coffee, sugar, brandy, opium, fine cloths and delicate foods were sent up regularly from the coast, while rice, vegetables and fruits were provided by large plantations outside the town. Every Arab household had its harem, and the town had an air of prosperity and wealth. Thousands of slaves were required to maintain these establishments, to work the land and provide personal retainers, as well as to staff the caravans, which set out every season. Then in the late 1860s, as the Zanzibaris advanced deeper into the Congo, they developed a further need for which only slaves would do. The so-called *wangwana*, or free slaves, made up the armies required for the conquest of new lands.

The traders themselves were frequently absent on long journeys for much of the year, and when they travelled they did so with their own armed forces. The *wangwana* were not so much 'free men' as slaves who had attached themselves to a particular leader in the lawless frontier districts of Central Africa. They regarded themselves as superior to the *washenzi* of the interior, the uncivilized Africans whom they tyrannized. The *wangwana* spoke a crude Swahili, they were nominally muslim and showed their allegiance to a particular master. They got little or no pay, but were allowed to loot the country as they went, taking slaves whom they either kept to sell, or gave to their leader in exchange for powder. The explorer Speke wrote that they were 'a loose roving reckless set of beings' who above all loved women and guns.[5] Men such as Tippoo Tib travelled with thousands of these warriors. While the more powerful Zanzibaris were less interested in slaves than in ivory, they still encouraged people hunting on a massive scale but left it mainly to their *wangwana*, because the *wangwana* would follow great leaders, and to take slaves was their privilege.

Tippoo Tib was perhaps the most successful in using these men. Following the victory over Nsama, he travelled west with a force of up to four thousand men, taking enormous quantities of slaves and ivory as he went. As well as being a brave and resourceful leader, he was ruthless, punishing villages and towns mercilessly when they refused to cooperate with him. Eventually, he succeeded in conquering the prosperous kingdom of Utetera in the eastern Congo, where he established himself as ruler, using it as a base for campaigning deeper into Katanga. He did it by a mixture of bravado and guile, but he was under no illusions about the real source of his power. 'In this country,' he later said, 'they knew nothing of free born men, nor at that time did they know of guns.'[6]

Guns, above all, enabled these men to open up huge stretches of new country in their relentless search for tusks. Farther to the north, one region in particular captivated the imagination of the Zanzibaris. Manyiema, a land of fabled wealth, was well known even at the coast. In 1871, Kirk wrote to the Royal Geographical Society that everyone had heard of it, although personally he had met no one who had been there.[7] It was known to be rich in ivory, while its people were peaceful and fine looking; they made good slaves.

The inhabitants of Manyiema had no idea of the wealth they possessed. In the past, they had used elephant tusks to support their houses, or prop up roofs, the items had so little value. As rumours fed back to Ujiji and Unyanyembe of the large stocks of ivory lying unused and cheaply available, traders began to move west in growing numbers, anxious to penetrate this Eldorado. And with them, despite the chaos and violence on the road, went David Livingstone.

Livingstone's journals of this period are a mixture of personal odyssey, geographical exploration and spiritual quest. His ostensible purpose, as he tramped thousands of miles through some of the most inhospitable country in the world, was to discover the source of the River Nile. But interwoven with an abiding interest in the life of the people around him was an obsession with his own spiritual journey, his relationship with his God, as well as a frequent sense of impending death. At times, his search for the great river had a mystical tinge. He wrote repeatedly about the triple fountains somewhere in Africa's interior, reported by Herodotus thousands of years ago. Improbable accounts of just

(*right*) David Livingstone in Africa. *(Corbis)*

(*left*) A slave gang being forced to march to the coast. *(Zanzibar Archives)*

(*below*) Slave-raiding in Central Africa. *(Illustrated Missionary News, 1873)*

(*top*) Seyyida Salme bint Said.
(Zanzibar Archives)

(*middle*) Seyyid Majid bin Said,
ruler of Zanzibar, 1856–70.
(Zanzibar Archives)

(*bottom*) Ludda Dhamji,
Customs Master of Zanzibar.
(Royal Geographical Society)

(*above*) Ivory consignment, Zanzibar. *(Zanzibar Archives)*

(*below*) Dhows moored in Zanzibar harbour. *(Zanzibar Archives)*

(*right*) John Kirk.
(*Royal Botanical*
Gardens, Kew)

(*below*) Cross-section of a dhow showing the slave decks, from *Dhow Chasing in Zanzibar Waters*.
(*author's collection*)

(*above*) Zanzibar slave market. *(Illustrated London News, 1872)*

(*left*) Hamali slaves at Zanzibar harbour. *(Zanzibar Archives)*

(*below*) Zanzibar early in the nineteenth century. *(Zanzibar Archives)*

(*above*) Tippu Tib,
photographed by
Kirk. *(National Library
of Scotland)*

(*right*) Henry
Morton Stanley.
(Corbis)

(*left*) Barghash
bin Said, ruler of
Zanzibar 1870–88.
(Corbis)

(*below*) Barghash
with Bartle Frere
and the Reverend
Badger. *(Corbis)*

Kirk as Consul General. *(National Library of Scotland)*

such fabulous outpourings began to convince him that the source of the river he sought was here in the eastern Congo.

The narrative of Livingstone's travels between 1867 and 1871 seems at times to be written by a man drawn progressively into a kind of hell on earth. For much of the period, he was helped and protected by one or other of the great Zanzibari traders. Sustained by their kindness and protection, he was frequently very ill, sometimes confused, and even close to despair. They provided him with medicine and basic creature comforts, and he repaid his benefactors with gratitude. He referred to them as the 'gentlemen subjects of the Sultan of Zanzibar',[8] men quite different from the *wangwana* whom he regularly witnessed dragging slaves to the market, and whose depradations were reported from the surrounding countryside. He was impressed by the Zanzibaris' piety, by their regular observances and prayers, regarding them as thoughtful men who spent time reflecting on their progress and what they hoped to achieve. They were, he believed, first and foremost traders whose involvement in slaving was relatively benign. He would seldom admit to himself that they employed others to do their violence for them.

Nevertheless, as Livingstone travelled west, he was aware of the increasing bloodshed. One *wangwana* leader boasted to him of the men he had killed during a raid. Livingstone said, '"You were sent here not to murder but to trade;" he replied, "We are sent to murder."'[9] The hunt for ivory was becoming intense as different gangs competed for tusks as well as for slaves, and when the local people resisted, they were easily picked off by the guns. Livingstone wrote that trading had been reduced to 'plunder and murder'. 'Each slave as he rises in his owner's favour, is eager to show himself a mighty man of valour by cold blooded killing.'[10] By early 1871, hardly a page of his journal does not mention the violence, the plunder and the bloodshed. 'The prospect of getting slaves overpowers all else, and blood flows in horrid streams . . .'[11]

By the middle of that year, he had reached Ngwangwe on the banks of the River Lualaba, the headquarters of Muhammad Dugumbe, a trader who, in early 1869, had already taken nearly 20,000 pounds of ivory out of the country at negligible cost. As the first Zanzibari to enter the area, Dugumbe considered the surrounding country to be his personal fiefdom, and there Livingstone remained under his protection. He built himself a small house, and for a few months he had some peace. Ngwangwe was a busy market town and regarded as free from conflict. Men and women brought in their wares on certain days, and as this was a place where agricultural trade was important, no one was threatened. However, in the country on the other side of the river, ferocious competition was taking place for the country's wealth. Fires could be seen at night on the horizon, and one day in July 1871, the violence came to the town.

In the surrounding countryside, a bitter difference had developed between Dugumbe's men and a breakaway group led by another slave leader. Villages had been dealing with both sides, and one of Dugumbe's *wangwana* decided it was time to demonstrate who was paramount.

Over a thousand people had come to market that day. The weather was hot and sultry, and a number of Dugumbe's men were already armed, an infringement of local custom. Livingstone had just returned from the crowded market centre when the first shots broke out. Random firing followed, and within a short period of time, people were being mown down in numbers. Some ran to the river to escape the slaughter, and falling into the water, were easy to pick off and then left to drown. The massacre appeared to have no reason to it. Nearly four hundred women and men were indiscriminately killed in a few hours.

For the first time, Livingstone witnessed at close hand the reality of what was taking place daily elsewhere, and he was traumatized by the experience. Unable to stop the killing, he found Dugumbe and appealed to him personally to put an end to the cruelty, and it seems that the Zanzibari protected a small number of people as a favour to the distraught European. Nevertheless, it was obvious that he had colluded in the massacre. By allowing his men to inflict this violence, he was demonstrating that his followers controlled the region. This was how things were done, and when Livingstone sought to intervene, Dugumbe strongly advised him to keep out of the conflict. His men had been ravaging the country for days, and many of the market people that morning had come from villages that had opposed them. Now it was the town's turn.

Dugumbe's involvement was hellish for Livingstone. He recorded it, yet he still could not bring himself to blame the man. The moral ambiguity of his own position was deeply painful, for he now knew without doubt the kind of men he had depended on and admired. Although under provisioned and ill equipped, he fled, setting off several days later for Ujiji, unable to endure the horror. He must have felt a deep shame – at witnessing something no one should have to see; at his own inability to protect the people in the market; and most of all, at his own complicity with the perpetrators of the atrocity. For months he had accepted their charity, blinding himself to the world they had created. He could not bear the knowledge.

He accepted some parting gifts from Dugumbe – a goat, gunpowder, trade beads and cowries – and made his way back by hard stages to the lake, where he hoped to find provisions from the coast awaiting his arrival. He passed through country devastated and torn by conflict. Plunder, rapacity and greed were evident everywhere. Whole villages along the way had been burnt out by parties of armed slaves, and deserted. Finally, he got to the port on the lakeside in late October 1871, only to have his hopes of finding the supplies requested the previous year dashed. There was nothing. The supplies had arrived many months earlier; however, Sherif, the Zanzibari agent in charge of the caravan, deciding that Livingstone was dead, had used them for his own purposes. When Livingstone finally arrived to claim the property, the man merely shrugged his shoulders – the supplies had been spent, and there was nothing to be done.

Livingstone was destitute, unwell, exhausted. Deeply shocked by what he had witnessed, he remained in Ujiji, a place he hated, unable to leave. Perhaps it had been naive of him to expect that these valuable provisions would remain untouched all this time, given what he knew of conditions in the country. Perhaps he was, in many ways, author of his own desperate predicament. He had journeyed deep into the most dangerous places, and was lucky to have escaped with his life. Now he faced failure and despair, and was unsure where to turn. Then, ten days later, another traveller reached Ujiji. On 10 November 1871, Henry Morton Stanley arrived in the town, and the celebrated meeting between the two men took place.

When Stanley arrived in Zanzibar several months earlier, with a brief from his employer to 'FIND LIVINGSTONE!', he knew how difficult his task would be. Bennett's paper, the *New York Herald*, had a record of publishing sensational scoops, and Bennett was convinced that the explorer's disappearance provided an opportunity for another dramatic success. Equally, Stanley was well aware that this story had the potential to make his own name, in Europe as well as in America. Born of a poor family in Wales, ill treated as a child before emigrating to the US, all his life Stanley craved success and recognition, and now he had his opportunity.

An energetic and driven man, who was often cruel in his treatment of others, from the beginning Stanley seems to have regarded Livingstone as a kind of prize to be hunted down, found and won. However, he had little idea where the Doctor might be located, and it was in this spirit that, on arriving in Zanzibar, he made immediate contact with Kirk. As the only man to have survived the full length of the Zambesi expedition without falling out with the Doctor, and regarded as having a unique relationship with the great man, Kirk was Stanley's best hope of establishing the explorer's last known location and so vital to his purpose. But Kirk seemed unwilling to cooperate.

On the second day after his arrival, Stanley was introduced to 'this much befamed man', as he described Kirk. He portrayed him as 'of rather slim figure, dressed plainly, slightly round-shouldered, hair black, face thin, cheeks rather sunk and bearded'. Kirk seems to have been immediately suspicious of Stanley. On being introduced, Stanley wrote:

> I fancied at the moment that he lifted his eyelids perceptibly, disclosing the full circle of the eyes. If I were to define such a look, I would call it a broad stare. During the conversation,

which ranged over several subjects, though watching his face intently, I never saw it kindle or become animated but once, and that was while relating some of his hunting feats . . .

The following Tuesday, Stanley was invited to a regular social evening at the Kirks' house. He was scathing in his criticism of Zanzibar society – 'the dreariest evening I ever passed'. However, at one point, Kirk took the visitor aside to talk about rifles, and Stanley asked 'carelessly' about where Livingstone might be. Kirk's answer was clear. Although nothing was certain about the Doctor's location, they were relatively confident that he was still alive, travelling in the interior – if he had died, Kirk implied, he would probably have heard about it. As far as he was concerned, Livingstone was not 'lost', and when Stanley inquired further, Kirk was disarmingly honest. The Doctor was a very difficult man to get on with, he said, and emphatically did not like to travel with other westerners.[12]

Stanley was discouraged, but also irritated. It seemed to him that Kirk was hiding something and he did not intend to relinquish it. Nevertheless, Stanley set about preparing for his expedition, and in February he assembled his caravan at Bagamoyo on the mainland opposite Zanzibar, where he found the last caravan to be sent out to Livingstone, dispatched in November the previous year, still detained and waiting.

Kirk had sent a total of three lots of supplies to Livingstone. In October 1869 he had sent the caravan under Sherif, which had then been looted in Ujiji. He had followed that up with reinforcements a few months later. He and Churchill had then put together a final caravan, which left for Bagamoyo in early November 1870, and this was the one that was still there in February the following year. The excuse given by the caravan leader was that sufficient carriers could not be found. Kirk, hearing of the delay that month, went across to the mainland and within twenty-four hours ensured that the caravan left.

It was not surprising that Kirk had not followed up the caravan's dispatch the previous December. Conditions then within the Zanzibar consulate had been desperate. Early in the month the building was almost under siege, while the consul himself lay on the roof dying. Kirk, attempting to deal with the crisis, had no opportunity or time to travel to the mainland. By mid-December, Churchill had left, and Kirk's overriding priority was to rebuild relations with the new sultan. The problems of Dr Livingstone, far away in the interior, were neither new nor very pressing. When he met Stanley, Kirk was exhausted, worn down by the crisis of the preceding weeks, and the picture of a wary, deliberate man is convincing. Relations with Barghash were only beginning to improve, and he had little interest in either the journalist or in what Livingstone was up to. He also knew the Doctor better than most, his eccentricities and his egocentric demands, and unwisely, he allowed his cynicism to show. He told Stanley that he thought Livingstone too old to continue with his travels. It was time for him to come home, he said, although there was little anyone could do to influence him.

He was right, but Stanley noted the comment and the cynical tone, and he bridled when Kirk told him brusquely that his horses would not survive in the interior because of tetse fly, later referring to Kirk as a dogmatic 'hobbyist'. However, Kirk was a serious scientist who knew Africa well, and the horses did die. To Stanley, though, it appeared that this man was determined to rebuff him, and he disliked him for it. When in February he met Kirk again in Bagamoyo, combining a shooting trip with dealing with the delayed caravan, he thought he had found a chink in the man's armour. This 'Livingstone's companion', he decided, was a fraud. The man who should have supported the great Doctor did not give a damn, and had allowed the caravan to loiter in Bagamoyo when it should have left months before. There was just enough truth in this to be convincing, which for Stanley was profoundly useful, because it became a key element in the myth he was constructing around Livingstone for his own purpose. The saintly explorer, abandoned in the wild interior by his friends, would be saved from disaster only by the heroic intervention of an outsider – Stanley himself. But such a myth needed a villain, a Judas. Kirk had supplied him with a candidate.

Kirk thought that he and Stanley had parted on good terms. During his stay in Zanzibar, Stanley had entertained his friends and hosts with constant talk of his prowess as a reporter, and how in the past he had outwitted his competitors. It did not take Kirk long to work out that the only reason a New York newspaper would fund an expedition into that part of Africa would be for the purpose of finding Livingstone, but he was unconcerned. 'I believe his ultimate aim is to meet with Livingstone,' he wrote to Rawlinson of the Royal Geographical Society. He trusted Stanley sufficiently to ask him for his assistance 'in saving the second lot of stores sent on to Livingstone . . .' 'My whole reliance is on Mr. Stanley; he will do his best,' he told Rawlinson. 'I feel assured, and I have given him full power to act.' He had no reason to doubt Stanley's motives, and when he heard later that the American had got involved in a war that had blocked the road to Ujiji, he was concerned that he would not manage to get through. 'He has, however, now met with a severe check; he has lost goods and men,' he wrote in January 1872. Stanley was apparently so ill he had to be carried on a litter, and Kirk worried that after such a disaster he might not manage to make contact with the Doctor.[13]

Kirk had underestimated Stanley's determination. Marching inland, he had reached Unyanyembe in four months, a record for that time of year. Driving his people ruthlessly, waking them every morning with a crack of his donkey whip, he abandoned those who could not keep up. Both his European companions died within months, but the harsh, violent African environment appealed to Stanley. In the interior, the exaggerated respect for firearms played to his own fascination with guns. They made a man very powerful, he discovered, and Stanley's sophisticated breech-loading rifles easily outperformed the primitive match-locks used by Zanzibaris and Africans. He delighted in describing his weapons, and how he used them. 'I toyed lovingly with the heavy Reilly,' he wrote,[14] shortly before recounting how he had applied it to an unfortunate giraffe. He knew well how he was perceived.

In Unyanyembe, Stanley had made his superior fire power available to the Zanzibari settlers who were then engaged in a war with Mirambo, a local leader who blocked the way west. Unwisely, Stanley had allied himself with them, and became involved in a disastrous battle. But eventually he marched round the resulting chaos, aggressively single minded on his quest. By now he had become obsessive, apprehensive that after such enormous effort and expense, the prize might still elude him. Yet when in November 1871, finally he entered Ujiji, Livingstone seemed almost to be waiting for him.

The Doctor turned out to be more rewarding than even Stanley could have foreseen. Although Livingstone was not lost, he certainly needed rescuing. He was in dire need of supplies, medicines and food, and only the support of the people in Ujiji had kept him from starving. He had been forced to endure the humiliation of seeing Sherif, who had effectively stolen his supplies, pass by and greet him daily. Ujiji was a slaving entrepôt on the lakeshore, with a regular market in people, but Livingstone was tied to the place, unable to move. Stanley not only brought him supplies, letters and company; he also brought him the freedom to travel again.

During the short time they were together, the two men developed a genuinely deep relationship, based upon a convergence of need. Livingstone was touched by the interest of a world faraway from his own, vividly demonstrated by Stanley's long journey. He realized, too, that this was was an opportunity to convey to a vast and receptive audience just what he had seen and experienced. For Stanley also, the opportunity was exceptional. Indeed, he wanted to bring Livingstone back as a kind of trophy, but the old man would not come, and instead they travelled together to the head of Lake Tanganyika, which for Stanley was almost as good. Then they returned to Unyanyembe together, where they parted, the 'good man's' letters and journals secure in Stanley's possession. It was a claim of future renown that no one could possibly deny him.

Livingstone's letters, however, were bitter. Stanley had inevitably talked to him of the delayed caravan at Bagamoyo, making clear what he thought of Kirk's poor support, preying on Livingstone's own paranoia. The imagined betrayals and treacheries of the Zambesi expedition all those years ago still rankled in the Doctor's mind. As then, he was more than ready to find someone other than himself to blame for his disasters. And Kirk, on whom he fancied he had placed a special duty of obligation, whom he considered his particular agent, this time did not escape censure.

A few days after Stanley's arrival, Livingstone wrote a long 'complaint' to Kirk, expressing his dissatisfaction and bitterness. About the Zanzibari agent entrusted with his caravan, he was justifiably angry. The man 'had divined on the Koran and found that I was dead', using this as excuse to plunder Livingstone's supplies, running riot with his goods, using his tent, and selling his brandy, opium and soap. 'I received of all the fine calico and beads you sent not a single yard or string of beads,' he wrote. From there, Livingstone moved on to blame the Indian merchants of Zanzibar, and in particular Ludda Dhamji. He hated these '*banians*' for financing the slave-trading caravans up country, and for using slaves to carry their goods, he wrote, although at the same time he exonerated the Arabs themselves, who did the slaving. Livingstone still could not face the truth about the men who had supported him, and yet he had to blame someone. So the Indians of Zanzibar and the slaves they employed became the particular objects of his rancour, and the phrase '*banian* slaves' recurs obsessively again and again in his writing. Finally, he held Kirk himself especially guilty for employing them, for entrusting his precious supplies with such undependable creatures.

There was little logic to Livingstone's tirade. He had overlooked the insecurity of the road, and the improbability that any supplies sent to Ujiji and awaiting him for over a year would remain untouched. The difference at the time between employing slaves or free men as porters was slight, and Ludda Dhamji, as he knew, was probably the most reliable of the merchants in Zanzibar. Livingstone had used him himself. Nevertheless, his complaint, the outburst of a bitter, destitute and disappointed man, ended with the ringing words 'I may wait twenty years and your slaves feast and fail.' It was a cry of pain, which was heard halfway across the world, for later that year, the letter, as well as several others, was published in the newspapers of London.[15]

However, it was a moderate document compared with private letters sent to his (and Kirk's) old friend Waller, to Sir Roderick

Murchison, president of the Royal Geographical Society, and to several other correspondents. In these, Livingstone blamed Kirk directly for the loss of his funds and, in effect, for his own failures. In the letter to Murchison, he was scathing about Kirk – 'that "companion of Livingstone", he was called . . .' He made bitter reference to the occasion 'when Zanzibar failed me so miserably' and it was obvious whom he had in mind.[16] In his letter to Waller, he stated contemptuously that Kirk should no longer consider himself 'a disciple of David Livingstone'. [17]

Kirk had never wished to be considered in this way. He had never thought of the Doctor as the Christ-like figure that Livingstone seemed to suggest for himself. He had always been wary of the man, and his capacity to humiliate those he considered guilty of betrayal. Moreover the disasters that had occurred to Livingstone in this his last journey were entirely predictable, as was his tendency to cast the blame on any one but himself. What magnified and distorted the argument far beyond their intrinsic significance was the intervention of Stanley. For him, the incident became a vehicle for his own self-promotion, a task he threw himself into with all his immense energy.

Stanley arrived back in Zanzibar in early May 1872 where he was welcomed and congratulated by members of the small European community, including Kirk. He also met the leaders of an expedition sent by the Royal Geographical Society to Africa with the express intent of 'finding Livingstone', a journey that Stanley was delighted to inform them was now without purpose. The leader of the expedition, Lt Dawson, uncertain whether to proceed or not, resigned, and then was not sure whether that had been the right thing to do. There was squabbling among the other members of the expedition, which included Livingstone's son, Oswell, who could not decide whether to go ahead or not. In the end, the expedition was abandoned.

Meanwhile, Stanley had brought with him Livingstone's papers as well as a letter from the Doctor, informing Kirk that funds sent to Zanzibar for his support should be handed over at once to Stanley. As the last person to have seen the great man, to have talked to him and heard his wishes, Stanley began to act as if he alone owned Livingstone. He was also efficient, and immediately organized a further expedition to carry back more supplies to the Doctor, showing up the squabbling British in contrast as poorly organized, ineffective and indecisive. Kirk attempted to retrieve some order but without success, and with Stanley his relations soon became frosty. Although Kirk had defended Stanley in the British press while he had been in the interior, they quickly disagreed, and then had a huge row about the reasons for the delay to the various caravans. Stanley's demand that only he should be responsible for spending the funds sent to Zanzibar was calculated to insult. Livingstone's complaint, and Stanley's comments on how the Doctor had been let down in his hour of need, indicated the direction the affair was taking.

Kirk was already angry at the document Livingstone had sent to him and which he in turn sent on to the Foreign Office. Then on 26 May he met Stanley again at the house of the US consul, just before he was due to leave Zanzibar. To Kirk's surprise, Stanley asked him whether he might take charge of the caravan he intended sending to Livingstone, since he was not sure he could manage its dispatch before leaving. Kirk replied coldly that he wasn't going to expose himself to any additional insult. Stanley then stirred matters further by explaining why Livingstone's criticisms were justified.

The conversation was suspicious. Stanley had no real problem with the caravan – it left for the interior the following morning – but he had managed to achieve extra evidence in Kirk's disfavour, and Kirk was aware of it. Three days later, Stanley left for Europe, arriving in Marseilles in July. His fame had run before him, and he was besieged by journalists as soon as he stepped on shore.

10: HARDLY TO BE FEARED

*The Arabs, taken as a whole, are a detestable race with scarcely a
redeeming quality; and it is a thousand pities that they should ever
have put their foul hands upon, and brought their paralyzing religion
to Eastern Africa.*

CHARLES NEW, *LIFE, WANDERINGS, AND LABOURS
IN EASTERN AFRICA*

*One morning they would see us burning the dhows which were
engaged in the slave trade, and the next morning they would see an
Englishman working factories and plantations with those slaves
safely landed; it was a question which puzzled far more acute people
than they . . .*

REVEREND HORACE WALLER, SELECT COMMITTEE ON THE
EAST AFRICAN SLAVE TRADE

During the early months of 1871, Sultan Barghash appeared to the
outside world to be confident, at ease with himself and satisfied
with what he had achieved. A photograph that was taken of him
some time after his accession shows him as a slightly overweight
man with a calm, relaxed expression. He lacks his brother's doubt
and torment; he might even be complacent. To visitors, he was
courteous and welcoming, and when Stanley attended him in
January that year, the journalist was disarmed at the gracious
manner with which Barghash invited him to precede him up the
grand staircase of the palace. Later, sitting opposite the sultan in

his audience chamber, with the Customs Master at one side, Stanley thought Barghash's demeanour gave nothing away except 'a perfect contentment with himself and all around'.[1] The sultan appeared urbane and well informed, asking Stanley about his travels, and appearing particularly interested in the great Muslim centres of Turkey, Persia and the city of Baghdad.

He was dressed simply in full turban and long dark robe, with only the gold hilt of his sword and scabbard giving away his wealth and position. His legs and feet, however, 'had a ponderous look about them, since he suffered from that strange curse of Zanzibar – elephantiasis.' The disease was endemic in the city, often resulting in grotesque swelling of the sufferer's legs and genitals, enlarging the scrotum to immense and disfiguring proportions. It was a humiliating disability, which Barghash was only partly able to hide beneath his robes.[2]

The sultan had reason to be content. By January, Kirk reckoned he had swiftly 'shown himself master of the situation'. Skilfully distancing himself from his more fanatical advisers, he had taken political control entirely into his own hands. He refused to pay bribes to the Gulf marauders, and corruption and bribery in the city soon became unknown. He was decisive, although greedy, and not afraid to offend conventional opinion by immediately auctioning off all the concubines and slaves belonging to his predecessor, an action that scandalized many Zanzibaris. Kirk thought his parsimony was a serious defect, which risked alienating some of his key supporters.

He has . . . one unpardonable fault in the eyes of his subjects and that is his want of liberality to the people of the coast and town many of whom have real claims upon him by oriental custom and from his position as their chief.[3]

Kirk was divided between reluctant admiration for Barghash's pragmatism, and distrust of his ultimate motives. To Hooker, he wrote that although the sultan was 'more tractable and pleasant to deal with in business matters . . . I know he is so for his own ends [and] still he is a man of very peculiar temper.'[4]

Kirk could not bring himself to trust Barghash again. The man was unpredictable and inconstant in his behaviour – 'without any steps taken on our part to conciliate him he has become respectful where before he was insolent and has set aside in great measure his Mtawa advisers on whom at first he relied and whom he made his tools . . .' Kirk expected to see Barghash change his policy according to circumstance, and as regards the slave trade, he had no confidence that Barghash would ever deliver on any promise he had made. He was a man 'utterly devoid of principle or honour'.[5]

At one point Kirk even suggested that an expedition from the Gulf with a hundred men could make themselves masters of Zanzibar, and replace the sultan. Perhaps he did it to find out just how committed his masters in India were, but it was a mistake, and he should have known better. Officials in Bombay had no interest in further involvement in East Africa merely to achieve a stronger treaty on slave trading, and Kirk was firmly discouraged from pursuing the idea further. While he had never been seriously considered as a candidate for taking over the agency, this rash suggestion must have finalized any doubts among his superiors, and private letters from Bombay soon confirmed what he had already suspected. A replacement was being sought elsewhere for the position in East Africa.

Already frustrated at finding himself yet again temporary holder of the post, Kirk could have given up, and he was sorely tempted to do so. He could have waited until he was replaced, and then taken whatever the Indian government offered him. Instead, he fell back on his own resources, once more adopting the role of 'locum', as he put it, and during the next two years, he developed it with skill. He used it to disguise the kind of man he really was, drawing on the fact that he had now been in Zanzibar for almost five years, and was so well known he had achieved a certain permanence in the town.

In March 1870, the town's corn merchants were accused of using false weights and measures in selling grain, and after endless argument failed to resolve the dispute, they came to the only person they trusted to solve the problem. Kirk listened patiently while they described to him the accepted practice, one notoriously easy to pervert. Finally, he proposed a new method of defining the standard, which would be transparent to everyone. The measure traditionally used, the *nepishi*, henceforth was to be strictly defined as equivalent to a specific quantity of water, so that every merchant could be held to it if requested. The proposal was unanimously accepted.[6]

Kirk was increasingly seen as an honest broker. He upheld British trading interests, but pursued no strong line or aggressive policy, and by 1871 everyone in Zanzibar knew why. Between the Indian merchant communities of Bombay and Zanzibar there was constant communication. Members of the same family often lived on both sides of the Indian Ocean, and it was how they conducted their trade. In Bombay it was well known among the Indian clerks that there was no confidence in the Zanzibar acting agent, the medical man who had encouraged Churchill in his disastrous intervention. It was understood that he was to be replaced as soon as possible, and it did not take long for the information to reach Zanzibar. Kirk was useful, and was respected. In the Admiralty court he handed out fair judgements, but he was hardly to be feared.

Kirk heard the rumours, and knew how they reduced and devalued his meagre authority. From London he got little support. Following the debacle of Churchill's brief return, there was no appetite for further action, and disagreement within the government meant that during the next two years Kirk received few clear instructions. London had no policy on Zanzibar, while India's attitude remained negligent and antagonistic to interference with the status quo. Caught in this trap, Kirk knew better than to stick his neck out. He was vulnerable, and once replaced was totally dependent on Bombay's goodwill. He had no money and a family to support. He could not afford to take risks. So, left to his own devices, he suppressed his views and became the impartial adviser, non-committal but available for advice. He was cautious and circumspect because he had to be.

The situation frustrated and galled him. He wrote to Hooker: 'I am again Acting Political Agent which is all the work of ten men ... the pay of one and the chance of being killed any day.'[7] But he became adept at exploiting the ambiguity of his position, even turning its uncertainty into an advantage. He became known for his probity, but also for the extraordinary extent of his knowledge. His Swahili and Arabic were fluent, people had confidence in his discretion, and because he knew so much they continued to come to him for advice. In late 1871, he said to a visiting businessman that there was probably very little that went on in Zanzibar of which he was not aware.[8] He received people's confidences, yet divulged little in return. That was how he survived. Knowledge became his weapon, and he used it, discreetly, but to effect. Most of all, he employed it in his relations with the sultan.

Barghash had inherited a state that was corrupt and had been chronically badly managed, and its finances were in desperate condition. The sultan's troops were ill disciplined and out of control, using their power to satisfy petty vendettas. Kirk wrote, 'The Swaheli population are in fact at the mercy of a brutal native soldiery and floggings are given without question of appeal.' Non Arabs were punished and sent to the stocks without authorization by the judges. In January, Kirk brought a particularly egregious case to Barghash's attention. He did not make his intervention obvious, but it gave the sultan, who had known nothing of the incident, a chance to appear a champion of the ordinary people. He was delighted to be able to take action, and 'thanked me in friendly terms for calling his attention to the existence of so gross a system of cruelty and one obviously liable to so much abuse.'[9]

Corruption existed in the sultan's own household. Slaves were vanishing although no one knew why or where they were going. Kirk was able to inform the sultan that, in fact, they were being kidnapped and sold via a senior member of the royal household. The slaves, deceived into assuming they were being offered a better life, were taken to dhows some distance from the city, and 'decoyed on board under fair promises of freedom on the coast where each might have his own garden and live at ease, instead of working daily carrying stone and mortar in town.' They were then shipped away and sold.[10]

Kirk continuously made himself useful, giving Barghash information and advice, and it was always free, offered without strings, as though their old relationship remained unaffected by

what had happened. The sultan, preoccupied with other problems, liked the arrangement, and in late January he even sent Kirk
a package of letters he had received recently from the Gulf, to ask
his opinion.

His Highness being desirous that the three first of these
letters should reach me unknown to his matawa advisers,
sent them by the hand of a confidential messenger and so
also were they returned with my acknowledgement and
remarks thereon.

Oman was now divided by civil discord, and Barghash found
himself beholden to both sides. His two brothers, Turkee and
Abdul Azziz, were in conflict with a self-styled Imam, Azzan bin
Kees, who had declared himself religious leader of the country.
Azzan was backed by the Mutawas, the same fundamentalists who,
in Zanzibar, had supported Barghash. The sultan's letters came
from both parties, each determined to draw Barghash into their
conflict, demanding a special duty of help from the new ruler.

The first three letters were from leading supporters of the
Imam, urging Barghash actively to assist them, and even
threatening him if he refused. 'If you bind yourself to follow the
Imam,' one wrote, 'he will continue the kingdom to you; but, if
you deny him, he will take it from you. Your wealth cannot protect
you from him . . .' The fourth letter was from Barghash's own
brother, Abdul Azziz bin Said, and it was just as pressing. 'While
you are at present sleeping at peace in your house, we are full of
trouble . . .' he wrote bitterly. He was concerned with the family's
many enemies and how they had betrayed him, but also about
money.

Pay . . . from your own pocket and I will pay you hereafter
. . . You of old have been my agent and are so still, nothing
more, so do not make a big name for yourself. I have drawn
on you for the sum of $500 . . . Pay it at once do not delay
as your brother in the beginning of Shawal is about to go
wherever God may will.

The letter ended with a dramatic statement of the family's continued dependence on Zanzibar for its survival.

> Either I shall live or die. I must do as our poet says . . . As you know Zanzibar is the fountain of money and we cannot get on without Zanzibar and moreover all my troubles have sprung from thence . . .

Religion and money – Barghash was under acute pressure from each.

The sultan naturally knew the British and Mutawas were old enemies, and that any Indian officer would be bound to speak against them, but Kirk was not a member of the British imperial caste; he was an outsider, free from any taint of 'policy' and Barghash trusted him because of it. So he was interested to know what Kirk advised, and Kirk played along. His reply was discreet but to the point. He warned Barghash that the Imam's claim to be master of Zanzibar would not go away, and he should therefore be careful before committing to him, for 'such pretensions will soon be followed by more substantial demands'. He signed off with the lines, 'Should it ever be in my power to counsel you further on this or any other matter of State, I shall always deem it a privilege to hold myself at Your Highness's orders.'[11] He was always available, and he was the sultan's friend.

Barghash was saved from making a decision when, not long afterwards, his brothers succeeded in regaining control of Oman, but Kirk had still proved his value. He was able to do so again a few months later, when the sultan's financial crisis abruptly spilled out into the open.

Barghash had inherited huge liabilities not only to his family, but also debts of half a million dollars incurred by Majid to Ludda Dhamji, the Customs Master. In late August, the sultan decided his only solution was to repudiate the contract with Ludda for farming the country's customs arrangements. Later that month, another merchant came to speak to Kirk confidentially. The sultan had approached him to take on the contract, he said. It was known to be immensely lucrative and he personally reckoned it was worth up to $700,000, but he was worried about the risk. There was concern about what the British might do one day concerning the slave trade, and the impact that could have on the country's overall commerce.

During the next month, Barghash and Ludda haggled and argued about the debt, the renewal of the contract and much else. Tempers became frayed. Ludda demanded immediate payment of the money owed to him, and Barghash retorted that the debt had been a personal one incurred by his late brother. Other merchants, sniffing profits, became interested and offered the sultan deals. Finally, Barghash sent a messenger to Kirk to plead for help. 'Tell the Balozi [i.e. consul] that in my passion, I forgot myself and said that I repudiated the debt and said to Ludda, go and take the tomb of my brother and his estates and ships.' The situation was out of control, and 'Ludda was mad', changing his mind from day to day. Neither man trusted the other, but Barghash could not find anyone to take the contract on better terms, while Ludda would not give up his debt. In the end, the only person they both trusted to sort out the mess was Kirk, and he persuaded them to reach a compromise.[12]

Merchants may have been concerned at the dangers facing the slave trade, but their fears had little impact on the scale of trafficking. During the second half of 1871, the business experienced an exceptional season. Stimulated by the enormous mortalities from the cholera epidemic, demand in Zanzibar and on the African coast appeared as strong as for the export market to Persia and Arabia. Kirk estimated that the numbers traded that season were the highest for six years – almost 23,400 slaves in total, including an estimated 2,000 mortalities.[13] The business was becoming highly specialized, as Zanzibar became the 'processing' centre for slaves, supplying a huge area. Some dealers made money from buying in untrained arrivals cheaply and in bulk. After 'breaking them in' and feeding them to better health, they would send them to market at higher prices. Others, responsible for shipping the slaves north, were skilled in the dangerous business of smuggling them out of the country. Kirk noted in his journal exactly how that was accomplished.

Two sets of books were kept. In one, the name of each shipper was registered, with the detailed number of slaves he undertook to carry, and this was privately used by the Customs House for tax purposes. In the other, the total value of a ship's cargo was calculated, without specifying its commodities, and a general permit was given based on its entire merchandise. In this second book, it was easily concealed that the dhow was engaged in slave smuggling. Those responsible for sending the slaves north were also skilled at spreading their risk. Slaves were rarely sent in large numbers on one vessel, but instead were shared across many different craft. 'In case of capture, the loss is distributed, and a sure profit left on the transaction collecting at the end of the year.' The dealer rarely identified himself, preferring to pay others to take the risk. 'Also an Arab never goes to the Sultan and declares many slaves but when shipping a number, engages poor people to come forward with their name and make the declaration for a small pecuniary consideration.'[14]

One way or another, everyone in the city was involved. Upper-class Zanzibaris might pretend that the crude business of trading in slaves was beneath them, but they still invested through others. For them, the market was also a kind of diversion, and they followed it in the way European aristocrats dabbled at the breeding and purchase of racehorses. Buying fine slaves was a leisure activity, and it fascinated them. Rich Zanzibaris would bid competitively for exotic individuals, endlessly discussing the finer points and prices of the rarest types. In April 1871, Kirk wrote:

> Yesterday it came to my knowledge that an Indian girl was being offered for sale by the slave Auctioneer and taken round along with Georgian females at night to the houses of the wealthy Arabs and that $250 had been offered for her.

The girl was extremely valuable, but because she came from India, Kirk could demand to see her. She spoke Hindustani, and told him her history. Dispassionately, he recorded the transactional life of a young woman who had passed through seven owners in as few years, bought and sold like a fine rare animal.

She had when young been sold in Bombay by her father Mohamed a Jemadar in the service of the Bombay government to a man who took her to Hyderabad in the Deccan. There she remained a long time when she was taken by one Sooroor to the Matulla in Arabia and there was sold to a man of Eastern Africa. At Lamo she fell into the hands of the notorious dealer Saed Auter an Arab of Shelher who sold her, I am told, to one of the Kadis here. Afterwards she passed to the hands of her present owner a young Persian who to make a profit put her in the markets.[15]

By mid-1871, there was little Kirk did not understand about the Zanzibar end of the slave trade, and its place in the city's social economy. He had now studied it for years with unremitting application. He not only knew the numbers involved, he had also done an analysis of the different tribal groupings, where they came from and how they made up the shipments. He was aware of which shippers specialized in the business, at what point in the season the slaving dhows left, and their destinations. He understood the sea risks they took, which 'honest traders' would not consider, and when to watch for them. He had calculated their profit margins. All this he recorded meticulously, and stored for further use. It was detail that no one else was interested in, and unless he could ever use it, it would remain untouched.

He came by all this information because, by 1871, the men at the Customs House and the merchants to whom he talked considered he could never be a threat to them. For Kirk was evidently not like other Europeans. A bearded, stooping, detached figure, he fell into a category they had not seen before – neither Indian Officer nor trader, and not a missionary; interested in commerce, but not in order to make money; interested in slave trading, yet not to condemn it; detached, yet prepared to help resolve disputes. He seemed intent on knowledge purely for its own sake, and so they told him what he wanted to know. He collected information on plants, and he collected information on slaves, and in the end they might have thought it was almost the same thing.

They may even have thought he was on their side, because there were occasions when Kirk went out of his way to support them against his own people.

Early in 1872, there was a public fracas between Captain H.A. Fraser, a British businessman resident in Zanzibar, and an eminent Arab. Fraser, who owned sugar plantations on the island, was able to use slave labour on his land despite being British, by contracting out through middlemen. Zanzibaris, infuriated by this evident hypocrisy, disliked him. In March, Fraser was accused of sending one of his servants to deal roughly with a slave belonging to an Arab, and after an argument, the two men came to ask Kirk to settle the matter. Almost immediately, Fraser began to abuse Sheikh Yoosoof, his opponent, refusing to sit with him. Kirk attempted to reason with the two men, and despite Fraser's barrage of insults, eventually managed to understand the details of the incident, pointing out to Fraser that he had been clearly in the wrong.

> Then I was interrupted by Capt Fraser in the most contemptuous and insulting manner abusing Yoosoof and saying that the British subject got no justice when they had a complaint . . .

Kirk refused to accept this.

> I then had to rise and inform him that I could not hear an arab in my court abused in this offensive manner and that he must go downstairs . . .[16]

Fraser refused, continuing his harangue, and finally Kirk was forced to go outside to speak privately to the Zanzibari.

Fraser never forgave Kirk for refusing to take his part, but the Zanzibaris saw the matter very differently. They were aware that most Europeans regarded them with dislike and contempt. Missionaries looked on the city with particular aversion – 'there is no morality in it, it is scarcely superior to Sodom,' wrote one. 'A black picture, upon which we can scarcely dare to gaze . . .'[17]

Naval officers, accustomed to harassing and plundering dhows along the coast, thought of Arabs and Swahili as vicious slavers without exception, and coming ashore, treated them with derision and disdain. In an evangelical age, Islam was seen by many westerners as repellent and backward, and Zanzibar's slave-dealing culture merely confirmed the city's status as an abhorrent place.

The Zanzibaris knew this, for it was conveyed to them unmistakably. One visiting sea captain, whose wife had been invited to visit Sultan Majid's harem, afterwards openly bragged about it as though it were a circus. Angry at such treatment, but powerless to prevent it, the Zanzibaris resented the British interlopers, and returned the contempt.

Kirk liked East Africa, and there was much he admired about its inhabitants, despite their slave trading. Perhaps he reflected that, until only seventy years earlier, Britain had supported a traffic far larger and at least as cruel. The ancient history and culture of the coast fascinated him, and he was unable to see the country as uniquely benighted and evil. The Zanzibaris noticed this, and they returned the respect, yet Kirk still felt he was a sham. He knew that he was respected, paradoxically, not for what he was, but for what he was not. He was not the acknowledged agent and consul, he was not a real *Balozi*; he was only a kind of shadow agent who would never be confirmed in the job, and who had little real authority. Yet he wanted recognition; he wanted to do what was necessary. He believed he had been given a purpose that he was uniquely placed to fulfil, and yet was unable to discharge. Throughout 1871, he became angrier and more bitter at the way he was even undermined by his own employers. In March, he wrote to Hooker:

> I am told by private letters from Bombay that the governor is determined to get in a Bombay man here, and he being the dispenser of the office I shall have the option of remaining ... without chance of promotion or looking elsewhere for myself.[18]

He expected to find his successor gazetted any day, some 'Indian' who had no knowledge of the place or its languages. Once they had done with him, he would be returned to Britain on the next mail boat, invalided out on half pay. Then it would be back to botany once more with little else to sustain him.

However, as the seasons changed with the arrival of the new monsoon, it seemed Bombay could find no one else to take the job. The Zanzibar agency had a curse on it, and in mid-1871 Kirk began to hear strange rumours. An officer stationed in the Gulf had been told he was to go to Zanzibar for the sake of the service, but his refusal was more adamant than most.

> You may have heard that the man, whom Bombay delighted to . . . name to supercede me in the Act, Agency, took a pistol and blew his brains out at once . . . The Arabs tell queer tales about him and say he was a muff . . . Zanzibar is well rid of him.[19]

Still, Kirk knew it was just a matter of time. They were running down the lists of possible candidates, and eventually they would find someone. He remained defiant – 'it will be a while before they can get me . . .' – but by late 1871 his letters had taken on a paranoid tone. He was angry at being passed over, at being underpaid and having to make his wife work as his clerk and at not being trusted, while hanging over him was the continual threat of dismissal. He felt he was being persecuted, and everything he had done would be discarded, unconsidered and wasted. 'They will turn me out without a cent . . .' He visualized his successor as he scribbled long, ranting letters late into the night. 'An Indian officer is pretty sure to make the common mistakes of his cloth and think he is a little Almighty . . .'[20]

He continued with his botany as relief, together with the obsessive recording of all the random details of his daily life. Odd personal anecdotes, economic data, facts on slave trading, the passing of the seasons – all were furiously crammed into his notebooks with an omniverous intensity, as though only by immersing himself in such detail could he keep control. On 11

October his third daughter was born. The same day he was invited on board a visiting French vessel whose captain abused the English, and then insulted Kirk, referring to the baby's birth as 'in his eyes but another enemy to France brought into the world'. On 24 October, he listed estimates of the capital worth of the four leading merchants in Zanzibar, and on 26 November he noted lengthy details on slave trading off the Somali coast. On 27 November he recorded that, 'the North Monsoon set in fairly today and blew steadily until sunset.' The following day he received from M. Suliman 'one Vulturian guineas fowl and one Egyptian goose . . .'[21] In the same month, he sent back to Kew a collection of plants, 'heaths, proteas and campasitae' brought down from Mount Kilimanjaro by the missionary, Charles New, who was the first European to climb through the 'the damp zones of forest that encircle the mountain' to the snow-capped summit.[22]

Yet this intense activity only conveys a sense of futility, as though he were hiding from himself the knowledge that all the effort was in vain. He kept on going because he had to. It was about then that he took his panoramic photograph of Zanzibar from the roof of the consulate, a 360 degree view of the city. He did it as an experiment – 'being out of . . . chemicals I have had to invent a process of my own,' he wrote[23] – but it seemed to encapsulate his outlook at the time. Turning round full circle, the view is always the same – a claustrophobic maze of square buildings, narrow alleys and flat, white roof tops, with no variation wherever one looked, except a minaret, the palace and the dhows lying moored in the harbour. It was as if there were no way out.

In July 1871, a private letter written by Kirk to Vivian, head of the Slave Trading Department at the Foreign Office, was published before a parliamentary committee in London. In it, Kirk had been openly dismissive about India's authority in East Africa. 'There is a very false idea as to the paramount claim of Bombay to the guidance of matters here. True, there are many Kutchees here, but Kutchees at best are not British Indians . . .'[24] Kirk had never intended the letter to be read in public, but he soon learnt the consequences of such disloyalty, and his dismissal now was certain. 'Unluckily a private letter of mine to Vivian has been published . . .' he wrote to Hooker. 'And Bombay is hunting me down . . . Well like your oyster I shall fight . . .'[25] Vivian had always supported Kirk but in December 1871, he wrote him a long letter in which he confidentially set out the government's position on the 'puzzling question of the East African slave trade'. It contained no good news.

The British government was disillusioned with its attempts to fight slave trafficking on the East African coast.

They look at the great expence [sic] which has already been incurred in our futile attempts to suppress the traffic (which they estimate at about £50,000 a year) and they point with considerable show of justice to the wretched results . . .

Further expenditure on ships and consuls was not considered justified, and might even, government thought, push up the price of slaves by making the smuggling more difficult. But most importantly, the men in Whitehall did not think that trafficking on the east coast of Africa should be judged in the same way as the Atlantic trade.

They seem to think that the case of the East Coast is not parallel with that of the West Coast, where the traffic was originally carried on in a great measure by British subjects in British vessels, whereas the East Coast Trade is carried on by Foreigners.[26]

Once again, British reluctance to force western habits on non-European cultures was the excuse. It was felt that Muslim slave trading was different, and instead of relying on repression, the government wished to give more encouragement to trade and steam communications as instruments of change. Commerce would prevail where force had failed. Vivian ended his letter regretting that Kirk's uncertainty of tenure had interfered with his ability to do his work, but unfortunately he could do nothing about that. The Treasury refused to share in the costs of the

Zanzibar agency, which continued to be India's affair. Kirk was on his own.

The Zanzibaris had a fair idea of what was happening. Gossip and rumour travelled fast among the trading communities of the Indian Ocean. They knew about India's indifference, and in conversations at the Customs House, they laughed out loud at the suggestion Bombay would somehow support an invasion just to abolish the slave trade.[27] They knew Kirk was under permanent threat of suspension, just as they knew he would not be suspended because no replacement for him could be found. That a man would rather go out and shoot himself seemed proof of this. To the Zanzibari merchants that season, Kirk's continued presence seemed the best possible situation, and they looked on the whole matter with wry humour. This doctor was their friend, he had no interest in acting against them, and his uninterrupted presence over the years was evidence of how they and their trade were untouchable.

On the night of 18 December, Barghash paid Kirk a confidential visit at the consulate. He intended to go to Arabia on a pilgrimage to the Muslim holy places, he said, and would be away three months. He would leave two of his trusted advisers as regents in his absence. He still enjoyed talking to Kirk, he could say things to him that were difficult to discuss with others. Kirk asked casually whether this was not the time to think about the succession, and perhaps even bring forward one of his younger brothers. Barghash was openly contemptuous. He had no interest in any of his siblings, he replied, naming each of them in turn, only to dismiss him. Majid, he said, had allowed them all 'to associate in the lowest company and grow up unable to read or write, without manners or education, in order that they might not be rivals to him,' and they were not to be trusted. 'There was not a son of Seyed Saeed who loved another,' Kirk wrote wryly.[28]

But beneath his calm exterior Barghash was also an angry man. He knew why Kirk had asked him the question. His elephantiasis had severely damaged him, and as Kirk put it, there was 'no chance from his mutilated condition of any direct issue.'[29] He knew he would never see a son of his as ruler, and he hardly cared at that point about the future. Later that evening, he said to Kirk, 'Wait till I die and then you will see strange things.' The comment was a typically bitter taunt – 'You may think I am bad, but there are worse to follow . . .'[30]

It was a long evening. The two men went on to discuss the slave trade, and Kirk as usual said he had no instructions. Barghash remarked whimsically that perhaps one day he might even abolish the system, since he had no intention of indulging the northern Arab marauders the way his brother had. But Kirk knew he was still playing a game. While from time to time, he might hand his 'friend' a small victory – an open slaver brought to court, a man imprisoned – these were the actions of a ruler dispensing gifts, and were not serious. His family were too involved, and even dhows belonging to Barghash himself were on occasion apprehended. The sultan had no intention of abolishing the business, however he might toy with the idea. He liked to play jokes, and that was the nature of their relationship – ambiguous, speculative, yet serious. The two men still got on well, and Kirk was useful to him, so Barghash was prepared to indulge him, and at times even taunt him slightly. Kirk always took it, trying to put himself in the other's position, to see things as he saw them, attempting to understand the man.

Shortly before Barghash left for Arabia, he called again to say goodbye, and presented six gold bracelets to Kirk's wife as a gift. Kirk, noting to himself that they were too valuable to accept, sent them back. 'He returned them and I sent them back again.'[31] It was the nature of their relationship.

11 : NOT WORTH THE CANDLE

The Northern Arabs generally sail in the night; they have houses in the town; it is notorious in what parts of the town they make their stay while they are collecting their slaves, and in the back parts of those premises they gather the slaves; then when they have a good opportunity they slip them on board the dhows secretly at night and the dhow goes out to sea.

REVEREND EDWARD STEERE, SELECT COMMITTEE ON THE
EAST AFRICAN SLAVE TRADE

On 10 July 1871, a British parliamentary select committee assembled in one of the rooms of the House of Commons to examine the question of the East African slave trade. It sat for three weeks, and its brief was:

> ... to inquire into the whole question of the slave trade on the east coast of Africa, into the increased and increasing amount of that traffic, the particulars of existing treaties and agreements with the Sultan of Zanzibar upon the subject, and the possibility of putting an end entirely to the traffic in slaves by sea.[1]

The chairman was Mr Russell Gurney, an MP and member of a renowned Quaker family which had taken part in the fight against the Atlantic slave trade earlier in the century. Gurney, a prominent humanitarian, had insisted on appointing the majority of the committee's other fourteen members, several of whom were active in anti-slavetrading and humanitarian causes. They were determined to bring before them a wide variety of witnesses, including two of the former consuls to Zanzibar, representatives of the India Office in London and missionaries returned from Africa, as well as retired naval officers from the antislaving patrol along the African coast. Their brief was to suggest a course of action for the government, but from the beginning their remit was confused. In addition, as always, public opinion and the views of the establishment were very mixed on the question of Zanzibar and its unpleasant trade.

Since the 1850s and 1860s, concern for fighting the slave trade had largely dropped out of the headlines, and widespread support for the movement had waned, largely due to several disasters around the mid-century. A catastrophic expedition to the Niger in West Africa,[2] and then Livingstone's own Zambesi expedition, had both seemed to demonstrate the futility of sending British people to tropical backwaters to die for a forlorn cause. The government itself was also ambiguous. Maintaining a fleet to suppress slave-trading activities in areas of little immediate concern to Britain was expensive, and at a time of fiscal austerity, hard to justify.

At the same time, in the aftermath of the Indian Mutiny, those concerned with imperial policy were very reluctant to interfere with established rulers who were favourable to Britain's interests. Politicians and diplomats had learnt that dismantling entrenched customs could be a dangerous business with unintended consequences.[3] When policy makers in either Whitehall or India cast their eyes at the East African coast, they felt considerably more comfortable dealing with a stable and established sultan than they might do dealing with unpredictable African 'despots'. Moreover, was not slavery an established part of Islamic culture? Maintaining order in the world was a high priority, and established hierarchies were often to be admired.

And yet there was pressure to do something. In 1870, Lord Clarendon had involved the humanitarian 'lobby' in his discussions on the slave trade, when deciding to put pressure on

Zanzibar. However, his initiative in forcing Churchill's return had turned into farce, and the consul's precipitate withdrawal had left the Foreign Office with its policy in tatters. Worse, the government was at loggerheads with the Indian administration, who informed London that if they were not prepared to pay towards maintaining the Zanzibar agency, they could have no part in running it. And the Treasury in London was quite clear that there was no budget for costs incurred in East Africa. A parliamentary committee seemed the only way out.

Proceedings did not go as planned. Members of the committee had not realized the difficulties in which they were involving themselves, and as the scale of the slave trade off East Africa became clearer, they became more and more uneasy. The amount of information they were able to receive on what was happening in a remote part of Africa thousands of miles away was remarkable, and yet the testimony of the witnesses was often confusing, and frequently contradictory. The more the committee members heard, the more complicated the matter seemed. The only thing that appeared to be absolutely certain was the scale of suffering undergone by thousands of people in this little-known part of the world. The harrowing accounts from government servants, seamen and missionaries all confirmed the horrors of this large-scale trafficking in people.

Yet this was clearly not a trade like the trans-Atlantic traffic from West Africa, where human beings had been purchased by British and other European shippers for sale to the American plantations. It was managed by independent states on whom Britain had little direct influence. It was not of recent origin, but had been going on for millennia. It was mixed up with legitimate commerce, was often hidden and not at all easily identified. Finally, it was intrinsic to the cultures of nations that Britain wished to maintain as allies. The situation was very problematic, and there were no easy solutions.

The full extent of what was happening came to the committee gradually. The Hon. C. Vivian was first witness, and as head of the Anti Slavery Department at the Foreign Office, he possibly had most to hope for from the discussions. Zanzibar, he said, was the centre of commercial activity in the eastern part of the Indian Ocean. Indeed, trade 'springing up' there was potentially capable of infinite expansion and of transforming the region. However, regrettably mixed in with this legitimate commerce was the extensive trafficking of human beings, and he estimated that the ruler of Zanzibar made some £20,000 per annum from that business alone.[4] Muslim attitudes towards this activity were unfortunate – 'they consider there is no harm in slavery at all.' As for bringing an end to it, he was deeply pessimistic. Any treaty with an Arab state was a waste of time, and as long as there was demand for slaves in the countries to the north, there would always be slave trading. It was impossible to stamp it out.

In case they had missed the point, Christopher Rigby, who had been consul to Zanzibar in the late 1850s, expressed the same negative view. The treaties Britain had signed with the country were 'mere waste paper', he said, and he also confirmed another concern that Vivian had mentioned. If the trade ever were abolished under pressure, it would be considered such a humiliation that there would be a revolution and the sultan would probably lose his life.

Henry Churchill, the last full-time consul to serve in Zanzibar, was equally cynical. The trade was there to stay he thought, 'because so long as the demand exists the supply will exist. I do not think anything in the world will suppress it, until you prevent Persia and Turkey from employing domestic slaves . . .' He introduced another complication. This was not commerce on an industrial scale, as it had been on the west coast, from where slaves had been shipped in vast numbers on vessels dedicated to the purpose. On the contrary, buying and selling people was part and parcel of the routine commerce of the region. Slaves were often exported in small groups as part of a consignment of other goods, although you could usually still tell them apart. For the 'raw' slaves in particular were 'marked like sheep. A part of the hair is taken off, and if you see 20 or 30 of them marked in the same way, you may be quite sure that they are for sale.'

Of all the witnesses, Churchill was perhaps the most defeatist and pessimistic. Still recovering from the illness and trauma of his last few months in Zanzibar, he spared the committee little. He told them his estimate of the number of slaves who were taken off the coast – between 17,000 and 18,000 a year, he thought, of which around 3,000 were retained in Zanzibar. He spoke of the enormous work the British consul faced, making do with just one clerk and a translator to assist him. He let them know how ineffective the naval patrol was, and the damage it caused to legitimate trade. On one occasion, he said, he had indicated a slaving dhow from the consulate window, only to see the British cruiser arrest the wrong dhow. He repeated the now familiar point, 'so long as the demand exists the supply will exist.' Everyone in Zanzibar was involved, he said. Everyone.

His responses even verged on the sarcastic as he listened to the naivety of some of the questions. Sir R. Anstruther seemed particularly slow at grasping the full impact of what he had been told. Questioning Churchill about a woman kept husking rice in Kilwa for a year, who had then been taken north and put in the Zanzibar market, the MP asked incredulously, 'Practically then she would be resold?' One can almost hear Churchill's weary tone, as he carefully chose words to indicate not only his agreement, but also the additional purposes for which this poor husker of rice might have been used. 'Yes,' he said. 'She would have passed through several hands.'

But it was the testimony of Sir John William Kaye, Secretary to the Political and Secret Department of the Indian Office in London, who perhaps most disturbed them. He had been in the post for fifteen years, and had been previously employed by the East India Company following military service in India.[5] He had immense experience, and his comments were dry and to the point, as he explained to the committee just how the Zanzibar consulate and agency worked. It was a joint enterprise, reporting to both the Foreign Office and the Indian government in Bombay, an arrangement that, he readily admitted, caused a good deal of inconvenience. The agent was primarily an officer of the Indian government, and British consul *ex officio*. He told them that the interest of the Indian government was mainly historical – to do with the Zanzibar rulers' association with the Gulf – and that in truth India would be readily shot of the whole affair if it could. As for the slave trade, given that the London government was not prepared to contribute a penny towards maintaining the agency in Zanzibar, India really did not see why it should pick up the tab for what was no concern of theirs.

The long argument between the two departments of state about who should pay for the agency gradually came into the open. On the one hand, 'The lords of the Treasury refused to pay a farthing towards it.' However, fighting the slave trade in Zanzibar, Kaye considered, was 'not a question in which the people of India are in any way concerned'. Indeed, 'it would be a misappropriation of the Indian revenues to devote money towards that purpose.' When asked why the London Treasury had not seen fit to contribute to the costs of the agency, he replied dryly, 'The views of the Treasury, I suppose, are that the game is not worth the candle.' So for several years these two great departments of state had squabbled about the costs involved, a total of £3,019 per annum.

However, it seemed that India's motives were not altogether innocent in the matter. When pressed on how helpful Bombay and Calcutta had been in assisting their Zanzibar agent to act against slavery, Kaye was not entirely direct. He would be surprised, he said, if 'the Indian Government had not thrown impediments in the way, or had discouraged the proceedings for the suppression of the slave trade.'

'So that this fearful traffic has latterly been increasingly carried on, owing to the action of Her Majesty's Government?' one committee member asked him in astonishment.

'Certainly, this would be the tendency,' was the smooth reply.

The committee, shocked to think that this awful traffic had persisted because of British internal disagreements and even negligence, for a brief moment thought a solution was within their reach. For a mere £3,019 per annum perhaps they could solve the problem.

Not so fast, Kaye told them. There still remained the question of the sultan. He would need to be compensated for ending his monopoly in the supply of slaves from the East African coast, and this was no trivial matter. But why would a civilized, educated man, such as Sultan Barghash, wish to continue with the cruel practice of selling into slavery every year so many thousands of Africans, he was asked. Kaye was unsparingly direct. Well, you see, he explained patiently, he needed the money. And in case these good men had missed the point, he forced it home. In fact, the sultan was not all that different from the British themselves, he explained. 'His continuing the slave trade is based solely on the ground that he cannot maintain his government without the amount of revenue which he receives from the duty on slaves.' He paused, then went on. 'Just as we uphold in India what we all know to be wrong, viz. the opium monopoly ... our only argument is that we cannot carry on the government without [it].'

Quite consciously, he told these pious, God-fearing men that the world was possibly not as they thought it to be. The British were not above condoning equally cynical practices. Zanzibar or Britain – there was less difference between them than the committee might think. However, the point about opium trafficking was passed over in silence – perhaps it was too embarrassing. The idea of a ruler who could profit directly from selling captives into servitude was quite offensive enough. 'He is a beggar on horseback,' exclaimed one member in horror and disgust.[6]

All this must have been acutely uncomfortable for the committee of humanitarians sitting in Westminster that July. For these men, the business of trading in African slaves was not merely one of the world's many unfortunate practices, to be deplored but tolerated, as Kaye suggested. It was almost the definition of sin itself, 'of all evils the monster evil', as an earlier campaigner against slave trading had once said.[7] It was also something they thought had been largely conquered half a century ago. With the abolition of Britain's own traffic, and then treaties with other powers on both sides of the Atlantic, they believed the practice had been pushed into the far margins of the civilized world. Now they heard that Britain and its Indian Empire had, in effect, condoned a trade, inferior in size but almost as cruel, on the other side of Africa, allowing it to flourish for the last fifty years. Even worse, witness after witness told them that there was really little to prevent this continuing for the rest of time.

The full horror of what this business involved was yet to be presented to them. During the next few days, two of the missionaries who had been active on the upper Zambesi during Livingstone's expedition presented evidence from their own personal experience.

It was Horace Waller who described to them in detail what the acquisition of slaves actually meant at the source of the trade. He told them how, when he was in Nyasaland, the whole country had been invaded by Yao incomers intent on gathering captives. While he allowed that once in the employment of an Arab master, slaves were treated relatively well, it was the suffering undergone in capture and shipment that was so dreadful. Prices for people in the interior were cheap, he said.

> When I first went there in 1861 … the ordinary price of a slave was two yards of calico; that is to say, for a boy of 10 years of age; a woman would fetch something more …

At the coast, the same slave might fetch $8. He then described the operation in some detail.

> The process of catching the slaves is this: the slave dealer goes into the country with so many muskets, and so many pieces of calico, and he finds out the most powerful chief, and he gives him spirits and keeps him in a state of semi drunkenness the whole time, and tells him he must have more slaves; he gives him muskets and powder on account, and the man immediately finds out an opportunity to settle some old outstanding quarrel with some other chief, and therefore a war breaks out.

And war, as Waller pointed out, always favoured the taking of slaves. In addition, if people were unable to cultivate their fields, if they missed the season, they were exposed to the effects of drought, and famine followed, and this also helped the slavers. A chief without adequate supplies of food would sell off his own people, and so the cycle of deprivation continued.

The more disturbed the country is, the cheaper slaves become; so cheap do they at last become, that I have known children of the age of from eight to 10 years bought for less corn than would go into one of our hats, and you may easily imagine where they are bought so cheaply, and where they fetch so large a price on the coast, it pays the slave dealer very well to collect as many as he can, knowing that he must lose a certain proportion on the way, but also knowing that the remnant he saves will pay him a very large profit.

He then gave the committee an image that was to remain with them. Struggling to find a means of describing the terrible attrition the slaves faced on their route to the coast, he referred to a common practice in England that July, which would be familiar to all his audience.

It is like sending up for a large block of ice to London in the hot weather; you know that a certain amount will melt away before it reaches you in the country as it travels down; but that which remains will be quite sufficient for your needs.

Waller's account was the most explicit description of the slave-raiding process the committee were to hear, and it shocked them. The comparison with ice melting was a graphic one, to be repeated many times, but the reasons for this phenomenon were also made abundantly clear. The progress of a caravan to the coast could take months as it meandered from place to place in its search for captives. As a consequence, 'the loss of life is very terrible indeed, owing to the hardships of the transit, and owing to the brutality of the drivers.' Famine and sickness were continual hazards. But in addition 'if there is anything like insubordination in the slave gang, the axe and knife are used very freely indeed, and an indiscriminate slaughter takes place . . .' Waller described how he had seen evidence of such killing. The slaves were virtually defenceless – 'they are all united in a long string, the men being yoked in heavy forked sticks, which are kept on the their necks from the time they are captured till the time they are delivered to the slave shipper . . .' Waller completed his testimony with the harrowing account of his own experience of famine on the upper Shire.

> When we were in the highlands in 1863 and 1864, in the neighbourhood of the Shire, all the population which was not swept off accumulated at the river; and it was a very frightful state of things there, because the people flocked to the river perfectly famished and perfectly mad with hunger, and they risked their lives for a few heads of corn. The river all day long was carrying down the dead bodies of those who had been fighting amongst themselves, like starving dogs quarrelling over a bone.

Edward Steere, another missionary who had also been on the Zambesi, had more to say about the next stage of the slaves' journey, once they had reached the coast. He explained to the committee that the majority of slaves arrived at the sea port of Kilwa, and from there were sent up the coast to the market in Zanzibar. The journey took between one and three days and the slaves were given a small portion of rice to survive on. If the passage lasted longer, as sometimes happened, many of them died, he said. He had lived in Zanzibar for several years, and he . . .

> . . . used to see the dhows coming from Kilwa with slaves: they used to go round our house close to our windows, the deck of the dhow would be entirely covered with slaves squatting side by side, so closely packed that it was impossible for them to move; there would sometimes be 200 to 300 in a large open boat . . .

Then from Zanzibar, once they had been sold, they were sent on up the coast to Arabia. This part of the journey could take up to thirty-five days, and at times the slaves were kept in the hold under conditions of great hardship. Steere was asked how they were taken. Under false permits made out for the port of Lamu, he said, although in reality their destination was elsewhere. It was all done perfectly openly. 'There was not the slightest attempt at interfering with it.' The licenses were legal, they were just for the wrong destination.

'It is a mere blind?' one member asked him.

'It is a mere blind,' Steere replied.

It was now becoming evident to the committee that something terrible was taking place on the other side of Africa, a disaster of apocalyptic dimensions, in a world utterly different from their own, which was nevertheless their responsibility to prevent. Yet again and again they were deprived of any practical solution. The question of a naval blockade, so effective in preventing the Atlantic slave trade, was raised and discussed. However, the naval commanders who gave testimony were just as cynical as the government officers. Indeed, they further confused the picture as they described their muddled attempts to impose a blockade on the slave dhows.

No one was quite sure why it was not working, but all were adamant that this was the case. Admiral Heath, who had been in charge of the fleet between 1867 and 1871 seemed particularly confused, acknowledging quite openly that he had been unable to intercept anything more than a tiny number of slave-carrying dhows. Asked by the committee how the dhows had evaded his cruisers, he said he was totally mystified. The question of informants among the translators and the men on the Zanzibar waterfront was raised, and under pressure, he finally admitted that 'the Arabs have very good information; I do not think they knew what I intended to do, but it is quite possible that they did.'

Then, once again, cruelty of the starkest kind was described. Captain Colomb, who had commanded one of the patrol cruisers, was asked what took place when a slave-carrying dhow was identified and pursued. The slaves were dispensed with, he replied.

Mr Fowler asked, 'By throwing them into the sea?'

'It would depend on whether they had a valuable cargo besides their slaves,' the captain replied. 'They certainly would sacrifice the slaves to save a valuable cargo, either by throwing them into the sea, or by knocking them on the head.'

Mr Kinnaird asked incredulously, 'They think nothing of knocking them on the head?'

From Captain Colomb: 'Nothing.'

Inevitably, the committee began to talk of putting forcible

pressure on Zanzibar and its ruler, for this seemed to be the only solution. Once again, they were frustrated. Vivian of the Foreign Office was reluctantly of the opinion that it was neither right nor legal for Britain to take the sultan by the throat and inform him he had to suppress the trade. One witness compared Zanzibar to Lagos, an island on the west coast of Africa, which Britain had seized in 1861–2, striking a death blow against the Atlantic trade. Perhaps Zanzibar could be seized in a similar fashion, or at the very least purchased. The idea was caustically dismissed out of hand, once again by the urbane Sir John Kaye. 'As to purchasing Zanzibar,' he remarked, 'you might as well talk of purchasing Germany.' This was an independent state with its own government; it was not for sale.

The issues seemed inconceivably complex, and nothing the committee was told seemed unambiguous or certain. Witnesses contradicted themselves. Distinctions between legal and illegal slave trading were confused. The reasons why the patrol was so ineffective were apparent to no one. The causes of the trade were obscure at times. The sultan's real control over his people aroused conflicting opinions, and witnesses held opposing views on the merits of forcing some kind of solution on him. During the proceedings many references were made to Livingstone and his reports from Africa, yet even here was an element of doubt. His expedition to the Zambesi had been controversial, and some members were concerned at just how accurate his reports were.

The committee members were desperate for a solution. They felt under pressure not just because of the terms on which they had been appointed, but also from a moral imperative. They had to do something. Not to do so would be to walk away from the Christian obligations that many of them took with great seriousness. Yet these dhows came south often on apparently legitimate business, as they had done for centuries. The demand for slaves was in countries over which Britain had little if any influence, and it seemed that every merchant between Central Africa and the heartlands of Muslim Asia was one way or another involved. How, then, did they prevent it?

Day after day, the committee grappled with the problem with an increasing sense of hopelessness, but one witness came forward who was radically different from the others. Sir Bartle Frere gave evidence in his capacity as a former governor of the Bombay presidency, and therefore a man who had once been nominally responsible for the Zanzibar agency. Whereas all the other witnesses presented difficulty and complexity, Frere was clear, specific and determined. Whereas everyone else had been cynical, he was optimistic about a possible outcome. He was the only witness to offer the committee what it desperately wanted, a clear and convincing way out of their impasse.

Frere was an ambitious man. After a long and distinguished career in India lasting almost thirty years, he had returned to Britain to take up a position on the India Council, a body that advised the secretary of state. He was passionately pro Indian, and had been particularly active in the civic and commercial development of Bombay while he was governor, setting up a municipal commission, which commenced a massive programme of public works, building and sanitation. Nevertheless, during his time there, he had frequently been in conflict with his superiors in Calcutta, and in particular with the viceroy at the time, Lord Lawrence. Frere had disagreed strongly with the prevailing policy, which avoided any interference in local practices, and this had damaged his reputation. Returning to Britain, he found himself languishing, barely occupied, in relative obscurity at his house in Wimbledon. The council met just once a week, and the real power lay in the relationship between the viceroy and the secretary of state. Frere felt himself redundant.

Tall, handsome and energetic, with a permanent limp, which only seemed to emphasize his vigour, Frere came to the committee room well prepared. Almost immediately he launched into a cogent exposition of his own views on the whole question of slave trafficking, which he felt had not been adequately explained to the committee. The problem was a direct result of British indecision and wavering – 'the oscillation of our own opinions in the matter'. He was forthright in his comments, using strong unambiguous words chosen to impress the committee. Excuses for slavery that had been put about in recent years were a 'cardinal evil' in his opinion. 'We need to make up our own minds with regard to what is to be done.' He presented himself as a man of action who knew what he was talking about. He believed in technology and commerce as agents of change, which by themselves could overcome many of the disabilities of under-developed countries. He himself had used such methods; as an example he described how a combination of steamships and telegraphic communication had managed to reduce a famine in Gujerat by quickly importing grain from Persia.

Frere also believed in native rulers, but thought they should be firmly shown the way. Men such as Barghash understood justice, but they also understood strength, and would respond 'by taking our advice and being a good deal guided by our wishes . . .' His philosophy when dealing with them was to employ 'frugal liberality' and to exercise forbearance. He had dealt with this kind of problem in the past, he said pointedly.

Frere mesmerized the committee as he expounded at length on exactly how the problem should be handled. He had no patience with equivocation or dithering of any kind, and he had no time for excuses about slavery's respected place in Islamic culture. Slave trading was wrong and that was all there was to it. To argue otherwise was moral cowardice. He spoke logically, and with precision, and he presented a total contrast to the tired and cynical witnesses who had preceded him. It is easy to imagine him striding back and forth across the chamber, holding the MPs' attention. They were desperate for a solution, and he was offering them one that was persuasive.

Frere did not want to destroy Zanzibar, an important centre of trade and commerce throughout the region. On the contrary, he wanted to carry its ruler with him, and he was totally confident that this could be done, if approached in the right manner.

Now if we get the Sultan's government . . . with us entirely, and act, as I think we are bound to act in those areas, rather in supplementing their defects, than in superseding their authority, and if we make use, as far as possible, of their authority, I think we should be able to get rid of a great many of those inconvenient limitations which very much harass and impede our naval officers.

As far as Sultan Barghash was concerned, Frere was entirely optimistic.

You must, to some extent, bring him over to your view, that this matter of slave trading is a bad one for him. I have no doubt that in time, he could be brought to see it in that light.

Frere had an anwer for every question and every uncertainty the committee posed to him. Questioned about how all this might be paid for, he was unconcerned. Zanzibar was a remarkable example of how commerce sprang up in the most unlikely places, and this would naturally continue. Trade itself would do the trick, he said, for as soon as the evil of slave trafficking was removed, so a more virtuous commerce would arrive to take its place. It had happened elsewhere, and he had no doubt it would happen here, too.

In fact, Frere was entirely free from doubt, and his testimony was peppered with the words, as again and again he told the committee how convinced he was. He had 'no doubt' that if slave trafficking were stopped, traders would attend to legitimate commerce. There could be 'no doubt' that the practice of slave trading was relatively new, and therefore would be easily contained in time. In his opinion, it really dated back only to the suppression of piracy earlier in the century.[8] There was 'little doubt' that attempts to enslave people were a response to an economic problem, also a matter that could be readily solved. Again and again he used the words, repeating clearly and forcefully his utter conviction that correctly handled, this problem was eminently solvable. By the time he was finished, few on the committee could have complained that he had not offered them a way out of their predicament. He even told them exactly how this should be done. A senior officer should be sent to Zanzibar 'prepared with some authority, and with the dignity of a special envoy to press these points ...' It was obvious whom he considered best suited for the task.

Throughout the hearings, however, one committee member remained less convinced than his colleagues by Frere's eloquence. Mr Kennaway, when informed that the Sultan of Zanzibar could be amicably persuaded to relinquish his profitable activities, and quietly give way to the demands of destiny, had a wry comment:

> You expect him to give up the 20,000 pounds which he is supposed to derive from the slave trade; that is a 'decree of fate' which a man does not submit to without a struggle.

Kirk had been referred to frequently during the committee proceedings. Churchill had told members that he had recommended his deputy for the job of agent and consul when he was forced to leave Zanzibar, remarking that Kirk's knowledge of the place was considerable. He was clearly the best man for the post. 'When in Bombay I recommended his appointment, but the Governor said that it had been decided . . . that medical officers should not fill the appointment of political agents.' As a consequence, he thought, Kirk would eventually leave the country for there was little point in him staying.

A letter from Kirk to the Foreign Office had been read out during the hearings, in which he had been particularly dismissive of India's authority in Africa.[9] He had also told Vivian that Barghash had no fear of force, for the sultan knew the British would always respect their treaties. Only economic pressure, Kirk believed, would tell therefore, but this was a view that Frere in particular dismissed when it was put to him. Nevertheless, Kirk had come out well from the proceedings, and the committee in its final report recommended strongly that he be confirmed in his post. But this was unlikely to have any effect since the Foreign Office still did not call the shots, and Kirk's letter had infuriated his Indian colleagues with its suggestions of disloyalty. They were not about to change their minds.

The committee's report was published on 4 August 1871, and its recommendations were optimistic, woolly and imprecise. The members loftily wished to ban slave trading in its entirety off the African coast, stating their confidence that legitimate commerce could take the place of trading in human flesh. To enable this they advised that a new treaty should be sought from the sultan, although the report did not say how this was to be achieved, beyond making vague comments on compelling Barghash to take additional measures. Needless to say, the government, having appointed the committee, did little to respond. A desultory attempt was made to interest other European powers, but without success. Gladstone, the prime minister, took the view that slave trading would decline gradually under the influence of legitimate commerce, and there was a general lack of interest in the country as a whole. The circulation of the *Journal of the Anti Slavery Society*, once a powerful voice, had declined dramatically, and although Livingstone's dispatches from Africa were published and read, he had not been heard of since late 1869.

At this point, Frere took the initiative. He had an instinctive knack of knowing how to exploit public opinion, and in early 1872, despite its diminished status, he got in touch with the Anti Slavery Society. In March, a meeting was held at Surrey Chapel presided over by Fowell Buxton, a noted antislaver, and Frere was the star speaker. Talking vigorously about the slave trade in East Africa, he roused the audience to renew its efforts and to reignite the old campaign. This was followed in May by a bigger meeting at the Friends Meeting House,[10] where once again Frere urged attendees to harry their MPs on this vital question.

He was a successful orator, and his efforts began to produce results. Towards the end of July, Lord Stratheden moved an address to the Queen in the Lords and virtually all speakers came out strongly against the trafficking of people off the African coast. The following day *The Times* carried a leader saying the foreign secretary, Lord Granville, had a duty to see that suppression would be carried out, and on 25 July the Anti Slavery Society arranged a meeting at the Mansion House. The Lord Mayor opened, and Frere again delivered a powerful address to a packed hall. Ten MPs were present, as well as leading antislave trade personalities including Buxton, Waller, Lord Stratheden, Kennaway, Rigby, Russell Gurney and Kinnaird. At this meeting, an old abolitionist in his ninetieth year was present, a man who had known Wilberforce and Clarkson, and who was next day quoted in the press as saying he was horrified to find that the slave trade was still continuing.

Thirty-five years ago I went to sleep in the belief the slave trade was finally dead and almost buried ... that the utter extinction of the traffic was a thing of the past. I now find a slave trade worse than anything that was ever known on the west coast of Africa is flourishing and still in vigour under our eyes on the east coast ...[11]

Frere, whose publicity skills by now were finely honed, suggested that this old man represented the feelings of the great majority of the people in Britain, and the following day a deputation of three peers, fifteen MPs and the secretaries of the main missionary societies called on Granville. Two weeks later, the Queen's speech referred to the government's intention to act against the slave trade off the east coast of Africa.

Frere, however, was not the only man in Britain who understood the usefulness of the press. On the same day as the Mansion House meeting, 25 July, readers of *The Times* and the *Daily Telegraph* were astonished to read over breakfast an astounding story, sent by 'special submarine telegram' the previous night from France. The explorer, David Livingstone, had been discovered deep in Africa by an unknown American. The story, in one paper referred to as the 'Incident from Ujiji', was explosive, and dominated the press for weeks. Together with interviews with Stanley, and quotations from Livingstone's letters, it filled column after column of the front pages. The reports were also accompanied by accounts of the indecision and confusion surrounding the collapse of the British rescue expedition, which only made the American's energy and ability more admirable.

After years of ignorance and indifference to Livingstone's fate, the story of his desperate wanderings, the terrible sufferings he had undergone and witnessed, and his final dramatic rescue were recounted in detail to a public avid for news. A long leader in *The Times* on 27 July eulogized Livingstone, adding 'we cannot conclude without expressing the admiration which every Englishman must feel at the enterprise and courage displayed by the American gentleman who has traced the illustrious traveller.'[12] The chronicle touched all who read it. It combined great heroism with Christian suffering; but it also involved treachery, for it included serious charges against the friend who should most have helped the lost explorer, and yet who failed him in his time of need. During long talks with journalists in Marseilles and again in Paris, where he was 'thronged every hour of the day', Stanley had given full vent to his accusations against Kirk. The use of slaves not free men, the neglect in forwarding letters, Kirk's shooting trip to Bagamoyo and the final refusal to assist Stanley in forwarding the last caravan – all were mentioned as evidence of his carelessness. Witnesses in Zanzibar were cited in support, one of whom, 'a wealthy merchant', was none other than Kirk's 'friend' Fraser.[13] Livingstone himself, Stanley said, had even asked for the acting consul's conduct to be investigated. In Paris, at a dinner given in his honour by American residents, Stanley openly referred to Kirk as a traitor.[14]

Kirk was immediately defended by a number of people in the press. Churchill wrote twice, Livingstone's son Oswell also wrote, as well as several others, including a Captain Parish who knew Kirk from Zanzibar. Waller, too, wrote in protest, and even went to see Stanley in his hotel to reason with him. However, the excitement and controversy continued for weeks, boosted by enormous press coverage when Stanley arrived in Britain on 1 August. From then until he left in early November, as he toured the country, he was rarely out of the news. Column after column was filled with Livingstone's letters, and Stanley was invited to address the British Association in Brighton, where over three thousand people, including Louis Napoleon and his wife, the former empress, listened to a vivid account of his travels.

Stanley basked in the adulation. He was the guest of honour at the Brighton and Sussex Medical Society, he was received at the Guildhall, and was presented to the Queen. A banquet was given in his honour at the Royal Geographical Society, and he was given the Victoria gold medal, its highest accolade. Sir Henry Rawlinson, its president, announced that 'Mr. Stanley's journey . . . is one of the most brilliant exploits in the whole history of African travel . . .'[15]

In October that year, Stanley made a short tour of Scotland, capitalizing on Livingstone's name in the country of his birth, and it was a triumph. On 23 October he was entertained to a banquet by the Corporation of Glasgow. On 24 October he visited Hamilton, where he met Livingstone's sister and daughters, and was granted the freedom of the borough. On 27 October he was met at Cathcart Street railway station, Greenock, by the provosts and magistrates of the town, and received an ovation from the crowd assembled to witness his arrival. On 30 October he was in Helensburgh, and the next day he arrived in Edinburgh, where he was 'entertained to luncheon by the Magistrates and Town Council', with 'invitations issued to about two hundred of the leading citizens, most of whom were present'.[16]

Throughout this time he kept up his attacks on Kirk, and in Edinburgh he devoted almost his entire speech to destroying Kirk's reputation. It was done very skilfully, and with an assumption of innocence and regret that he had ever been drawn into such a matter. He did not have any quarrel with the man, he said. 'I do not charge Dr Kirk with any wilful neglect, or any feelings of jealousy, that is far from my mind.' Nevertheless, after hearing what Livingstone had to tell him, he could not keep silent.

And if I experienced certain feelings of indignation – if I was sensitive and susceptible when Livingstone repeated these things to me – you will understand . . . [He built up a picture of Livingstone as the abandoned saint, a] poor man, sitting down with the sentence of death almost written on his face . . . To this man in Central Africa, with the dark midnight of barbarism around him, suffering even on the verge of the grave – a 'ruckle of bones', as he said himself – I who met him at Ujiji – I, the susceptible and sensitive Yankee – said 'Doctor . . . I will explain the thing to people . . .'

And explain he did, contrasting his own sensitive and generous spirit with that of the man in Zanzibar.

The gentleman who has got his fame and position as the friend of Dr Livingstone, [who] left him in Africa, silent, alone, deserted, and almost at death's door . . . If Dr Kirk wishes to be the friend of Dr Livingstone, all he has got to do is to prove to Dr Livingstone that he is his friend.[17]

But Livingstone had already proved he was certainly no friend to Kirk. His individual letters by now had reached their destinations, and the one to Sir Roderick Murchison, the late president of the Royal Geographical Society was particularly bitter. In them, he accused Kirk of laziness, and of only desiring the salary and status of consul. He, Livingstone, had 'made' Kirk, he claimed, yet the man felt no gratitude.[18]

On 4 November, an important antislavery meeting took place at the Mansion House, convened by the Lord Mayor to express public feeling for the immediate suppression of slave trading in East Africa. It was already known that Sir Bartle Frere was due to go to Zanzibar to negotiate with the sultan, and he was present, as were many others identified with the movement. Stanley sat beside the Lord Mayor, and made a long speech about the horrors of the trade – not something he had normally been concerned with. He ended with a final jab at Kirk. Frere was sorely needed in Zanzibar, he said, not least because of the poor relationship between the current British agent and the sultan.

Stanley left for the United States on 9 November, and his account of his travels in Africa, *How I found Livingstone*, was published later that month. It became an instant bestseller, selling tens of thousands of copies and running straight to a second edition. It was a racily written account, produced at great speed, and it renders vividly Stanley's energy and vigour as he crossed the difficult dangerous ground between the coast and Ujiji, where he finally claimed his prize. His search is presented as an obsessive, almost holy mission, and Livingstone himself is repeatedly described in terms of cloying sentimentality and adulation. 'Lips that never lie . . .' 'The man has no guile . . .' 'He is as near an angel as any living man.'[19] Here was a saint in crisis, resigned to his fate, betrayed by one who should have saved him. For threaded through the book, repeated again and again, are references to Kirk's unforgiveable treachery.

It was always a partial account, for Stanley did not really find Livingstone the way he presented him. In his journal written at the time he freely admitted that the Doctor's 'strong nature was opposed to forgiveness and that he was not so perfect as at the first blush of friendship I thought him.'[20] Nevertheless, Stanley had by now firmly laid the foundations of the Livingstone myth. It was a moving story, which was completed by the old man's lonely death at Lake Bangweulu in May 1873, the transport of his body to the coast by his followers, its journey to England, and the final procession through weeping crowds to its burial in the nave of Westminster Abbey. This was to become for the Victorians an immensely powerful and uplifting narrative.

At that point, Stanley did in a sense own Livingstone. He carried the explorer's last known words, for no European or American was to see Livingstone again. He had told a powerful story, which only he was able to do, and he had told it well. The American and British public were fascinated. The learned societies and the government were bound to listen, for it came with the sanction and authority of Livingstone himself. But for Kirk, it represented shame and disgrace.

Sir Bartle Frere left England for Africa later in November 1872. His lobbying and mastery of publicity had served him well, for he had secured from Lord Granville the grand title of Special Envoy under the Great Seal, and a handsome salary. Public pressure on the government had grown throughout the summer, and although the Indian authorities resisted, Frere had used his connections to secure cooperation from Calcutta for his mission. Sending Frere to Africa had now become the only way out of an insoluble problem for the government, and Frere knew it. He had negotiated for himself a brief that allowed him virtually complete freedom in his discussions with Sultan Barghash. He also carried instructions to establish the truth of Stanley's accusations of negligence on the part of John Kirk, acting agent in Zanzibar, in failing to support Dr Livingstone.[21]

12: A LOAD UPON THE CAMEL

His Highness replied, 'We are in your hands, if you persist all the caravans will die and die through your instrumentality, and I would not wish it so.

SULTAN BARGHASH TO SIR BARTLE FRERE

On 29 March 1872, Barghash arrived back from Arabia, travelling by one of the first steamers to be seen in Zanzibar harbour. Two weeks later, on 15 April, a cyclone crossing the Indian Ocean carved its way across the island, wrecking everything in its path. It was entirely unexpected since Zanzibar lay to the north of the normal cyclone zone. The storm began during the night of the 14th, with heavy rain and a strong wind from the south south west. By next morning it had increased to a gale, rapidly reaching hurricane force, and by midday the air had turned completely still, the barometer had plunged and there was a fine clear sky. Then the full storm broke with abrupt violence, as the winds shifted in a great circle from north north east to north, to north west and then west north west, raging throughout the day. Torrential rain turned the narrow streets of the town into deep torrents, and with the exception of one steamship, all craft in the harbour were swept to destruction.

The British consulate, standing close above the shore on Shangani Point, took the full force of the gale. The first gust of the storm drove in the windows of the building, breaking open doors

231

and throwing furniture against the walls. As the sea rose over the shore, great sheets of water drifted in through the broken windows, and filled the building a foot deep. Kirk wrote:

> The sea was driven with such force as to undermine and sweep away the whole embankment of stone and double row of wooden piles that protect the foundations of the English, German, and American Consulates, and throw down an immense wall four feet thick with foundation eight feet deep in front of the garden, which was in great part washed away ... The Consular boathouse and two boats have been entirely destroyed.

At the storm's height, Kirk's office was burst open by the howling wind, and a solid chest of teak, which he used to store documents, as well as the bureau where he held his correspondence, were ripped open and gutted of their contents.

> Next morning I recovered in the street many Government orders and confidential memoranda, together with the bulk of my mail that should have gone the next day ... In my own quarters, which are behind the Consulate, windows were burst open and carried away, while the floor of the drawing-room was covered a foot deep with water in which books, pictures, and china, with tables, chairs, etc., etc., formed a confused and sodden heap.[1]

Wherever the cyclone had passed, there was nothing but wreckage. Whole plantations of cloves and coconuts were flattened, houses and villages demolished, and dhows moored in the port were destroyed. Boats were lifted inland and laid down haphazardly across the ground and among the trees. It was as though a great hand had passed across the island, and the vegetation was shrivelled and charred. 'The island had the appearance of having been scorched with fire, or as if the burning blast of the simoom had passed over it,' wrote Christie.[2] The agricultural economy was ravaged, and many of the richest citizens contemplated the ruin of their estates. Moreover, the disaster had come at a difficult time. Wars in the interior meant the ivory trade was also in crisis, and the Customs House looked like making a loss that year. But the trading in slaves seemed unaffected. In the season of 1871–2 it gave every appearance of continuing its remorseless growth.

In January 1872, Kirk had reported on the previous season's numbers.[3] It had been an exceptional year, the largest in terms of shipments since 1866, with twice the volumes of the preceding year. The main reason, he thought, lay in the deaths from cholera, not just in Zanzibar but all along the coast. Supplies of labour needed replenishing, and between May and December 1871, 14,392 slaves had been shipped out of the port of Kilwa into Zanzibar, with a further 3,000 shipped from elsewhere. Of these, nearly half continued to Arabia and Persia.

Yet the market was still volatile. A few months later, on 22 May 1872, Kirk wrote:

> Never since coming to Zanzibar have I seen so many large Dhows come in crowded with slaves and seldom have the slaves imported been landed in a worse state but the speculation is little likely to prove profitable unless they can be smuggled off Somali land or Arabia for the Hurricane which ruined the Arab plantations has placed it out of the owners power to purchase slaves and lessened enormously the demand for labour.[4]

Slaves had become a burden to the estate owners. Unable to feed themselves because of the destruction to their crops, they depended on their masters for their daily food supplies. However, the markets to the north were still proving robust. In Somalia prices were high, and the annual fair at Berbera off the Somali coast went on for months, creating a huge demand. From there, many slaves were shipped on up the Red Sea, across to Arabia and into the wider world.

Throughout that season and on into early 1873, Kirk recorded endless evidence of the trade's expansion. Occasionally, he was able to obtain a conviction against dealers, but these were rare.

> On discovery that Ottomano Lamo and his son both implicated in the shipment of slaves last season to Brava in the Dhow ran ashore by the boats of HM ship 'Columbine', and against whom I held good documentary proof were in town purchasing slaves, I applied for their arrest sending the proof before HH [i.e. Barghash] . . . Both have been placed in heavy slave irons in the fort where they will be kept for a time and on being released fined. Their houses when searched contained 41 slaves which have been confiscated.[5]

Sometimes the numbers were large – towards the end of the year, a dhow with 133 slaves on board was caught – but more often they were pitifully small, and again and again the victims were children. A young boy, hauled out from under the sacks of a dhow apprehended in March 1873, had been bought in Kilwa by the *nakhoda* as a small investment. He was a Yao from faraway inland. In April 1873, two boats were caught manned by Somalis, and some of the slaves were thrown overboard to avoid capture. In May an Indian man called Arnasallo living in Bagamoyo was arrested for casually killing a female slave in his possession. One of his other slaves told the court that he beat his slaves daily with a stick. Arnasallo was fined one hundred dollars.

At times Kirk seemed overcome by the weary hopelessness of it all. In July 1872 he had been ill for almost the first time, suffering from dysentery and malaria. He wrote:

> There is I am sorry to state every sign of the slave trade being on the increase and worked under an organised system which it needs organisation to meet, and to any one on the spot the means . . .[6]

But he did not have either the means or the organization.

There was also a fundamental contradiction to the court's activities, which was evident to everyone in Zanzibar, not least to Kirk himself, and which made it often appear a futile and absurd charade. These cases, tried in a hot airless room of the agency building, where interpreters and judge explored arcane infringements of an alien law, were held in the midst of a city dedicated to the very practices under trial. Few understood the court's rationale – why some cases of slave catching and shipment were legal and some not – and few even cared. The court itself appeared to be nothing more than the freakish whim of powerful western intruders who indulged in it for their own selfish purposes. Sometimes slavers were tried and convicted, while simultaneously other slavers passed within sight of the court with total impunity in their dhows. And a few miles away the slave market in town prospered without interference.

There were times when Barghash assisted the consulate in its efforts, partly from goodwill and partly from his own desire to control the anarchic slaving raids from the north. But for him, slave trading was only part of a wider problem. By late 1872 the Customs Master Ludda Dhamji had died and Lukmidias, his successor, was losing control over the coastal ports and inlets. The Customs House was not yielding the profits it had in the past, some of the merchants were refusing to pay duty, and overall smuggling was on the increase as larger numbers of slaves passed outside the official system.

Nevertheless, by September 1872, prices had risen to record levels – as much as $40 per slave[7] – and in January 1873, dealers on the waterfront were openly bragging about the good season they were enjoying. And on the 12th of that month, an imposing squadron of three British cruisers and a steam yacht sailed into Zanzibar harbour. They dominated the waterfront by their sheer presence, and everyone on the island knew that they conveyed a special envoy from London with the specific intention of bringing to an end forever the island's traffic in slaves.

The city opposite which Frere anchored still showed marks of the battering it had taken the previous April. Since this was high season for visits by travellers from the Gulf, the harbour was filled with 'a wilderness of dhows', but above the town, the wreck of a frigate belonging to the sultan was visible, like 'a waif left from last year's hurricane'. Roofs were still damaged, doors and windows blown in, and the whitewashed walls of the large seafront buildings were stained with 'great patches of discoloured decay'.[8] The same day as the squadron's arrival, shortly after sundown, Kirk went out to meet the envoy on his yacht, the *Enchantress*, and not long after he was followed by the sultan's wazir, Nassir bin Saeed, who invited Frere to visit his master on the evening of the next day.

Kirk had been prepared for Frere's arrival. Since late 1872 he had been receiving letters from friends in England informing him of the extraordinary effect of Stanley's return from Africa. He was also fully aware of the impact this had for him personally. H.W. Bates, the assistant secretary at the Royal Geographical Society, wrote that they were doing their best to defend Kirk from 'the cruel charges' being spread against him in the press. But 'the arrival of Stanley, skilfully heralded by Telegrams and all the arts of the newspapers' special correspondents, raised the enthusiasm of the nation on behalf of Dr. L. to the highest pitch.' Stanley, Bates wrote, was 'a popular hero', and 'the consequences have been a furious attack from almost all quarters against all the supposed critics and enemies of Livingstone ...' Contesting Stanley's version of events was hopeless 'whilst public opinion treats him as a demigod and obliged to be right in everything'.[9]

In November, Oswell Livingstone wrote to Kirk, telling him he had been forced to intervene in public to warn 'that scoundrel Stanley' to take care about what he said.[10] Hooker, too, wrote saying how disgusted he had been to meet Stanley at a public reception. Lieutenant Dawson, leader of the aborted Livingstone rescue expedition, had been reprimanded for his conduct in abandoning the search. In September, he wrote to Kirk telling him how he had attempted to defend him. Stanley, he wrote bitterly, had been presented with a gold snuff box and was due to meet the Queen. Dawson also sent Kirk an implicit warning about Frere's visit, advising him against expressing the slightest criticism of Livingstone. Frere knew everything, he wrote. 'But I thought it better to warn you that Dr. L. is a saint in England, and were he living the life of fifty Arabs put together it would not matter. He is the people's darling so make him yours ...'[11]

Livingstone had become untouchable, and yet some spoke out. The dispute had spread to the Indian press, when Fraser, the Zanzibar sugar planter, had written a malicious letter reaffirming Stanley's accusations. There was a swift riposte, not from Kirk, but from a long-standing British merchant, called Pollock, who had lived in Zanzibar and knew the whole story. On 6 July 1872, Pollock wrote to the *Indian Statesman*, accusing Fraser of outright lies. He pointed out that Fraser and Kirk had been good friends until a few months previously when Fraser had been shot at by some Arabs, and in the ensuing case had turned violent and been asked to leave the British consulate. From then on he had been an enemy of Kirk's. As for Livingstone, Pollock wrote, he was 'a somewhat perverse and crotchetty old gentleman who has been playing at "hide and seek" for a number of years, has put people to a great deal of expense and has had a fit of sulks upon him of unusual duration.'[12] He went on to remark that Livingstone had never had a better friend than John Kirk.

In the face of all this, Kirk was forced to assume a dignified silence. The Indian government did not permit its employees to respond to comments in the press. He did write to Granville, on 9 May 1872, explaining his position in clear unemotional terms, and this, as well as other letters, was printed in the London press.[13] But he must have known that among Frere's duties in visiting Africa would be an investigation into his own conduct, and when the great man arrived, anchoring the *Enchantress* opposite the British agency, Kirk would have been aware of the kind of scrutiny he would receive from the various officials on board.

Frere's mission was substantial. The special envoy had brought with him a team of attachés, advisers, private secretaries and Foreign Office officals, including a British Hindu from Bombay and the former Diwan of the Rao of Kutch. However, the most important member of the entourage was Frere's confidential adviser, the Reverend George Percy Badger, a white-bearded, elderly scholar, prone to frequent attacks of gout, and famed for his extensive study of the history of Oman and his deep knowledge of classical Arabic.[14] He was to act as the key intermediary between Frere and Sultan Barghash, whom he had met on a previous visit to Zanzibar twelve years earlier.

The mission had come well prepared. On board was an extensive library of books, including several recent works by explorers and travellers, such as Burton, Livingstone, Baker, Speke and the Frenchman, Guillain. Frere had also ensured that they carried an enormous quantity of files containing official correspondence on the slave trade, numerous commercial reports, confidential documents and orders in council, together with the various rules and regulations affecting consular courts.[15] At some stage along the way, the yacht had also acquired a monkey, which made a habit of stealing dispatches and eating them on deck.

In the course of a year, Frere had achieved much. The resurgence of interest in Livingstone, and the press hysteria that followed, had been of immeasurable assistance to his own campaign, and he had exploited it well. But he had also raised expectations to a very high level. Identifying himself with the anti-slavetrade cause, and capitalizing on the public frenzy, he had managed to make himself virtually indispensable to the government. He had effectively written his own brief, securing in addition a very substantial salary, merely submitting it to Granville for approval. Yet behind the evangelical and policy concerns, the envoy had his own private agenda.

Frere intended that his trip to Africa and the Gulf should be a tour de force. For many years, he had believed that Britain's involvement on a larger and more energetic scale in and around the Indian Ocean was both necessary and inevitable. Perhaps, even, a further extension to the Empire was possible, covering the petty states of the Gulf, and extending through the territories along the East African coast. Prior to his departure and during his trip, Frere was clear that achieving this had become his own overriding ambition.[16]

Frere's methods, however, did not attract universal approval, and there were some who were not easy with his approach. Lord Argyll, the secretary for India, expressed his reservations, suggesting that while Frere was full of interesting theories, he was not always the most practical man.[17] And Lord Acton, an astute observer of political life, liked Frere, but thought him 'a dangerous agent'. Acton wrote:

[He] is a strong and able, and a plausible man . . . It is true that his strength is akin to obstinacy and self-will, that he is rather too plausible, and that he will gain his ends by crooked paths when he has tried the straight in vain.

Frere was indeed persuasive and plausible. He had managed to present himself to the committee and to the British public as a modern man, enlightened and tolerant; certainly not one of the old 'Indian' school, who would rely on compulsion in dealing with traditional rulers. He implied that his gift was his ability to persuade. Yet at heart, Frere was still an 'Indian'. He had spent thirty years on the subcontinent, and he was instinctively accustomed to exercising the power behind British rule. His use of 'persuasion' had always been from a position of strength. Acton, like many in Britain at the time, distrusted the habits of such men. 'Indians are not generally a healthy element in the body politic,' he went on to write. 'And [Frere] has the constant vice of Indians, belief in force.'[18]

Frere did not see himself in this way. On his trip to Africa, he was determined to avoid any use of force. On the contrary, he intended to be idealistic and principled. Yet from the beginning that 'Indian' vice still managed to suggest itself, for status and position were absolutely vital to him, and he could never conceive of any negotiation that would not be from a position of superiority. His title of Special Envoy under the Great Seal seems to have been invented to give the impression of immense importance, and on his voyage, he carried with him the whole panoply and inheritance of the Indian Empire and its overwhelming concern for rank and power. It was his past, it had created him and he could never forget it.

Frere had left Britain, confident in the knowledge of the impact public support had given him. By the time he left the country, the anti-slavetrade campaign in the press had worked itself up into a frenzy. The dinner held on the eve of his departure at the Royal

Geographical Society was attended by more than two hundred people and widely reported in the national news. Throughout his long voyage across Europe and down the African coast, Frere, determined to maintain this advantage, ensured that regular dispatches and letters were sent back to London reporting on his progress, so that the mission was rarely out of the news. He even arranged for the new monthly packet boat service to Zanzibar to be increased in frequency while he was there, so that his reports would be more frequently read. Beginning his trip overland, he had called in to Paris, where he met the French foreign minister, M. de Remusat, who assured him of his support. The Italian foreign minister did likewise, and in Rome the Pope was happy to grant Frere an audience.

In Brindisi, Frere joined the *Enchantress*, a handsome 800 ton steam yacht that the Admiralty had put at his service, and from there sailed on to Egypt where he had a number of meetings with the Khedive Ismail. The khedive, an enlightened man who was in the process of aggressively modernizing his country, was initially encouraging on the whole question of slavery. In Egypt, he told Frere, the practice was in decline, with minimal slave numbers entering the country from the south. Frere, chatting to residents in Cairo, unfortunately discovered otherwise. An English school-teacher told him that prosperity had increased the demand for personal slaves at every social level. Indeed, the khedive's own mother was actively looking to acquire a number to supplement the dowries of her granddaughters. Slightly chastened, the envoy continued through Suez to Africa proper.

Frere had taken considerable care to prepare for his mission. He had tried to portray himself as a disinterested fighter against an ancient evil, deserving the support of all civilized nations. However, when he arrived in East Africa, he discovered not everyone saw his mission in the same light. The morning after his arrival in Zanzibar, he sent members of the mission to visit the German, French and American consulates. To his surprise and annoyance, none of them showed the slightest interest in his assignment. They had no wish to accompany him on his ceremonial visit to the sultan's palace that evening, and Mr

Schultz, the German consul, was particularly dismissive, remarking that personally he was unconcerned about the abolition of slave trading; nor did he consider that recent activities of British cruisers off the coast were primarily motivated by combatting slave traffickers, whatever they might protest. His implication was that Frere was empire building.

Frere's dignity was seriously upset. 'None of these representatives of the Foreign Powers have as yet called on me,' he noted sniffily the following day. In the meantime, he had somehow persuaded the officers of a visiting American ship to accompany him, and together with all those on board his own small fleet, he had managed to assemble a procession of forty-eight British and Americans. That afternoon, they landed and marched along Zanzibar's seafront to the sultan's palace, all wearing full uniform and with Frere at the head of the column. Later, he sent his own description back to London.

> The narrow streets which lead from the Consulate to the Sultan's palace were thronged with a crowd of Arabs and Negroes, such as I am told has never been before collected in Zanzibar, but they were all perfectly respectful and orderly, and the work of the Sultan's guard of Arab and Persian soldiers with which the streets were lined was but a sinecure.

Barghash met them about thirty yards from the door of this palace, which Frere noted smugly he had never been known to do before for any visitor. Customary greetings were exchanged with Frere and then with each member of his escort, and guns were simultaneously fired in the harbour, and responded to by one of the British cruisers. The party then proceeded into the palace to the sultan's audience chamber.

> According to the etiquette of this country, I preceded His Highness; he seated himself at the end with his five brothers and two of his ministers . . . on his right hand, while we were placed on his left. After the usual complements and inquiries had passed on both sides, I presented the Royal letter. On

receiving it, His Highness rose all present following his example, and according to the eastern custom raised it to his head as a mark of veneration.[19]

From the beginning, Frere behaved as though he thought he were visiting an outlying corner of the Indian Empire. He may have considered his mission that of an impartial fighter for the rights of oppressed Africans, but that was not how it appeared to Zanzibaris and other 'foreigners'. Britain, already regarded as an overweening and threatening power across the Indian Ocean, was regarded with suspicion. In Zanzibar, where a fragile balance had existed for years between the interests of the various powers, Frere's arrival was inevitably suspect.[20] His insistence on such overwhelming pomp and display only made it more so.

Following the sultan's visit to the *Enchantress* the next day, attended with full etiquette and a royal salute of twenty-one guns, Frere let it be known that he would continue to reside on his personal yacht during the course of his visit. A 'large and commodious house on the waterfront' had been generously offered to him by the sultan, but Frere decided not to avail himself of it, ostentatiously declining this hospitality. The house, he thought, would prove more useful for the Reverend Badger to live in, as all direct contact with Barghash during the negotiations would now be through him. A special envoy, he intimated, should not have to subject himself to the meanness of life in an Arab city.

This was to be Frere's style. As befitting his exhalted status, he would keep himself remote and unconstrained by any need to negotiate directly, leaving the aged and scholarly Badger to do the real work. While Frere issued lofty instructions from his yacht, which Badger would industriously translate into Arabic, the rest of the mission waited anxiously and with little to do. Badger would hurry round to deliver to the palace his master's latest thoughts, and in due course translate and carry back Barghash's reply to the seaborne envoy. Sometimes letters crossed, and inevitably the result was confusion. Although the sultan's palace and the envoy's yacht were each visible from the other, separated only by a short stretch of water, they could have been in different countries, and this was presumably what Frere desired. The British fleet in the harbour was intended to convey a sense of power, high rank and dignity. Above all, it signalled a refusal to compromise.

From the very beginning, Kirk was excluded from negotiations. As the envoy and Badger developed their discussions, there is no evidence that they consulted Kirk for advice at any point, and the combination of Frere's self-regarding arrogance and the Reverend's bumbling and dithering must have depressed and irritated him.[21] Frere was everything Kirk had always feared and disliked about the Indian governing class, but he was vulnerable, and under suspicion, and he knew it, so deliberately he kept a low profile. Just as deliberately, he made a point of helping Frere wherever he could. In particular, he supplied him with endless quantities of information – on the country, its people and its history; on Zanzibar's commercial and economic activity; on slave trading off the East African coast, and much else. This was data that only he knew, but which Frere was able to use in the constant stream of reports he sent back to London, enabling him to pose as an authority on the region. Meanwhile, Nelly entertained the mission at the consulate. With Frere she became an instant hit, flattering and charming him with her lively personality. Bored with weeks at sea, the various members of the mission were delighted with the company and the social distractions she arranged for them.

However to the Zanzibaris, this must have only confirmed what they had always felt. Frere's visit showed them the reality of British power, and the acting consul had little to do with it. In the next few weeks, as Kirk played virtually no part in the discussions, it was clear to them he was barely relevant to their fate. Even his own masters seemed to ignore him.

During the first days after the mission's arrival, Badger had a number of meetings with the sultan, and was surprised to find how much Barghash had changed since he had last seen him twelve years previously. The sultan possessed a library of Arabic books published in Cairo, and displayed an inquiring and educated mind. He was particularly well informed on the foreign policy of Egypt, which he worried might have ambitions on his own territories. However when Badger presented him with a draft treaty abolishing all trading in slaves, Barghash was immediately unwilling to cooperate. He pointed out to Badger the dire state of his country following the damage wrought by the cyclone. Hundreds of people had been reduced to poverty, he said, and it would require years to recover their losses. Did Badger not realize that to ask the country to give up its access to new slave labour would be to invite ruin. He had consulted his council, and this was not the time to cripple his state further.

The main problem was economic, for slaves and slave trading were intrinsic to Zanzibar's economy, and Barghash was not only referring to the commerce up to the Gulf, which technically did not exist. Slaves were still vital for manning the caravans to the interior, they were needed to work the plantations, and they kept the city's essential functions going. And because slaves did not breed easily, new imports were continually required.[22] So Barghash could not conceive of ceasing to deal in them. Abolition was impossible, he said.

For several days, the two men endlessly debated the matter, while the sultan presented one reason after another why he could not sign the treaty. He and Badger talked about religious doctine, and the position of slaves under Islam. The sultan was also well informed. The Portuguese, he said, had been given several years by the British to abolish slave trading. Why, then, should the Zanzibaris not be given the same flexibility? Finally, he resorted to pleading. Could not Badger, as an old friend, help make his cause with the envoy? He was moved almost to tears as he contemplated the terrible position in which he found himself.

But Frere, anxious for a quick conclusion, was getting impatient. Receiving Badger's notes of the conversations, he energetically despatched back to shore his responses, sometimes dashing off several letters a day. There was to be no change to the draft of the treaty, he wrote, and absolutely no compromise. He began to make threats. If Barghash did not give in, he hinted that the Egyptians might actually be encouraged to move farther south. Perhaps the sultan should even consider whether the hurricane had been an instrument of divine providence. As Barghash continued to prove obdurate, Frere began to propose increasingly eccentric ideas. If the sultan were concerned about needing labour, it could be provided in other ways. For instance, he suggested, perhaps a 'Magna Carta for free workers' emigrating from the mainland by special steamers, and certified by British consular officers at every port, would deal with the problem.

Badger, reading this bizarre plan, said he would rather not write it down in Arabic as the sultan might misunderstand the envoy's intent. By this time, Badger was becoming a little panicky at the lack of progress. His gout was distressing him, and the pressure from Frere was telling on his nerves. At a meeting on 17 January, he began to plead with Barghash to give way, and perhaps noting this, the sultan started to recover his poise. That evening, with a hint of irony, he commented to Badger, 'Of course, the exhalted British Government is strong and we are weak and it can do with us what it pleases . . .'[23] Britain could compel submission.

It was a clever comment, because Barghash had understood his opponent's dilemma. Although Britain was perfectly capable of forcing the issue, it was a route the British wished to avoid. Britain could not be seen to break its treaties with this small and vulnerable ally – the damage to the country's reputation would be too great. Badger, irritated by the sultan's sarcasm, replied tartly that he wanted a direct reply to take to the envoy. I cannot give you one, said Barghash, adding, with exquisite courtesy, it would be too rude for the envoy to read. However, he did say that he respected the British 'too much to believe that they would resort to force and plunder unjustly . . .'[24] and was therefore anxious to offer a compromise. If he gave in, his councillors and clan chiefs would never accept the defeat, and would assume he had given up the cause. He suggested, therefore, that Frere might assist him by personally meeting his council; perhaps that way a compromise could be found.

The unfortunate Badger agreed to pass this back to the yacht, but Frere tartly refused to consider the idea. This was something entirely beneath him. He would deal with Barghash as the monarch of his people, as befitting his rank, but he could not consider sitting down and debating the issues with the various clan heads. Make the sultan give way, he wrote back. Tell Barghash that if he refused, he was prepared to use the British fleet to blockade the coast, and even monitor the status and identity of every slave leaving the mainland.[25] There was to be no compromise.

Barghash, who knew better than the envoy just how difficult that last suggestion would prove, may not have found the threat very convincing. In any case, he was curious to establish just how serious the British were, and an opportunity to test this soon presented itself. On 25 January, to Badger's consternation, he received a message from the sultan attached to a cutting from the *Bombay Gazette*. It was an article in which a correspondent had suggested that the mission to Zanzibar would never be successful, and that the only real answer was to annex the island by force. Was this, perhaps, what the envoy had in mind, Barghash inquired innocently. Badger, embarrassed, scribbled on the paper, 'the writer of this is a babbler, therefore pay no attention to his folly . . .' and hastily sent it back.[26] So, once again, he confirmed to Barghash that force was not an option the British wanted to follow.

It was Barghash who decided, finally, that they were getting nowhere, and he should have a personal face-to-face meeting with the envoy. They agreed to visit the British agency for the purpose on the evening of 27 January.

Barghash arrived on his own; Frere, true to character, came with several of his team, including two of his aides plus Kirk and Badger, who by now was suffering severely from gout and was unable to walk without pain. Barghash told Frere he had sought the meeting for a reason; he needed something to tell his councillors, and he wanted to know whether any compromise were possible. For example, would Frere perhaps provide any financial inducement if the Arabs agreed. No, replied Frere, not until Barghash signed the treaty could he talk about such matters. So, responded Barghash, it really was then simply a matter of force. 'Your hand is most powerful, and we cannot resist.'[27] Not at all, responded Frere. He did not wish to carry his treaty by force.

He wanted willing compliance. To Barghash, this was quibbling.
He became emotional.

> Then why destroy us, as we are assured you will by insisting
> on your treaty? The Arabs . . . [are] a poor people, and
> trusted in the honour of England, whom they could not
> resist.

Had he not always helped England? When had he obstructed the
treaties signed by his predecessors?

> Have not my soldiers taken slaves by force from the houses
> of their masters? Have I not suffered in silence the outrages
> of your cruisers, even the burning before my very eyes of my
> own dhows uncondemned and innocent . . . How can I do
> more? I cannot with the force at my command prevent
> thieves and kidnappers carrying on their trade.[28]

The anger and resentment of years poured from him. It was hot
in the agency, and he paused for a moment to take a glass of water.
Frere, thinking he was at an advantage, pointed to the glass. Just
as Islam insisted on its adherents drinking water, and forbade the
taking of intoxicating liquors, he said, so Barghash should know
that his religion forbade the taking of slaves.

Barghash listened, and the comment seemed to encapsulate the
gulf between them. Yes, he said, he agreed.

> It is good; I asked for this interview to assure myself if there
> was no middle course open to me, which you might have yet
> kept back. I do not want you to go back to England
> unsuccessful through my acts; but in your success lies my
> ruin. A spear is held at each of my eyes, with which shall I
> choose to be pierced? Either way it is fatal to me.[29]

Frere had no idea what the sultan was talking about. He did not
seem to understand that Barghash faced a danger that was
enormous and complex – not only the perceived ruin of his

economy, but also the disaster that would envelop him personally if he were seen by his people to give way to British demands. He could not act on his own – he did not have that power. Offer me some middle way, he asked, something I can take back to my people to show I have not just surrendered to everything you demand. But Frere, focused only on getting what he wanted, did not hear.

So the meeting ended. Barghash concluded:

> Do what you like. We will never give up your friendship. We could submit to be cut in bits by degrees for your sake; but you come by the right of the stronger to cut off at once the life and the head of the weaker. I have troubled you much, and kept you long . . .[30]

Frere did not enjoy being accused of bullying. He was used to getting what he wanted but liked to have his victories dressed up as amicable agreement, and Barghash refused to play this game. Politely, he told the Englishman he knew what he was doing, and they might as well acknowledge it, but having now discussed the matter with Frere personally, he no longer trusted him. When Badger was sent to him again the next day, he merely listened to his platitudes and his promises. The envoy wished 'to carry out this measure in a friendly way', said Badger again; he did not wish to purchase agreement. Therefore the sultan 'must be content to trust to the Envoy's reserve' and sign before discussing any pecuniary assistance.[31] But Barghash no longer had any belief in the envoy's 'reserve'.

On 1 February, the two men met officially again in the sultan's audience chamber, but on this occasion no minister appeared to conduct the envoy formally to the palace, and he was compelled to walk unattended through the public streets. When he arrived, he was kept waiting before the sultan finally saw him. Annoyed at the implied insult, Frere delivered another harangue on how Barghash's country would be at risk if he did not give way. Of course, said Frere, he did not wish to make threats, but he really could not understand the sultan's position . . .

At that point, Barghash interjected, asking politely in what way did the envoy not understand. Badger, translating, was forced to say somewhat lamely that it was 'the drift which the Envoy did not understand'. Well then, Barghash resumed patiently, let me explain again. 'It is quite in your power to destroy us, but you ask us to destroy ourselves, and that we cannot do.'[32]

Barghash had openly called Frere's bluff, and Frere didn't like it. The mood in Zanzibar by now was very tense. People sensed that the negotiations were getting nowhere, and Europeans were becoming unpopular. It was reported on the waterfront that the sultan had said 'he knew the English would come with plenty of ships and do plenty of talk, and then go away and do nothing.' Nevertheless, although members of the mission were being mocked in the town, people were uneasy. No one knew what would happen next.[33]

On 3 February, Frere departed on a temporary visit to the coast, and while he was away, Barghash sought a private meeting with Kirk. Kirk had had no direct involvement in the negotiations during the previous weeks. Once, when the wazir had asked him to intervene, he had refused; now the sultan tried to involve him again. Badger, who had not accompanied the envoy to the coast, insisted on being present, but it was Kirk the sultan wanted to see. He was desperate for a way out, and he needed Kirk's advice.

When they met, Barghash addressed him at once, speaking slowly and deliberately. 'When you find you have heaped a load upon your camel that it cannot pass the city gate, do you not lessen the burden and gain your object?' he said. 'Now lessen this heavy burden . . . be it ever so little, and we are your servants, and you will gain all you desire . . .'[34] He was asking Kirk to help him find a way through the impasse, but Kirk knew he could not respond. Frere was an obdurate and forceful personality. He would never have tolerated any intervention in the course of the negotiations while he was away; nor would he consider anyone else seizing the initiative. The agenda was his, and however much Kirk may have disliked his methods, he had no alternative but to accept them.

He could not alter Frere's position, but he could change the conversation. So rather than answering directly, in a quiet and low-key way, he turned the discussion to the economics of the situation. Instead of citing morality or threatening force, Kirk began to speak to Barghash about business, about credit and the state of the clove estates. He knew what he was talking about. Many of the estates were heavily mortgaged, and following the hurricane, were in considerable difficulty. This was what really mattered, he told the sultan, and it could get worse if the negotiations broke down. He flattered Barghash. The sultan could not shut his eyes to the fate that must befall his people if such misfortune struck; he had been placed over them as guide in times such as these. If the negotiations failed, there might be a collapse in the credit of the Arab landowners, and many would be compelled to sell or further mortgage at ruinous prices. They were already heavily indebted to Indian merchants, and these debts could be enforced. If things got even worse – say, through a trade blockade – that could perhaps result in a rising of the slaves. Such a disaster had been known to happen elsewhere. It would, Kirk said, be 'an object unanticipated in the present negotiations, [but] brought about with a violent convulsion and the utter ruin of the Arab race in these parts.'[35]

Barghash listened intently to Kirk's speech, and it was clear he believed him. The island was already suffering from the aftermath of the cyclone, and the prospect of futher catastrophe worried him deeply. Would Kirk be prepared, he asked, to repeat this to his council, for they would never believe it if it came only from himself. If Kirk spoke to them, they would credit what he said. And immediately the full council were led in – they had been waiting in an adjoining room. Slowly then, Kirk repeated once again that the real danger they faced was not force, but the long-term destruction of their prosperity. Britain would not seek to stir up the slaves, but if the economy did not improve, it was inevitable that eventually they would rise against their masters.

One member of the council, Hamed bin Suleiman, turned to Kirk. 'We are led like blind beasts,' he said. 'It may be to corn, it may be to chaff.' They knew they were in a bind, and faced a terrible choice, but they trusted Kirk to advise them. For a few minutes, it seemed as though a deal were possible, but then they began to bicker and argue about how much money they might need, how many slaves the island required to maintain its economy, and how many years' transition could be bargained for. The meeting broke up in disarray, but as they took their leave, one of Barghash's oldest councillors, Seyyid Suleiman bin Hamed, a man who had advised the family for generations, laid his arm on Kirk's.

> In the most earnest manner, with tears in his eyes, [he] said, 'I have heard nothing of what has passed, I am now old and deaf; but, if the Government press this matter, I myself will live to reach London, and Paris, and New York, and claim a hearing and justice for the Arabs.'[36]

These men knew Kirk well, and they trusted him. It was Seyyid Suleiman's daughter (who was also Seyyid Hamed's wife) whom Kirk had rescued from shipwreck on Latham's Island almost four years previously. They would have remembered that, as well as other occasions when Kirk had taken their part.

Moreover, Kirk knew that the key did not lie only with Barghash. Persuading the other communities in Zanzibar's complex mosaic was vital, and in particular the council needed to be brought over, but the negotiations were beyond his control. On 8 February, Frere returned to the island and three days later Barghash made his final response to the envoy. He would not sign the treaty. 'Your friend understood what you stated,' he wrote. He disliked giving such a categorical refusal, but he could do nothing else on account of the hardship and ruin that such action would bring to his people. Zanzibar would therefore remain with the situation as it was. Strict enforcement of the old treaties would do them no harm, but if Britain were to violate its old agreements, then 'we are helpless, and shall take patiently whatever God may decree . . .'[37] Once again, he was calling the envoy's bluff.

Faced with such obstinacy, Frere did nothing for a few days and then sailed to the mainland again while he reflected on the matter. Leaving on 15 February, he decided this time to go to Kilwa, the port from which the largest number of slaves were sent to Zanzibar each year. He wanted to see the place for himself, and arriving a few days later opposite the town, he went on shore personally with some of his aides. Seeing a number of 'British Indian subjects', he immediately approached them, informing them he wished to discuss the subject of slave trading. He also intended to inquire at the local Customs House to establish what the statistics on trafficking were. However, to his surprise, these 'Indian subjects' had no desire to speak to him. Indeed, they clearly resented his intrusive behaviour, and did not recognize that they were beholden in any way to this self-important European officer. They told him they knew nothing about slave trafficking, and if he wanted to learn about statistics, he was advised to return to Zanzibar, which was where all the records were kept.

Colonel Pelly, Frere's ADC, was sent into the town to locate Barghash's governor, whom he eventually found resting in his house. When Pelly asked him to come and attend the envoy, the *wali* replied that, on the contrary, it was up to the visitor to attend him. 'Let him come here and sit here, I will not move to see him,' he remarked.[38] Frere then decided he would try the Customs House, but a group of armed Arab soldiers immediately positioned themselves at its door, indicating that entrance would be strongly resisted.

Frere was outraged. 'The demeanour of all the Arab officials was unmistakeably insolent and defiant as that of the Indian traders was impertinent,' he wrote in his report back to London.[39] It did not seem to occur to him that this was a foreign country where he had no right to act in the way he had, and that perhaps his own behaviour was at fault.

It may have been this final insult to his dignity that influenced Frere in his next move. From Kilwa he sailed briefly to Madagascar, and then, on 12 March, he returned to Zanzibar in the midst of a dramatic thunderstorm.

Darkness spread like a veil over the island, black banks of storm clouds rolled up, strong, raw gusts of wind swept along in company with a beating downpour of tropical rain.[40]

For half an hour the squall raged, the iron roofing of the sultan's new harem was wrenched into the air and some twenty small dhows were driven on to the beach. As the storm eased, the *Enchantress* emerged from the fog, bringing the envoy back into harbour, but this time he did not remain for more than a few days on the island. On 14 March, he held a farewell dinner in the British agency for his staff, together with Kirk and his family, before finally sailing away from Africa to the coast of Arabia, leaving Kirk once more in charge.

The envoy had never expected such a result, nor that he could possibly fail in his mission to 'persuade' Barghash to give up his trade in slaves. He was also well aware of how his failure would be regarded back in Britain. The mission had been expensive, and its progress had been continuously reported in the British press. In addition, his own career and dignity were at stake. Resentful at his personal humiliation, and refusing to accept that he had been outmanoeuvred, his thoughts turned to the only solution remaining, that 'constant vice' of the Indian Empire – compulsion by force.

Part Four

UNSAFE TO SPECULATE

For Zanzibar Arabs, even of the highest class, the speculation in slaves seems to have the same sort of attraction which horse-dealing has for an ordinary Yorkshireman. They examine and discuss the points, bargain and bid, and, if they purchase an animal they like, they keep it till tired of it, and then exchange or sell it . . .

I was assured that in Arabia, though respectable Arabs will purchase slaves when they want them, it is considered disreputable to purchase them for re-sale, or to sell them except as a punishment or upon dire necessity.

It may be asked what, beyond the blunted moral sense caused by the atmosphere of a baracoon, is the cause of the special popularity of slaving ventures in Zanzibar? It is probably, in the higher classes, mainly due to the gambling element of risk – the uncertainty whether the result will be a great success or a total loss. In some cases there would be an additional attraction similar to that of smuggling or poaching for many classes in Europe, in that the venture was attended with danger, and was secret . . .

BARTLE FRERE'S REPORT TO LONDON

13: NOT WITHOUT EMOTION

To the lower classes in Zanzibar a slave is a safe, easy, and profitable investment, and they will talk, even when slaves themselves, of investing a windfall of money in a slave or two, just as a native of India would of investing it in a pair of bullocks, or in bangles for his wife . . .

BARTLE FRERE'S REPORT TO LONDON

In April 1873, hundreds of *hamalis* and other dock workers crowded round the harbour in Zanzibar to watch the spectacle of a young elephant being led along the Customs House wharf. The animal was over six foot tall and already growing short tusks. As he passed, the crowds pulled at his tail and tugged at the ropes by which he was led down to a lighter on the water below before being ferried out to a steamer bound for Bombay. The elephant seemed to take all this with complete equanimity, and passively endured being hoisted into midair from the lighter on to the deck of the *Punjab*, where he was placed close to the donkey engine. This he regarded with fascination, refusing to let the engine be covered with a tarpaulin, and removing it each time it was put in place.

The elephant had arrived with a caravan from the interior the previous year, having been sent to Zanzibar by Mutesa, king of Buganda, as a special gift to the sultan. The sultan had no use for him, though, and after some months, decided to send the animal to India as a uniquely African present for Sir Philip Wodehouse, governor of Bombay. Sir Philip, reluctantly accepting the gift, offered it to the viceroy, who politely declined. Eventually the animal was bestowed on the prime minister of one of India's rulers, who in turn passed it on until the creature came to end his days as an inmate of the Bombay Zoo.[1]

The young elephant was in many ways like Zanzibar itself – awkward, unwanted, embarrassing, a responsibility the British wished to avoid, were compelled to accept, but just did not know how to handle. Sultan Barghash seemed really determined to be Britain's friend, as his father had been, and indeed wished to continue to pay tribute to Britain's power – except that the particular homage Britain desired, he resolutely refused to render, and that was his right to trade in African slaves. It was intrinsic to his city's very existence and always had been, and even when the British Empire sent one of its most distinguished representatives to demand compliance, he still said no.

During the two months Frere had been in Africa, he had worked hard at acquiring as much information as possible, applying himself to the task of building a deep and extensive knowledge of the area. The *Enchantress* was a fine yacht, but sat deep in the water, so its ports could rarely be opened. As his cabin moved back and forth in the intense heat, Frere could often work only by holding on to his table with one hand and both his feet. There, tormented by his pet monkey, he managed to write a series of long and exceptionally detailed reports, which were sent back on a regular basis to London, and together formed an implicit statement of his larger ambitions.

He analysed the trade within the region, the history of the Arab conquest, the weakness of Zanzibari control of the mainland, the society and culture of the Indian community, the complexities of the slave trade and the culture of slavery itself. His reports were sprinkled with suggestions on how British control might benefit the region. Yet for all his analysis, he never quite understood Zanzibar's relationship to the interior, and he totally misunderstood Barghash. The sultan's indirect and ambiguous way of speaking irritated him. At one moment he thought him a decisive and independent ruler; at another, he despised 'his cunning smile'. And in the end, he failed to get his agreement on banning the trade in slaves.

Frere could have had few illusions about how this would be received, both by the government and by the British public. He had deliberately stoked up expectations in England and abroad by his endless barnstorming and use of the press. Following his departure for Africa, his evangelical friends continued to fuel public opinion with lurid accounts of Arab atrocities against peaceful innocent Africans. In late 1872 and early 1873, members of the Anti Slavery Society toured the Midlands and the north of England, speaking to large audiences in city after city, building on Frere's own leaks to the press on the mission's progress.[2] Illustrations appeared in the papers showing slavers at their bloody work, putting further pressure on the government.[3]

Granville, desperate for a solution, had given his envoy virtual *carte blanche* in his conduct of the negotiations. Frere was permitted to offer financial inducements if necessary, and strict adherence to the terms of the draft treaty was not entirely necessary if an acceptable compromise could be achieved. Granville just wanted a solution he could plausibly sell. But Frere, determined on complete submission, had wilfully ignored these options.[4] Continually facing Barghash with a take it or leave it proposition, he had never thought for a moment the sultan would turn him down.

Confronted with failure, Frere sent a valedictory despatch to the foreign secretary from his yacht some days after leaving Zanzibar. In it, he placed all blame on Barghash's unwillingness to compromise. Usually trenchant in his arguments, Frere's report on this occasion was specious and evasive. He suggested that the sultan had turned down his offers of financial assistance, although he had made none. He accused Barghash of bad faith, and alluded to shadowy and unspecific intrigues by the French consul in Zanzibar. He even blamed the sultan for listening to his own advisers. Frere could not admit that, ultimately, he had fallen short of what he had undertaken to deliver.

Returning from the coast on his final visit to the city, he had been furious to find everything he had said to Barghash during the previous weeks completely ignored, and that 'the abomination of the public sale of slaves in the slave market' still continued. He was unused to such casual disrespect, and arriving in Mombasa a few days later, frustrated and angry, he took matters into his own hands. On his own authority, without consulting his superiors in either London or Bombay, he issued orders to the commander of the British squadron that had accompanied him, imposing draconian sanctions on the island and its coastal territories. Henceforth, he ordered, all vessels leaving the coast and suspected of carrying slaves were to be immediately seized by the British navy. They were to be brought to the Vice Admirality court in Zanzibar where the slaves would be interviewed to establish if they were *bona fide* domestic servants, or being transported for sale, even within the sultan's domains. If the latter, they were to be freed at once. The court would also require the owner of the slaves to pay substantial security, which was at risk of forfeiture. Only after he had issued these orders did Frere send a further despatch to Kirk telling him to inform the foreign secretary in London about what he had done.

Kirk and Frere came from very different worlds, yet by the time the envoy left Zanzibar, the two men got on surprisingly well. Partly this must have been due to Kirk's deliberate decision to subordinate himself to Frere's egocentric personality, assisting him whenever he was able. But the whole mission had been impressed at how Kirk had managed to keep the agency running effectively, without support and for so long. Nelly's role was also significant. Her bravery and her ability to raise a young family in the heart of Zanzibar's chaotic and unhealthy city had surprised and touched the group of officers and gentlemen. Frere seems to have been completely charmed by her, and the subsequent correspondence[5] between the two of them indicates a genuine friendship. But ultimately Frere realized that his own ambitions completely depended on Kirk's continued presence in Africa. When he left Zanzibar, it was clear any possible hope of saving the mission's reputation depended on Kirk, and with it possibly Frere's own career. It may have been with a slight feeling of desperation that the envoy finally entrusted Kirk with full authority to continue the discussions with Barghash after he had gone.

Before he left, however, there was still the embarrassing matter of the Livingstone inquiry. In a note back to London, Frere dealt with this in typically peremptory style, almost dismissing it as a matter barely worth consideration. He knew that Kirk could not be completely exonerated without implying criticism of Livingstone himself, which even Frere could not afford to do. He therefore finessed the issue, simply by pretending the problem did not exist. In his note, he allowed that the necessary goods had not reached Livingstone, but maintained this was due entirely to the failure of the porters. As for the Doctor's harsher criticisms of Kirk, Frere refused to credit them, declaring airily that Livingstone had only 'imputed to Dr Kirk no more than companionship with himself in the misfortune of putting their trust in men who deceived'. Both men were therefore blameless. Indeed, Frere concluded, 'Dr Livingstone never had here, possibly not in any part of the world a truer or warmer friend than Dr Kirk.'[6]

Honour satisfied, Frere was eager to press ahead with his own plans, and without consulting Kirk's superiors in India, he immediately proceeded to announce his official promotion as full agent and therefore consul in Zanzibar.[7] Without the slightest qualms, he also appointed two assistant agents, enlisting in the service a former Indian Army staff officer, and a gentleman traveller 'of good education', who both happened to be there at the time.[8]

In London, the news of Frere's aggressive actions seems to have hit the government like a bombshell. The perception of Britain forcing a small defenceless nation to do its will was bad enough, but the special envoy had exceeded his brief, acting entirely without authorization. In addition, his actions were illegal. A declaration signed with France in 1862 agreeing to respect Zanzibar's sovereignty had been seriously flouted, and Frere's instructions to the navy to interrupt shippers within Zanzibar waters were at once referred to the Crown Law Officers for their legality. They advised that Frere's directions 'imposed terms upon the Sultan not imposed by the Treaty of 1845', and that consequently in carrying them out, the actions of British naval officers would not be protected under law.[9] The cabinet met to consider the matter; it did not like what Frere had done, but it did not wish to back down. It had given its envoy a free hand and he had used it.

In Zanzibar, an uneasy calm had fallen on the city following the special envoy's departure, as it took measure of what would happen next. Barghash was in good spirits; when Kirk had seen him on the eve of Frere's sailing, he was typically ambiguous, even playful. Hearing of the misconduct of his officials at Kilwa, he expressed regret, and said he would write to the governor and make an example of him. As for the slave trade, he said it was becoming troublesome, and it would be in all their interests to get it out of the way before it damaged the rest of the island's commerce. He compared his own position to that of a spoilt child who had to take a dose of medicine, but once forced to take it, all would be well. Kirk did not believe him for a minute. Barghash was adept at voicing aloud his intentions of doing one thing while planning something entirely different.

Meanwhile, the new slaving season approached, and more than three thousand slaves, many of them children, were gathered at Kilwa ready for shipping to Zanzibar. Kirk, having received Frere's orders, was faced with the unenviable task of trying to put them into action. He had always doubted whether force on its own was the ultimate answer. British cruisers would never detain ships carrying the French flag, which many slavers now used, and coastal blockades could easily be frustrated unless the Zanzibari authorities helped.[10] Also, Frere did not seem to have thought through the practical implications of his actions. Thousands of slaves would have to be looked after once they had been released in Zanzibar, and on 3 April, Kirk wrote the envoy a tactful letter, pointing out that he would now need an additional establishment to cope with them. Once freed, they 'could not be prudently landed or given over to residence in Zanzibar, where their free status would not be respected as legal'. In no time, they would be re-enslaved. The only answer, therefore, would be to send them on by steamer, either to the Seychelles or Natal, involving additional cost to the Indian treasury. Extra staff, medical facilities and housing would also be required to manage the liberated slaves.[11]

The situation was threatening to become an administrative and political disaster, but if Frere had ever considered such practical necessities, he had brushed them aside, leaving Kirk to manage the crisis. So it was Kirk who, in early April, conveyed the news to Barghash that, from 1 May, Captain Malcolm of the Royal Navy had instructions to arrest every dhow carrying slaves along the African coast, including within Zanzibar waters.

Both Kirk and Barghash had played this game of threat and counter-threat before, and perhaps that gave the sultan confidence. Encouraged by conversations with the French consul, he must have been aware of the weakness of the British position. The squadron sent by Frere to monitor the slavers at Kilwa consisted of just two cruisers, and was unlikely to remain there forever. Some dhows would eventually evade them, others would adopt the French flag, slave caravans could even be marched up the coastal land routes. So as the new slaving season approached, Barghash calmly announced that arrangements would proceed just as they had every previous year. Nothing would alter, and on 1 May, a notice was posted at the Customs House announcing that, as usual, the shipping of slaves could proceed unhindered.[12]

Nevertheless, the build-up to the crisis had had an effect. The Kilwa shippers knew about the cruisers waiting out at sea, and the dhows obstinately refused to set sail. They were scared of the warships, which would see them leaving, and they considered the risk too great. Everyone was waiting to see which way matters would go. In Zanzibar, Kirk heard that the slave wholesale dealers intended visiting the sultan the following day 'to ask whether in renewing the usual permission to import and ship slaves he is prepared also to protect their property and enforce restitution in event of seizure.'[13] The situation was tense.

Kirk had always known that Barghash could never give in simply on his own authority. The sultan was not as absolute a ruler as Frere thought. He depended on his advisers, on representatives of leading families and on the trading community.

He also still depended on the Mutawas. Years earlier, Kirk had noted in his journal a list of the six key Mutawa zealots who exerted influence on Barghash. They were a shadowy group, who did not appear in public and had little support among the island's easygoing Muslims, but they were feared. Since Frere's visit, Barghash had once again turned to them for advice and backing.[14]

Elsewhere, Barghash's wider support was starting to fragment. The Indian community were alarmed by the damage the slave trade threatened to their overall interests. The intricate relationship between slaves and other commodities, particularly ivory, meant that general commerce was beginning to suffer. However, a week after the onset of the new season, Kirk visited the slave market, which had recently been moved, and discovered no shortage of slaves, despite the Kilwa blockade. They were simply coming in from a different part of the mainland, and the market was doing brisk business in its new location.

Other parties in Zanzibar's network of business interests were also becoming concerned, though. On the evening of 20th May, Kirk received an unexpected invitation to visit the American consulate. A new consul had been recently appointed, a man called Webb who represented the Boston trading house of F.R. Webb. Sales of American cloth were big business in Zanzibar – the cotton bales were one of the main staples of the inland trade – and Webb was worried about the future. American fabric was used to barter for slaves, and also for other products, especially ivory. Webb was aware of the damage disputes on slave trading had done in the past to commerce in the Americas. He did not expect to be in Africa long, and did not want to see his firm's business collapse while he was there. So when Kirk arrived late that evening, he found Barghash waiting for him also. Webb was trying to craft a compromise between the two.

The three men argued about slave trading and its prospects all evening. For the first time, Barghash openly admitted that the slaves who arrived in Zanzibar were far more than his country needed. He conceded that, at most, a total of 5,000 a year were required for local consumption, and at least 12–13,000 were re-shipped for export elsewhere, but he still considered it was his right to do so.[15] Moreover, he was extremely annoyed at continued British interference in his affairs, even though he was dismissive of their chances of success. With only two small cruisers off the coast at Kilwa, how could they expect to influence matters for long, he asked Kirk sarcastically. More ships would arrive, Kirk said, and the impact had already been significant. He told Barghash he knew that slave shipments from Kilwa had been paralysed, with only the smallest of efforts. He had also talked to the Customs House and learnt how bad the duties on slave imports were so far that season.[16]

Barghash laughed. If trade failed, he said, the blow would fall on everyone. The British Indians and the American shippers would suffer just as much as his own people. The cotton trade would be ruined, he told Webb. As for the Arabs, they might simply decamp to the mainland where they could run their affairs as they chose. Slaves could easily be transported north by land, beyond the reach of the British warships. This was not an empty threat. There were already reports of slaves being marched overland from Kilwa, up the coast to Somalia from where they could be exported.

They parted that evening without settling anything, but Kirk knew the window of opportunity for him to reach agreement would not remain open much longer. In London, the government dithered, and Kirk was not sure which way they would go. A long-term blockade of the African coast would create problems with the French, and have unpredictable results. Backing down would be equally damaging. For Kirk, either option would mean the end of years of patient work. He waited for a decision.

On 24 May, the British agency hoisted the flag to commemorate the Queen's birthday, and as though to indicate that matters continued perfectly as normal, Barghash 'dressed his ships and fired a salute of twenty one guns at noon' in honour of the occasion. Aware that Kirk would be holding a formal dinner that night, he sent round a gift of 'a sheep roasted whole, on a gigantic charger borne by slaves, pillars, pyramids of fruit, and piles of confectionary'. That evening, Kirk's little daughter, a favourite of the sultan's, was out walking with her nurse near the palace.

Barghash, spotting her, called her in for a chat, and she came back home, 'laden with Indian toys, most of them curious specimens of zoology, and provided with enough sugar-candy and sweet-meats to disorganise a young lady's boarding school'.[17]

Barghash was determined to be friends, but he was also determined to win. Two days later, he paid a visit to the consulate, and the small English community, including several missionaries, were gathered there to meet him. The sultan arrived with his usual retinue of Persian and Baluchi guards, and the conversation initially was desultory. They talked about the Queen and the length of time that she had been on her throne, until Barghash spotted an Arabic translation of the Bible lying on a table. It was a good book, he remarked in front of the assembled missionaries. He knew it well. Were they not aware that it authorized slavery as an institution? No one laughed at the joke. Barghash, always happy to exploit the embarrassment of Europeans, went on to talk urbanely about trade and then religion. He would like to visit Mecca again, he said.

Slave trading was deeply embedded in Zanzibar's life and culture – it symbolized the country's dominance of the interior; it was sanctioned by history, custom and religion; and it was an intrinsic part of the island's commercial activities. Yet Kirk was sure that for the Zanzibaris, trade came first and, in the end, nothing else mattered as much. Whether Arab, Swahili or Indian, he believed there were few in Zanzibar who cared about politics or religion as much as they cared about making money. As the threat to slave trading began to affect the island's other commerce, the ivory trade in particular began to suffer, and that was the island's life blood. Kirk knew this, he understood the opportunity it presented, and in the next few weeks he pressed the point remorselessly. And because he knew so much about the country's commercial activities, he was listened to.

On the Queen's birthday, a deputation of mainly Indian merchants came to the agency to present their congratulations, and Kirk took the opportunity to discuss the situation with them. He told them clearly that in his opinion the slave trade was likely to be ruined, and that they might as well accept the position. He did not threaten them, even though he was now the official agent. Instead, he tactfully conceded that, of course, they were not directly involved, but in his opinion, selling to dealers goods that were used in exchange for slaves could now be a very risky prospect, and he really would not advise it. In fact, 'the articles that purchase slaves [were] unsafe investments in which to speculate,' he thought.[18] Quite consciously, he preyed on their concerns about the future. His message to them was, if you trade goods with slave dealers, you will lose your money. Slave trading was bad for business as a whole.

Meanwhile, the blockade on Kilwa was putting a severe strain on the small squadron. Evidently, it could not be kept up for long. Kirk, knowing how weak the fleet was, had nevertheless been sending back reports attempting to reassure the Foreign Office. Matters were under control, he told them. Then on 2 June, he finally received the foreign secretary's decision. However, not one but two notifications arrived on the mail boat from Aden. The first was the government's formal reply, informing Kirk of the illegality of Frere's move, but this had been overtaken by a cable sent to Cairo, where it was decoded by the British consul there, and then sent on by the same mail. The cabinet, concerned about its popularity in the country if it backed down, had changed its mind, and decided it would effect a complete blockade of Zanzibar unless the sultan agreed to come to terms.

Kirk could gauge from this just how ambivalent the government was. Moreover, his spies had told him that the French consul was seeking to exploit the crisis by having the situation referred to international arbitration. The British government was a weak one, and Gladstone, the prime minister, was known to have little interest in the slave-trade question. As impartial judge of a dispute between Britain and the island state, the French might stand to gain what they had always wanted – their own protectorate in East Africa.[19] Kirk now knew he had little time to affect the outcome of the crisis. He asked for a meeting with Barghash for the following day.

For years he had constantly involved himself with the island's trading communities, Arab as well as Indian, as conciliator, adviser and broker. Now was the time to turn this knowledge and these skills to his advantage. In his communication to the sultan, Kirk requested that the council of advisers might also be present at the meeting, the same men with whom he had talked early in February.

Kirk arrived at the palace on the morning of 3 June, and in front of the assembled advisers he slowly read out the British foreign secretary's cable. He emphasized the British government's determination, and then patiently explained what a blockade would mean for Zanzibar. Once again, it was business he had come to talk to them about, not politics. He spoke as their adviser, not their enemy. A blockade would destroy the country's trade entirely, he said; all of it, not just the traffic in slaves. He had talked to the German and US consuls, and even the trade in their ships would be affected; even those of the French. Britain, unfortunately, felt that strongly about the matter.

But this was not the way to obtain a treaty, retorted Barghash. This was force. It was, said Kirk regretfully. Then, deliberately turning to the council members, he abruptly added an unexpected and new twist. He knew them all, and he was certain they would have already advised Barghash to resist any further pressure. Now he told them that he had requested their presence for a very specific purpose. He was sure that if Barghash refused to agree terms and a blockade led to economic disaster, they would turn on the sultan and hold him responsible. But he, Kirk, was not prepared to let that happen. In fact, he intended, he said, to 'place responsibility [for any decision] on their shoulders lest at any future time it should please them to turn on their chief and accuse him of want of foresight in not yielding at such a crisis.' In that event, he would deliberately ensure that 'their personal assistance at this interview was ... a matter of public notoriety.' He would make it known throughout the city that they were equally to blame.

Kirk understood too well the fractious nature of Zanzibar politics, and he had laid his trap with care. Twice he had set out the economic dangers before them, and now he told them their personal penalty if they went ahead. Their own necks would be on the line; and they believed him. 'As I finished speaking, when the Sultan turned to his advisors and said "Now, shall I give him the word agreed upon this morning?" all whispered in audable chorus "No."'[20]

None of them had expected this, least of all from him. By defending the sultan before his own council, Kirk had changed the debate entirely. He had stripped away the defence Barghash's advisers had thought to protect themselves with, and he had given the sultan a weapon. The only way out was to agree to terms, Kirk told them. Still the same honest broker, the wise counsellor, but for the first time showing a harder edge than ever before. Then, respectfully he left them.

One further hurdle remained. At that crucial meeting in the sultan's palace, there were some important absentees. Barghash's Mutawa advisers had not been present, and without their involvement any agreement would be valueless.

That same evening, 3 June, Kirk received a message that Barghash wished to call on him at the agency. Kirk could not see him there because he had guests, but he replied that he was happy to attend the sultan again at his palace. Later that night, he walked alone the half mile along the waterfront, past the walls of the old fort, past the Customs House and the rows of dhows in the harbour. It was late and the waterfront would have been quiet apart from odd groups of people, children and beggars, but behind the grand buildings the town would still have been noisy and full of activity. Finally, he reached the royal residence. Later, he wrote how during this period he knew he was being constantly watched, possibly with the intention of putting him out of the way, but he discounted the danger to his life; he did not think of it.[21]

He arrived at the great pillared entrance hall to the palace, and ascended the stairway once more to the audience chamber, and again he found himself facing the same council, the same advisers, only this time they were accompanied by the three most influential Mutawa leaders. Kirk named them: 'they are Hammood bin Hamed bin Muselline El Farahi – "Alui of the fanatic portion of the sect of the Ibathia" – Seyed Hamood bin Hamed and Mahommed bin Sulemian maderi.' These were the fanatics who constituted the secret Mutawa Council, they were his enemies, and they hated him and everything he stood for.[22] He had now forced them into the open where he could meet them face to face.

Kirk immediately realized that the main council had given in. Their own vital interests threatened, the game with them was over. It was why the others were there. Barghash, squeezed on both sides, had brought the Mutawas to meet his British 'friend', but Kirk knew that they, too, were effectively beaten. The meeting itself was evidence of it, for otherwise they would not have deigned to appear. He had been right; against the potential disaster of economic collapse, the arguments of extreme religious belief carried little sway. However, they still had to be part of the final bargain, and so Barghash had brought them along to confront their enemy.

They tried to evade the issue, and they haggled with Kirk in an attempt to prove he had not the authority to carry the deal, but he refused to give way. He kept in front of them the simple choice they must make – accept or refuse. Barghash asked for a delay in imposing the blockade while he went to Europe to discuss the matter, but Kirk had prepared for this, too. He surmised that, once in Europe, Barghash would make Zanzibar a pawn between Britain and France. The blockade would be called off, and the opportunity would have gone. He advised Barghash not to leave, telling him that a British cruiser, unfortunately, would prevent him.

Finally, they said they did not have a copy of the treaty, and Kirk did not have one, either. So late that night, in the shadowy corridors of the palace, they scrabbled about looking for the version in Arabic that had been left by Badger several weeks earlier. It was eventually found among a pile of papers in a box, stored away. Barghash had never thought of it since, but now it was brought out and discussed. However there was another clause to add to it, Kirk told them. He would not have either the council or Barghash telling him in months to come that this agreement had been imposed upon them. The sultan had to sign willingly, accepting the implications of all that he was committing to. He could not wash his hands of the matter as his father and brother had done.

The final agreement was arrived at with great politeness and respect. 'So, it is done,' said Barghash. 'I will sign it tomorrow.' He knew he had been beaten at the game he had prided himself on playing. The years of subterfuge had finally come to an end. The following day, 6 June, the sultan did sign the treaty, and a young naval officer, a Lieutenant Hamilton, was immediately summoned ashore and handed the document. He was to go to London, Kirk said, without breaking his journey. He was not to let the treaty out of his sight until he had personally handed it to Lord Granville or one of his secretaries. There was only one copy, and it was in Arabic, but it could be translated in London by the Reverend Badger.

Two days later, on 8 June, an order from the sultan was posted at the Customs House, and was read with great interest and discussion.

> To allow our subjects who may see this and also to others, may God save you, know that we have prohibited the transport of raw slaves by sea in all our harbours and have closed the markets which are for the sale of slaves through all our dominions. Whosoever therefore shall ship a raw slave after this date will render himself liable to punishment and this he will bring upon himself. Be this known.[23]

Kirk, too, read the declaration and pointed out to the sultan that the agreement between them was not only to cover raw slaves, or *bagham*. The trading in any slave should now be forbidden. So the order was altered to apply to slaves of any kind, and once again posted where all might read it. Kirk noted:

> When reposted a large crowd assembled at the Custom House and read it not without emotion, but the public have accepted the situation and know that the final act has been that of their chiefs and not of the Sultan individually.[24]

Three days earlier, the slave market in Zanzibar, the oldest institution on the island, had been finally cleared by the sultan's soldiers, and the auctioneers were forbidden ever to return.

14: THE KISIJU ROAD

*It must be borne in mind that we are engaged in a campaign with
an enemy who has little to lose and everything to gain in his contest
with us; who is therefore ever on the alert to take advantage of our
mistake; whose information is far superior to our own; and who by
the very necessities of the case, must excercise ceaseless craft,
vigilance, and activity.*

JOHN KIRK, MARCH 1875[1]

If Barghash had signed under pressure from Frere, he would have
been murdered within twenty-four hours, he told Kirk. Now 'he
laughs and says that if anyone is to be killed I am the one.'[2] For
no one now could blame the sultan. The heads of all the major
clans had signed away the slave trade of their own free will; they
had openly agreed to its abolition. But Kirk would apply that
agreement with a relentlessness and determination they could
never have foreseen.

It was to the Indian traders that he first turned his attention.
In late 1873 he travelled the length of the coast, using his new
deputies to visit every town and commercial centre. Town criers
were sent through the streets announcing in loud wails that the
holding of slaves by 'British' Indians was illegal and henceforth
would be punished. At a set time, the local merchants were given
notice to report in person with a list of their slaves to be freed.
Kirk visited Mombasa in October, and did the roll call there

himself, standing by the local Customs House where so many slaves had been sold and bought, and personally writing out notes to free them. Later that month, he was in Malindi, and then Lamu. He contacted individual slaves, talking to them privately and getting them to testify against their masters, and he pursued those Indians who would not comply, without mercy. Agents were appointed for the protection of the freed slaves. In November, after returning from the north coast, he wrote that he had liberated 479 individuals, 'not a bad haul out of these coast towns'.[3]

Kirk was interested in the Indian merchants for a specific reason, for he was finally able to put his understanding of the business to good use. The Indians had always been the financiers of the trade, and now he began to put pressure on the supply of credit. Mortgages issued on slaves were cancelled, and when goods had been advanced against slave-dealing operations and the slaves freed, he refused to allow the value of the goods to be reclaimed. His aim was to force the slave dealers to repudiate their debt, and thus make lending on their operations too high a risk. If he could prevent transport by sea, and if he could starve the business of investment, he was convinced he could kill slave trading as a commercial activity. Without markets and without funding, it would die.

At Kilwa on the south coast, though, matters were very different. This was still the main source of new slaves from the interior, and when Kirk visited the port in mid-1873, he found the local slave market had been closed but the trade had not gone away. Now it was merely conducted secretly and in private. He was treated with respect, and allowed to go where he wished, but the town had lived off the traffic for too long, and the old families who had prospered over the ages were not going to give up their privileges easily. Thousands of captives, held ready for export, had been sent inland and concealed just prior to his arrival.

Nevertheless, Kirk was optimistic. Since the prohibition, only two large shipments had managed to leave for the north, and prices locally had plunged.

> As the result of my diligent enquiries not in town only but by the reports of secret agents along the coast I am enabled

to state that hitherto the traffic may be said to have been closed notwithstanding the fact that there are at Kilwa about 4,000 slaves now offered for sale at the reduced rates of from half a dollar to three dollars a piece . . . The losses I am told have been great . . .[4]

The business clearly was in trouble, and Kirk was told that slaves, unable to travel by sea any longer, were already being transported legally up the coast by land to Somalia from where they could be sent elsewhere. He had already been to the Somali coast earlier that year, had seen the caravans and realized that transport overland was the fall-back solution, but he was convinced that it would not pay. Far too many slaves would die. He wrote:

From my short experience of the heat, the sand, and the rocks of the country near Brava, and Kismayo, and the jungles that are behind, I cannot think it will be found possible to transport slaves by that route, without enormous loss on the way . . .[5]

His spies, travelling with the caravans, reported that mortalities were indeed high.

Meanwhile, his work among the Indian merchants was already having an effect. Credit was becoming scarce, and in Zanzibar he noticed . . .

. . . beads and cloth that before were accepted without question are now subjects of litigation on sample, quality, time of delivery and a thousand other objections that while the slave trade flourished no one looked to. This indicates the firm conviction among the merchants that these sorts of goods will now entail a loss and prove how widely all classes of the commercial community were indirectly profiting by and tacitly sharing in the slave trade.[6]

Squeezed on all sides, starved of capital and threatened by arrest, economics and force together would surely prevail. Nevertheless, as he prepared to go on leave in December – by then he had been in Zanzibar for over seven years without a break – Kirk told his deputy, Frederic Elton, to travel south to Dar es Salaam. He wanted to find out exactly how the land route from Kilwa was developing.

Kirk had underestimated the resilience of the Kilwa traders, as well as their ruthlessness. Slaving was deeply ingrained in the town's culture, and when Elton reached Dar that January, he heard much to disturb him. Several people warned him not to travel any farther south along the notorious road through Kisiju, for white men down there were hated, and the slavers were well armed; if he met them he would be killed. But Elton did continue south, and he discovered that the road from Kilwa along the coast was now in full use. Almost daily, large gangs could be seen passing through. As the road wound farther north, it extended inland leading all the way up to the coast at Lamu. It had been well prepared, and there were reports of Arabs coming back down from the north with orders to buy.

The route deliberately bypassed the major towns and the sultan's forts, instead crossing remote creeks, and diverting through mangroves and other difficult country. It had been well provided with watering places; and cooking trenches, spare gang irons and slave stockades were evident in the villages along the way. At the waterways, ferries had been specially arranged. Men said the conditions were hard, and as Kirk had surmised, the mortality rate was evidently terrible. Travelling south that season, Elton reported that '"places of skulls" mark the various roads upon which the traffic continues to flourish and skeletons lie thick scattered on the beach . . .' An old Akhida, an Arab from Sheher, who was well used to slave trafficking, said that 'he had never seen anything so shameful, it was only killing men not trading.'[7]

On his second day out of Dar, Elton met a caravan. The slaves were chained in gangs of sixteen, and at first their guards passed on the track without comment. Then one of Elton's servants, a boy of twelve who was wearing a sun helmet, running ahead through the long grass, was taken for a *msungu* (i.e. European) attempting a covert attack. Elton shouted out that they were officers of the sultan, and had no business with the caravan. It was too late and chaos followed. Water jars, bags of rice, slave irons and boxes were all thrown on the ground as the caravan retreated into the bush, and slaves and slave drivers ran in every direction yelling and screaming.

> One gang of lads and women, chained together with iron neck-rings, was in a horrible state, their lower extremities coated with dry mud and their own excrement and torn with thorns, their bodies mere frameworks, and their skeleton limbs slightly stretched over with wrinkled parchment like skin. One wretched woman had been flung against a tree for slipping her rope, and came screaming up to us for protection, with one eye half out and the side of her face and bosom streaming with blood.[8]

Elton could do nothing for her; he had no authority to stop caravans trading by land, and the slave gangs eventually moved on.

The caravan had come all the way from Nyasa, and later that day they passed two more, each with several hundred slaves. On one occasion, there was a stand-off between Elton and one of the chain guards, who was prepared to shoot him. Elton repeated that he had come to deal with the Indian merchants and no one else, and there was no violence.

Finally, that afternoon he reached the little port of Kisiju, a village that had now become a major stopping place for the caravans heading north.

> A square in the centre of Kisiju is set apart for the accommodation of the caravans, cooking places are built, huts for the wet weather, spare chains and rings in readiness, and an old Arab [is] in charge who receives a reward for apprehending any runaways, and gets everything in order for the arrivals from the south . . .

The land trade was bringing prosperity to the local people along the route, and Kisiju was doing particularly well.

Its inhabitants do a large stroke of business in buying half dying children, fattening them up and re-selling at a profit, the place being full of walking skeletons.

Elton estimated that 1,280 slaves had been marched up from Kilwa that week, through Kisiju and towards the northern ports.[9]

While in England, Kirk received the reports of the overland transports along the coast, but he still refused to believe this was permanent. Once the stock of slaves held in Kilwa had been sold off, he said, he was sure the land route would cease to be used. However, he knew well that in Zanzibar he had only begun what would be a long and difficult job. During his stay in London, he met his boss, the new foreign secretary, Lord Derby, and asked him for instructions on how he should pursue his work when he returned to Africa, because he knew that closing the market in Zanzibar was just the beginning.

However, W.H. Wylde, head of the Consular and Slave Trade Department at the Foreign Office, was doubtful whether Kirk would get much help. Derby didn't care 'a farthing about the suppression of the slave trade from conviction,' he later warned Kirk, 'but he takes it up because the public insist on carrying it out.'[10] Antislave trade feeling in Britain was still strong. Frere's mission had been regarded as a great success, although the government was well aware it was only because of Kirk's handling of the crisis. Moreover, in early 1874, the abolitionist movement had received a further boost. In March, news had been received from Zanzibar that David Livingstone was dead, and his body had arrived on the African coast. It had been formally identified in Zanzibar, and instructions were sent to have it conveyed to England.

The result was an almost unprecedented outpouring of national mourning. When the steamer bearing the corpse finally arrived at Southampton on 15 April, crowds were already at the docks waiting. A band played the Dead March from Saul. The coffin was conveyed by special train to London, where it lay in the map room of the Royal Geographical Society for two days before finally being interred in Westminster Abbey. As the funeral procession wound through the London streets, thousands turned out to watch. Ten mourning coaches followed by a line of private carriages, including that of the Queen, followed the hearse to the Abbey. The coffin was carried into the nave by eight pall bearers among whom were both Stanley and Kirk. Politicians, explorers, geographers, philanthropists and missionaries, diplomats and civic fathers all crowded to atttend the service, which was given by Dean Stanley, the eminent churchman, while Jacob Wainwright, the African convert who had come with the body to England, stood by the grave. The moving account of how Livingstone's corpse had been preserved by his faithful servants, and then carried back to the coast, was by now well known. The nation's most saintly hero had returned after his weary pilgrimage, and the cause for which he had given his life, the fight against slavery, had been sanctified by his death.

The government, surprised by the scale of the public response, could have had no stronger evidence of how deeply the country felt about this human trafficking. Yet Derby still dithered – within the cabinet there were conflicting views – and Kirk had no instructions right up until the night before he left to return to Zanzibar. But his last day in London was productive. During a final interview with the foreign secretary, he worked hard on him, persuading him to back his ideas for fighting the slave traffic. Derby, still reluctant, eventually handed the responsibility over to Kirk to work out for himself. 'I am simply instructed to follow my own old policy in politics and act in judicial matters as I have done,' he wrote to Hooker on his way back to Africa.[11] He had been given a free hand, and it was now up to him to solve the next stage of the problem.

Kirk knew that if he failed, or if he made mistakes, he alone would carry the blame, yet he did not hesitate. Derby had given him latitude to follow his old policy, but during the next five years, he applied himself to nothing less than the destruction of slave trading throughout the East African coast. All the pent-up energy from years of restraint was released in an explosion of constant unremitting activity. It was as if he had become a different man, but Kirk had not changed. He was the same, still unemotional and logical, but now driven by a purpose for which he had spent years preparing. He knew who his enemies were, he knew how they worked, he even knew how they thought. He had spent years studying them, he understood their business, and now he set out to destroy it. He used the information and knowledge he had acquired, and he used it ruthlessly.

Kirk knew also that his success depended entirely on Barghash. Only through him could he obtain the cloak of legality with which to fight the slavers. Yet Barghash would never agree to be a mere puppet, and nor did Kirk want him that way. The sultan had to be credible with his own people; he had to appear to agree with the measures Kirk proposed, but Kirk was afraid that Barghash would never be strong enough. He had signed the law, but if Kirk ever had to denounce him for refusing to uphold it, his policy would have failed. So, instead, he set out, quite consciously, to corrupt the sultan.

During the next few years, he made sure by every means he could that Barghash depended on him just as he depended on the sultan. He built up Barghash's authority with support that only Britain could offer. An order for a 700 ton steamer was placed with the British India Company, 300 new Snider rifles and two Gatling guns were sent for his troops, his vanity was flattered by an invitation from India to attend the Viceregal Durbar. He even received an invitation to make a state visit to Britain, an honour he had always craved. But all this had its price – support for Kirk in his war with the slavers.

Moreover, it was a double-sided bargain that Kirk had made, for if such costly gifts and honours were to be provided, Derby and the British government also required satisfaction; but their price was political. They needed visible progress in the war against slavery, as a return to the British electorate. Once more, Barghash was key to the bargain, for if Kirk could offer him up as a good and noble monarch in the fight against evil, everyone would be pleased. But the British had to believe in him.

Kirk had agreed with Derby that Barghash should visit England as soon as possible, and he was barely back in Zanzibar before he had to leave again to accompany the sultan to London. The royal party set sail from Africa on 9 May, arriving in England a month later via Cairo and Portugal. Disembarking at Gravesend with his extensive suite of advisers and councillors, a secretary, a painter, four cooks, two barbers and a cashier, Barghash was welcomed by the ineffable Badger, before proceeding by launch up the Thames to Westminster Stairs. There a group of distinguished personages and members of parliament stood ready to greet him, while the Fusiliers' band played the national anthem, and a guard of honour of the Coldstream Guards presented arms. The first to step forward was his old friend, Sir Bartle Frere, who perhaps had something to do with the constant coverage given by the press throughout the visit.

During the next three weeks, *The Times* and other papers devoted column after column on almost a daily basis to 'the Seyyid of Zanzibar'. The mission's apparent success had given a significant boost to Frere's political career, and Barghash's visit was taken as further tribute to this resounding achievement. It was seen as a moving personal testament to Britain's civilizing influence across the globe, and during his stay in London, Barghash was constantly attended by the most distinguished politicians, military officers and high-ranking civilians the country could provide. He was fussed over by members of parliament, geographers, churchmen and missionaries, for everyone wanted to be seen in his company. Within hours of his arrival, he was visited in his hotel by Lord Derby, and Lady Derby held two receptions in his honour. A long list of the good and the great, including Disraeli, the Lord Mayor and the Archbishop of Canterbury, called upon him privately. The Reverend Badger was in constant attendance, making long speeches, which he assured everyone represented the Seyyid's deepest thoughts. Within days, Barghash was received at Marlborough House by the Prince of Wales and his consort, together with their German cousins, Prince and Princess Louis of Hesse. After prayers, he was photographed by Messrs Maull and Co. of Piccadilly. Lord Salisbury held a grand dinner in his honour, the Prince of Wales gave a garden party for him at Chiswick, and he took a special train to Windsor, where he was received with his full entourage by the Queen. He went to the British Museum, spent the evening watching 'Around the World in Eighty Days' at the Princess's Theatre, and visited Brighton, where he was shown the aquarium by the mayor, having travelled there by the 4.30 from Victoria. As his open carriage paraded through the crowded streets, he stood up and solemnly bowed to the cheers.

Back in London, he went to the Central African Mission, where he endured an address from the Bishop of London, to the Alexandra Palace Horse Show, where he was received by the Duke of Edinburgh, and on the afternoon of 19 June, to Sir Bartle Frere's at Wimbledon for tea. The same evening, a special fireworks show was put on for him at the Crystal Palace, and the sky was lit up with the Arabic words '*Ya Fattah*', which *The Times* assured its readers meant 'the Opener'. Barghash rose to his feet in wonder, and the whole audience did likewise out of respect for this enlightened monarch, who had done so much to banish the evil of slave trading from Africa.

For this was what the visit was really all about. The British were, in fact, congratulating themselves. In Barghash, they believed they had the ideal oriental prince, a true partner in their great expanding empire. Hailed as a man 'with the dignified and courteous bearing which is inborn in true Arabs of every class',[12] cheered by large crowds everywhere he went, attended by military bands on every possible occasion, he even received the dedication of an oriental love song from its composer, a Mrs Alfred Phillips, specially translated for the occasion by the Reverend Badger.[13]

Barghash had done what the British wanted, he had seen the light, and during his visit he played his part to perfection at every turn. He expressed surprise and admiration at all the wonders he saw. His appreciation of the hospitality he was shown was boundless. When the Anti Slavery Society thanked him for his efforts, but pointed out that slaves were still transported by land through his territories, he answered with tact and grace. To the Church Missionary Society, he announced:

We are aware that your Society is zealously engaged in spreading the light of godly knowledge among the ignorant in Africa. That is a praiseworthy object and such as will meet with a recompense from God . . . What we have done we have done for God's sake, and, God willing, we shall continue to do so . . .[14]

When he was later received at the western gate of Westminster Abbey by Dean Stanley (in his Oxford gown), readers of the press reports could almost believe the Seyyid had become a Christian.

Barghash continued to visit all that was civilized and industrious in England. He took in military manoevres at Aldershot, once again as guest of the Prince of Wales. He attended an assembly of the Royal Geographical Society at Burlington House, visited St Thomas's Hospital, where he was deeply affected by the lines of patients, and dropped in to the House of Commons to hear Sir Harcourt Johnstone move for a repeal of the Contagious Diseases Act. He inspected the Royal Arsenal at Woolwich, where he witnessed the 40 ton Nasmyth hammer in action, and afterwards was said to have remarked wryly, 'I have seen the Gate of Hell.'[15]

Barghash's London visit was rounded off with an evening at the Italian Opera in Covent Garden, where Meyerbeer's 'Africaine' was staged as a compliment, and the next day he proceeded on a tour of the provinces. Once more, he was received, feted and cheered by crowds of townspeople, and dined by the foremost citizens of each city he visited. In Liverpool, once centre of Britain's own slave-trading activities, and in Manchester, he was congratulated on his far-sighted policies, and his suppression of the traffic in human beings.

Behind the scenes, though, everything did not go always entirely as planned. Kirk, mentioned in the press merely as the Seyyid's constant companion, maintained a low profile during the visit. For him, it was vital that the trip should go well, and he worked hard to ensure any mishaps were avoided. Some of his difficulties were easily overcome. Lord Stanley of Alderley,[16] an eccentric member of the House of Lords, and a Muslim convert, was eager to involve Barghash in a pan Islamic political agreement together with Turkey and various other countries. Kirk intervened, and Lady Stanley was annoyed at having to cancel the reception she had planned in the Seyyid's honour. The royal family, however, proved a little more problematic.

The reason was due to the re-emergence of Salme, Barghash's half-sister. Since leaving Zanzibar, she had been living in Germany, where she had taken up the title of 'Princess' following the death of her husband, Ruete, in a tram accident. After years of hardship, Salme and her children had been rescued by the German royal court, partly because of her exotic background, but also perhaps because of German political interest in Africa.[17] Salme was now anxious to regain what she considered her personal inheritance in Zanzibar, and thought her new friends could help her. Representations were made on her behalf by the German imperial family through their London ambassador, and during Barghash's visit to London, she decided to visit Britain, hoping to arrange a meeting with her brother, and perhaps even a return to Zanzibar.

The British and German royal families were closely related, and Princess Christian of Schleswig Holstein, Queen Victoria's daughter, took up Salme's cause. Under pressure to act, Kirk was finally persuaded to raise the matter with Barghash. The sultan responded curtly that he did not wish to hear his sister's name mentioned in his presence. She had dishonoured his family, and her apostasy, under Muslim law, had annulled any inheritance. The incident threatened to poison the visit. The British royal family were upset, and Barghash and Kirk were excluded from the royal enclosure at Ascot. The same day, Barghash was further insulted when two military gentlemen accosted Kirk in his presence, and 'began dilating on the disgraceful way in which the Sultan was treating his sister'.[18] Kirk told them to mind their own business, before being informed by a detective that they were the Duke of Cambridge and Count Gleichen, yet another member of the Anglo-German imperial clan.

Salme, meanwhile, was staying privately in London,[19] planning how she might contrive to meet Barghash on one of his frequent public appearances, when she received a request to see a rather grand individual who had turned up at her friends' house. Sir Bartle Frere was polite, solicitous and anxious to establish the reasons for her visit to Britain. Finally, he came to the point. He was there to offer her a choice – between attempting a reconciliation with her brother, or the restoration of the rights of her children to their property in Zanzibar. If she chose the former, she would sacrifice her ambitions for her children. She could not have both. Salme, after much agonizing, finally committed herself to avoiding Barghash during his stay if her children's rights were restored, and Frere departed.

The promise was never made good, and the incident left Salme bitter, and even prepared to be of use to Britain's enemies.[20] However, the danger of showing Barghash publicly in an unfavourable light had been avoided. Frere and Kirk, although allies, had very different motives for ensuring the visit was a success, and that nothing should disturb it. For Frere, it was a matter of personal reputation and career; by now, his name had spread as far as the United States as the man who had put an end to the inhuman traffic in slaves in the Indian Ocean.[21] For Kirk, however, the issue was more complex. He needed the government and the public to believe in Barghash, but equally he needed Barghash to believe in Britain, and he wanted nothing to disturb this calm and equable relationship. Fortunately, he was successful. Again and again, the Seyyid was lauded for his 'suppression of the slave trade', an object that he agreed was certainly most desirable, and when he finally departed from Britain in mid-July, his reputation was secure. Yet it was a fiction, a triumph of successful public relations.

Barghash journeyed with his party to France and from there they travelled to Egypt. While in Cairo, he and his closest advisers decided to indulge in some luxury shopping before their final return to Zanzibar, purchasing eight expensive Circassian concubines for their harems, six of whom were for the sultan personally. In order not to arouse attention, the slaves were sent on discreetly to Jidda to await shipment for Africa. Unfortunately, one of them, reputedly the most beautiful and costly, on learning that she was destined to fulfil the pleasure of the ancient councillor, Seyyid Hammud, attempted to commit suicide in Jiddah by throwing herself from a high window into the street below.[22] The incident caused a scandal.

Kirk did his best to hush up the affair. He knew that Barghash had not changed his opinion on slave trading but he still needed his support; how badly became apparent on their return. In early 1876, Kirk finally admitted that the land route from Kilwa to the northern ports was a reality, and not merely a temporary expedient. Slaves in large numbers were being taken overland, and the loss of life was terrible. Despite this, the new arrangements functioned well and the dealers made money.

'There has never been such a good year,' said one owner of a long string (of slaves), 'there is great demand and no duty levied by the sultan, the $2 ½ which went to him before for slaves shipped by sea, we save, the land journey is worked at a profit!'[23]

So in July 1876, Kirk persuaded Barghash to issue a proclamation outlawing the trafficking of slaves by land, and giving him the authority to pursue the caravans farther onshore.

Kirk was successful only because in late 1875, shortly after the sultan returned from Europe, he had proved his worth to Barghash in ways neither could have foreseen. In November that year, Egyptian forces invaded the southern Somali coast at Brava, territory nominally claimed by Barghash, although the sultan's writ had never been strongly applied that far north. Barghash had long feared the khedive's imperial ambitions, and he immediately wrote to the officer commanding the invasion force demanding its withdrawal. However, the situation was confused, so later that month Kirk personally took a British cruiser, the *Thetis*, and sailed to Brava himself. Anchoring off the town, he sent ashore a demand that, as British consul, he should be allowed to speak to the local Indian traders. The Egyptian officer commanding the occupying troops at once contested his right, and when the *Thetis* levelled its guns on the town, the Egyptians said they would meet force with resistance. There was a stand-off.

The Egyptians had already occupied other points on the Somali coastline, and had other warships farther south. Nevertheless, Kirk landed on the beach that afternoon with the captain of the

Thetis. They were met by Egyptian troops lined along the sand, and ordered to stop. Kirk was questioned about his identity. He told the Egyptians brusquely that it was none of their business, and brushing them aside, walked on into the town, where he was constantly challenged by the occupying military. He delivered letters to an Arab trader, and eventually re-embarked on the *Thetis*, but during the course of his visit ashore, he had been able to establish useful information for his report back to London. All commercial activity on the coast had been interrupted by the invasion, he wrote. In addition, the Egyptians were actively encouraging slave trading once more in the area, something, he assured the Foreign Office, Barghash was committed to abolishing ... Indeed, he asserted, it was the sultan's intention to do away with slavery entirely on the Somali coast, in order to block finally the route from the slave-hunting grounds of East Africa to the Middle East.

Kirk's tactics worked. By evoking once more the spectre of the slave trade, he persuaded the British government to put pressure on the khedive, and Egyptian forces were withdrawn. Kirk had demonstrated to Barghash just what he could do for Zanzibar when it was most threatened.

Everything Kirk did depended on his relationship with the sultan. He could pursue the slavers under cover of the law, but he could not risk the sultan distancing himself from his actions. Yet Barghash knew when he was being manipulated; he refused to act as Kirk's mere instrument, and the relationship was a volatile one. The sultan hated to obey the man he had once patronized. In 1876, Kirk wrote:

I have now for months watched that man's temper and moods and just let him have from day to day the freedom ... I thought good at the time ... One day he had to be congratulated and given credit, then he got a sharp word, but it had to be dropped outside to reach him from others, and I had to keep all this to myself. Even the assistants did not know the game ...[24]

The game involved a constant pretence – 'a slender thread of duplicity, more or less visible' was always present in their relationship. Barghash was Kirk's creature, but it was vital he did not seem so. He gave Kirk his support, but he gave it reluctantly.

He fully knows that the least spontaneous energy displayed in furtherance of our views will alienate the wavering allegiance of his distant subjects, and bring about the forfeiture of a position to which he still fondly clings . . .[25]

And every day, Barghash's position was slowly being eroded. He craved prestige as much as power, although he did everything he could to maintain the semblance of power. Nevertheless, real authority in Zanzibar was increasingly being wielded elsewhere.

For the next five years, Kirk harried the slave traders along the east African coast mercilessly, without respite and with every means. His will and determination were prodigious, and the sultan's authority was always the cover within which he worked. He used force, and he used his knowledge of the trade's economics, and when these proved insufficient, he used even more radical weapons.

Throughout 1876, the trade centred on the island of Pemba to the north of Zanzibar, and Kirk sent ships there to watch the creeks and inlets. Sometimes he accompanied the sailors personally. In February 1876, they captured a vessel with 102 slaves on board, while another two escaped by landing their slaves in the surf, and taking them off through the bush. The master, crew and slave owners of the captured boat were all handed over to Kirk for trial, and were found guilty. Their punishment was deliberately shocking.

After hearing the case I had the six slave owners, of whom three were pure Arabs, together with the dhow Captain secured in their own slave chains, and marched for exhibition through the streets. Thereafter having communicated with His Highness, they were flogged in public before the palace, the pure Arabs and negroes being treated alike and all flogged in a manner that will leave its mark for life.[26]

Kirk knew what he was doing. In a society where honour and respect for rank were unconditional, such 'degrading personal punishment of pure born Arabs of Arabia' was bound to cause agitation. Kirk was also aware of the pain it caused Barghash to see high-ranking Zanzibaris treated this way and in his name, and Kirk had to put pressure on him to take the action. It did not stop the trade, but it had its effect.

... the infliction of corporal punishment in public is driving the slave trade into the hands of the lowest classes and so far making it every day less and less reputable and more within our power to deal with. A few years ago the best Arab in Zanzibar would think it no disgrace to head his slaves. This is no longer so ...[27]

Public disgace made people see slave trading as a route to dishonour and loss of dignity. It was a dangerous tactic, but it worked. Kirk knew who the principal slavers were, and he targeted them mercilessly. Sometimes they were shot attempting to evade arrest, but the most senior men, once caught, were branded in public. The prospect of being flogged and thrown into the common jail was a terrible deterrent.

In early 1877, Kirk caught the most senior slave dealer on Pemba. The Arab community on the island were alarmed, and at once made strenuous efforts to prevent any further action. Forty of the most influential men came across to Zanzibar to wait on the sultan to plead with him for their friend's acquittal, and Kirk noted that 'with this object every sort of pressure was brought to bear.' He resisted the pressure, and insisted that the man was put in irons and sent to prison. It was not long before the chiefs of Pemba were approaching Kirk personally, to discuss in a friendly manner how the problem could be resolved. Kirk said, with grim satisfaction, that he was happy to meet them, and would accept the invitation pressed upon him to visit the island as their guest. He wrote:

And I doubt not that this occurrence will be the means of greatly increasing our influence over the most persistent and influential slave dealers with whom I have had to do.[28]

Kirk was playing a strangely ambiguous game. He wished to destroy slave trading, but he did not wish to destroy Zanzibar. So even as he squeezed the men behind the trade, those who financed and profited from the business, his relations with them remained cordial. These were the men, Indians and Arabs, who formed the backbone of the country's economy, and after it was all over he would still have to deal with them. He wrote to Wylde:

I am on the best of terms with all the capitalists who import slaves, that is who find the money or in the end buy them. I live with them, shoot with them and [we] quite understand each other. I well believe they would help me catch a slave gang if we came across it . . .[29]

For them, it was business. Slaves were still just another commodity, and Kirk understood that. It had always been just business.

Nevertheless, his tactics of forcing the trade down the social scale had their dangers. The slave gangs were now run by men who were poor and desperate, and who had nothing to lose. They were 'fatalistic to danger', he wrote, and they hated him. In March 1877, while he was at Malinde on the coast, it was only by luck that he avoided a group of eighty men with guns who were out searching for him. He was known as a good shot, and would deliberately show off his skill at times when it suited him. He joked:

If I had not an exaggerated reputation all along the coast as a clean shot, there is small doubt some of the villains who do the trade would pay me off, so that it really does good to drop a buck or kill a hippopotamus sometimes.[30]

However, despite being tough, even ruthless, Kirk could never control the trade in the interior, and at Kilwa, where the main slave routes reached the coast, the dealers still ignored the sultan's word. He wrote to Derby:

> In Kilwa and its neighborhood, there are however a large number of natives so demoralized by long contact with the slave trade in its worst form, that they never will change their mode of life and these at present form a dangerous element to be repressed by force alone . . .[31]

In 1876, Kirk had already taken two hundred Zanzibari troops down to Kilwa to quell a threatened rebellion, but when he got there, he found the slaves and dealers had vanished, taking protection deep in the swamps of the River Rufiji delta, where they were easily concealed. Kirk thought there might have been as many as six thousand slaves hidden in the marshes. The old slave routes from Nyasa were still being supported, and Kirk learnt they were protected by Barghash's own governor.

Saeed bin Abdullah, the governor of Kilwa, was a powerful man. Not only did he control a lucrative and important part of Barghash's territories, he was also directly related to the sultan. He was an Arab of the most senior rank, and he considered himself above the law. In late 1876, Kirk persuaded Barghash to recall him to Zanzibar in an attempt to neutralize his activities, but the trade from Kilwa still continued. Then on 9 February the following year, Kirk had his opportunity.

A gang of slaves being marched from Kilwa up the coast were spotted by one of Kirk's spies as they were shipped by dhow off the port of Pangani on the coast near Zanzibar. The slaves and their immediate owners were arrested and brought to Zanzibar, where Kirk personally interrogated them. Five of the eight owners proved to be 'petty speculators', but of the others 'three were found after a long and tedious examination, in which these men did everything possible to hide the truth, to be agents and confidential slaves of Saeed bin Abdulla the ex governor of Kilwa . . .'[32] The men finally admitted that their chief was continuing to support the purchase of raw slaves from the interior for onward trading, and Kirk now had the evidence he needed.

Later that month he risked everything he had achieved in one extraordinary confrontation, and he set it up with care.

Saeed bin Abdullah was a member of the Sultan's council, although he had not been present at the agreement to sign the treaty in 1873. Nevertheless, Kirk was determined to make good his threat to hold the most senior Zanzibar families to account, and bind them personally to what had been agreed. And he intended to do it publicly where all might see, within the sultan's palace. He chose a day in mid-February when he must have known that the former governor would be seated by the sultan at the 'public durbar'. This was a position to which he was entitled by right, as one of the royal family and a man of importance. For even though the reason for his removal from Kilwa was common knowledge, he had been formally accused of nothing. That day, Kirk entered the durbar hall without advance warning, and he had with him the men who had been in charge of the captured slaves, as well as the depositions and evidence he had collected. He also had with him 'an old slave of Saeed bin Abdulla taken from his chain gang'. In open court, in front of the sultan and his advisers, he confronted the former governor with this man, and demanded that the slave be allowed to speak.

Embarrassed in front of his ruler and his peers, there was little the former governor could say.

When confronted with the domestic slave he had put in the gang to be sold and with the testimony of his own confidential slaves who now turned against him [Saeed bin Abdullah] had nothing to say in his defence but to try to cast the blame on his agent, a clerk who is absent from Zanzibar.

No one believed him. To all those present, it must have been a shocking occasion, a contravention of everything their society was and had stood for. A common slave from the chain gang, one of the lowest forms of life, had appeared at the sultan's court and dared to accuse a member of the ruling family of holding him and his kind as chattels for sale.

Kirk did not describe the tension in the durbar, and made no comment on how Barghash reacted. He only wrote with typical understatement that 'nothing could have been more opportune than finding him [i.e. Saeed bin Abdullah] in Durbar for all present saw that the evidence was unanswerable.'[33] He had deliberately chosen such a high-risk course because that way he could show everyone in Zanzibar that even the highest born were culpable before the law. The former governor was at once arrested and placed in slave irons, and then removed to the common prison. There he found himself confronted by the very men who had acted as his agents in driving the slave gang overland from Kilwa. In order to humiliate him even further, Kirk made an appeal on behalf of these men to the sultan. He claimed that as slaves themselves, they had only been obeying their master, and would have been flogged or sold off had they refused. They should therefore be freed from prison and released from their servitude, so that they would not be further exposed to their master's anger. And that was what happened.

Kirk knew that in treating Saeed bin Abdullah as no more than a common criminal, Barghash had been pushing his own authority to the utmost, but no one in Zanzibar was fooled. Everyone realized that the author of the man's disgrace was Kirk and not the sultan, and it was against Kirk that any anger was directed. People now understood that their own slaves could report against them with impunity, and that no one was safe from accusations of slave trading. If they were involved, the consul's spies would inform on them. In Zanzibar's new order, people trusted and feared Kirk more than their own leaders and masters.

The ruin of Saeed bin Abdullah changed the whole tenor of slave trading in East Africa. The system of organized trafficking through Kilwa had been dealt a blow from which it never recovered. Other officials were removed, and by August 1877, Kirk could write that . . .

. . . the foreign slave trade from Zanzibar territory has been for practical purposes totally abolished, that which took thousands of slaves to south Somali land is equally a thing of the past and we have to do now with the limited land traffic alone.[34]

Arabs travelling up the coast reported that the price of healthy slaves had dropped so far that the long-distance trade was no longer worth the effort. Indian merchants now refused advances to slave traders on any terms.

Nevertheless, Kirk continued to punish the local traffic unremittingly – in November 1877, a dhow was captured with a hundred slaves and sixteen Arab and Baluchi dealers on board – and by mid-1878, work in the Admiralty court was merely 'technical', with few cases concerning raw slaves from the interior. By the end of the decade, Kirk was able to write to Wylde that the 'slave trade for all practical purposes [is] over and done as far as ever will be while slavery exists.'[35] Intermittent dealing in small numbers up and down the coast continued until the end of the century, but the transport of slaves to the Middle East had been cut off, and the centuries old supply lines from East and Central Africa had been virtually terminated.

Kirk had done what his masters in Britain had required. He had not done it out of moral fervour, or deeply held religious conviction, or even from emotional outrage. He did it because he considered slave trading a kind of social contagion, which was debilitating and ruining a vigorous and energetic society. From the start, he had been pragmatic, efficient, clear in his diagnosis and precise in his application. Once he had decided what was necessary, he had been determined and often fearless in his course of action.

Kirk had sought little credit for himself, but in the capitals of Europe his work had attracted attention. In April 1879, he received a letter from Leopold, King of the Belgians, complimenting him on his achievement. It was to be an omen for the future. In the wider world, powerful interests began to look upon Africa with a very different agenda. The fight against slave trafficking was about to be adopted cynically by those who would use it as disguise for far less altruistic purposes.

15: BARGHASH THE UNLUCKY

There are mysterious Germans travelling inland . . .

KIRK TO GRANVILLE[1]

Zanzibar was changing. Kirk put it down to the impact of the new monthly mail ships. Towards the end of the 1870s, the numbers of westerners coming to the city were increasing rapidly. Many were adventurers, others were explorers and missionaries. There was talk of a road from the coast down to Lake Nyasa. Speculators sought concessions on the mainland, and some of the newcomers were almost farcical. 'Already we have visited high class and proficient swindlers,' Kirk wrote. 'Now we have received a German who with his wife proposes opening a cafe chantal and casino. He comes last from Bombay and Yokohamo, but is before time here . . .'[2]

As the torrent of wealth from hunting elephants continued to pour out of the interior, many of the new men were attracted by the lure of ivory. One of the biggest markets had developed in the United States, where in the Connecticut river valleys, whole towns depended on manufacturing ivory products. At its source, though, the business was still mainly controlled by Zanzibaris, from their trading posts deep in the Congo. In 1879, Kirk noted:

Zanzibar traders have now pushed their ivory expeditions so far west that the product cannot be brought frequently to the

294

[East African] coast, there is a large Zanzibar colony now at these distant stations and it may be more easy to convey their ivory and to work the country by steamers on the Congo.[3]

The traders from the coast seemed impregnable in their remote settlements at the centre of the continent. But in Europe, there was increasing interest in Africa's wealth, and the idea of challenging the Zanzibari monopoly on the ivory trade seemed more attractive as time went on. Some in high places even talked of justifying commercial conquest with a renewed fight against that old demon the slave trade.

In September 1876, King Leopold of Belgium held a conference in Brussels, with the ostensible purpose of encouraging an international movement against slave trading, and from this was born his African International Association. Three years later, Stanley was back in Zanzibar, this time on Leopold's behalf, setting off once more for the Congo, while the previous year, a Frenchman, Debaize, had also left for the interior. In 1880, Leopold made a proposal for a Belgian 'colony' in Africa. The same year, the Scots businessman, Mackinnon, sent a representative to Zanzibar to propose a company for exploiting the interior, and another Frenchman, Rabaud, did likewise. German and French expeditions set out in 1880, intending to establish ivory trading stations in Unyanyembe, there was another Belgian expedition, and several Christian missions were established. Joseph Thomson explored the highlands of what was to become Kenya, Count Teleki pushed north into Turkana, and in 1884, Harry Johnstone went inland to explore Kilimanjaro. There were many others.

Meanwhile, along the coast, much of the energy had gone out of the Zanzibar enterprise. Breaking the slave trade had not just deprived it of a source of wealth. The export of slaves had always been more than a mere business; it had been the symbol of Zanzibar's domination of the mainland, and part of the country's reason for existence. Black Africans taken from the interior, by force or by purchase, compelled to change their identity and become Muslims, and then sold into servitude – this had gone on for longer than Zanzibar itself had existed. Deprived of that ancient right, the coastal people's confidence in their superiority to the 'barbarians' of the interior had been dealt a severe blow. Life went on as before, but without its old vigour. In 1874, an Arab on the coast told one of Kirk's deputies,

> One day resembles another with its money making, and external gossiping, and perservering. Idling and ample regrets follow relations of the past prosperity when Seyyid Majid was King, and caravans headed by flags and men giving guns swaggered through the streets to receive royal presents, and men of high estate from Zanzibar spent their wealth open handed. But nothing is done, Bargash is pronounced 'the unlucky', and tomorrow is a counterpart of yesterday.[4]

Barghash 'the unlucky' increasingly depended on outside support for his authority. Kirk, writing of 'the decadence of the Arab power', thought that the city's rule in the more distant parts of the coastal belt existed only on sufferance. The collapse of the slave trade had brought about the decline of other institutions. The hold the Customs Master had traditionally exercised over all coastal trade had weakened, and in 1876 the sultan had given up any pretence of ruling the Zanzibari settlement inland at Unyanyembe. When yet another war erupted between Zanzibari traders and the local Wanyamwezi, Barghash took a critical step and recalled his governor, leaving the settlers on their own. The fight against the slave traders had also had other long-term repercussions.

At every level, it had increased Kirk's personal influence. In combating the slave traffickers, he had established an extensive 'system of informers and frequent visits' all along the coast, and years after the slavers had been defeated, the system remained in place. The control he had maintained over the Indian merchants to prevent their funding of slave trading led to his involvement in a host of other disputes. He spoke on Barghash's behalf to the local *walis*, he accompanied punitive expeditions by Zanzibari troops to Mombasa and Kilwa, he advised Barghash on how to deal with the adventurers and concession seekers who besieged him. By the end of the decade, there were few aspects of Zanzibar government with which he was not concerned.

In breaking the power of the slave trade, Kirk had created for himself an almost mythical status far beyond Zanzibar itself. He was known by reputation to chiefs and rulers deep within the continent. With some, he exchanged gifts; others sent him invitations to visit them. His relationship with the Yaos of southern Nyasa was more problematic. Determined to prevent any revival of trafficking, he watched the port of Kilwa closely for any new slave arrivals. When caravans continued to come in from the main Yao dealers, Kirk sent them a tough message in Swahili, even though they lived hundreds of miles away and far from Zanzibar rule. He could not prevent them enslaving their neighbours, he informed them, but if they continued to send slaves to the coast, he would free the captives, he would impound their caravan goods and their agents would be imprisoned.[5] They took heed.

During these years, it was accepted in Europe that Britain's influence in East Africa was paramount, but Kirk knew how fragile the Zanzibar state was. Its informality made it vulnerable in the modern world. He attempted to get British support for establishing internationally accepted boundaries to Barghash's territories, and at one point Barghash himself even seemed willing to make his country a British protectorate. But London was reluctant to get further involved; a policy of influence without responsibility seemed to offer everything that was needed. No other power could establish colonies in the interior while the coast from Delgado Bay in the south to Lamu in the north was under Barghash's control. He had guards and officers in virtually every port. Seyyid Said's genius in establishing commercial hegemony along the seaboard was more than ever apparent, for any trading operation in the interior needed to negotiate customs dues with the Zanzibar ruler, and any colony would require access to a port to make it viable. Zanzibar's historical dominance still held good, as long as Britain remained its friend.

Kirk was determined to bolster that dominance. His reliance on Barghash to implement the measures against slave trading had changed the nature of government in Zanzibar. The new policies were not popular, and as slavers from leading families were punished under the sultan's name, Barghash had inevitably become a more autocratic ruler. Kirk wrote to Derby:

> It must be borne in mind that ever since he has given way to our policy he has had to exercise a personal authority unknown before and at variance with the fundamental system of government among the Arabs of Oman . . . He was always supposed to be supreme but he stood almost as an equal among the heads of the various Arab families.[6]

But Barghash could not rely any longer on his elders and advisers, and his existing troops were not dependable, so Kirk arranged for the creation of a new military force, comprising African soldiers rather than the traditional Baluchi mercenaries. It was better disciplined, and equipped by Martini Henry rifles, supplied from Britain. It was also commanded by a British former naval officer.

Kirk did not flaunt his power but all were aware of it, within the city and beyond. He had remade Zanzibar, its society, its law and the way it was governed, and that gave him an influence even larger than the interests he represented. His prestige extended deep into the continent; explorers and missionaries reported that in the Zanzibari settlements on the lakes and in the Congo, he was regarded as a 'sort of second Sultan'.[7] He was identified clearly with Zanzibari regional supremacy, and his aim was to use British might to ensure it. Outwardly a mere consul, he was the indispensable link between the two, for through his influence on the sultan, he was the means by which Britain controlled access to a subcontinent. His position seemed all but unassailable, and a certain arrogance in his words and actions during these late years became apparent. Perhaps that was what led to his downfall.

Over the years, the life of the African coast had become Kirk's own life, and he recorded it endlessly in photographs and in his journals, which continued to be crammed with a stream of information on everything he came across. Commercial data was mixed up with geographical observations; the finances of Indian traders followed information on sea lanes and lighthouses; the ownership of land mixed with the origins of words. The use of cattle, population distribution, the productivity and value of slaves, botany, the pay of sailors on dhows, and the management of the sultan's economy were all noted in quick urgent staccato entries. The thread was the same – the curiosity of a voracious mind, constantly inquiring, assimilating and using every piece of information it came across.

Joseph Thomson, an explorer who came through Zanzibar in 1879 on his way to the interior, gave a brief portrait of Kirk.

> We found him almost buried in the midst of his newly arrived letters and newspapers. On introducing ourselves we met with such a hearty welcome . . . Mrs. Kirk, who presently appeared, also charmed us by her graceful and hospitable reception. We were forthwith invited to take up our residence with them . . . Before returning to the ship we met four children of Mrs. Kirk's, and were much surprised at their healthy appearance. They looked as vigorous and lively as if they had never been out of England, and yet they had never left Zanzibar, where they were born.[8]

Kirk was immersed in his life in Zanzibar. A short way out of the city, he had his 'country house' at Mbweni, where he had developed a botanical garden, and where he experimented with plants. Botany was still his passion. He did research into the local growth of rubber, corresponding with Kew and contributing to the development of the crop in West Africa. He continued to work punishing hours – 'I cannot live without work, and am not happy. Here I have a little too much,' he wrote to Wylde, and by 1878, his health was beginning to suffer. 'I am so weak I cannot manage a smile.' The climate of the African coast, which he had once enjoyed, he now thought was 'as vile as any on the face of the earth', and he complained about his teeth. Yet intellectually, he was at the peak of his powers.[9]

Kirk was not in favour of European settlement in the interior. He hoped rather for an East African state under Zanzibar rule, allied to Britain.

> As to Central Africa being an outlet for European colonisa-tion I am satisfied that there is no region within the tropics of Africa fit for colonisation in the sense in which we . . . use the word.[10]

Nor was he overenthusiastic about the proliferation of Christian missions, although he took care not to say it openly. On arriving at the CMS Mission outside Mombasa in late 1873, he had scribbled in his journal, 'Mission station. O heavens, is this teaching the heathen? Paddys, pigs. If this is a place, give me a good native village.'[11] He may well have thought Islam more suited to Africa, for as he travelled up and down the coast, the ruins of mosques and ancient Muslim tombs never ceased to fascinate him. Remote, absorbed in his own view of Africa, perhaps without realizing it, Kirk had lost touch with new currents of thinking far away in Europe. He knew the world was fast changing, but underestimated the scale of change. Africa, in becoming part of the outside world, had become more interesting to the outside world, although the wrenching dislocations that this would bring were apparent to very few.

In 1882, the most dominant figure of the interior, returned to Zanzibar. The ivory trader and adventurer, Tippoo Tib, came back to the coast that year at the head of an immense caravan, bringing with him much of his hoard of ivory accumulated during decades of trade and plunder in the Congo. While in Zanzibar, the trader wrote to Kirk asking for advice in his relationship with Stanley, whom he had been helping faraway in the Congo. Kirk was unable to assist, but the two men met, and Kirk took a photograph of the great warrior. Unusually, it shows Tippoo Tib armed and in full ceremonial dress, self-consciously the Arab chieftain. It is almost a romantic portrait, as if the photographer were deliberately recording an image of power that had already begun to fade from the continent. Perhaps Kirk even saw the Arab as an archaic figure, to be recorded for posterity. He might also have recognized in the other man a distant parallel with himself – both of them briefly in positions of dominance, before being overtaken by the tide of continental change.

Tippoo Tib, however, had not yet given in to the future. A few years later, he had a meeting with Barghash. By then, the trader had fallen out with Stanley. Fully aware of Belgian ambitions pressing on Zanzibari interests in the Congo, Tippoo Tib offered the sultan a deal. If they acted fast, he said, they could still maintain control over the richest part of the continent. He, Tippoo Tib had the arms, the men and the money, and with Barghash's backing could establish a colony in the centre of Africa, which would hold the Europeans at bay. But the fire had gone out of Barghash. He knew how little power he had, even in his own city. So he listened, and then replied, 'Hamed, be not angry with me; I want to have no more to do with the mainland. The Europeans want to take Zanzibar here from me: how should I be able to keep the mainland? Happy are those who did not live to see the present state of affairs. You are a stranger here still but you will see how things are going . . .'

Tippoo Tib then said with resignation, 'When I heard these words I knew that it was all up with us.'[12]

Carl Peters was a young German who was consumed by a passion to glorify his country with possessions overseas. Like many adventurers who arrived in Zanzibar in the 1880s, he was ambitious, unscrupulous and prepared to take high risks, but unlike most, he also had large political aims. In September 1884, he and three companions travelled to Africa in the guise of mechanics and under false names, and arriving in Zanzibar, set off for the interior. They had been warned by the German government to expect no official protection in their enterprise. Nevertheless, they headed inland towards the region of Usagara, and there, during a period of three weeks, signed a series of twelve treaties with chiefs of varying importance, surrendering to their company sovereignty over 2,500 square miles of territory. Peters' treaties appear to have been flimsy. Missionaries in the area claimed they were signed with men whose authority was questionable, but they served their purpose, and became useful in a trial of strength that was only just beginning.

Kirk knew little of the expedition, and when he heard that one of its leaders had died, thought it had proved a failure. But in early 1885, Peters returned to Berlin and presented Bismarck with his results, and on 3 March, the German Chancellor, asserting that the territories were clearly beyond the limits of the sultan's 'Reich' and therefore unoccupied, announced their formal protection under the German Empire. This new protectorate was clearly a threat to Zanzibar since it was located directly across the island's principal trading routes into the interior, which connected the city to its settlements in Unyanyembe and farther west. Equally, Zanzibar blocked easy access from the sea to Germany's new territory. Without a port it was not viable, and Kirk, as soon as he was informed, realized that conflict between the two was inevitable.

Barghash at once countered the German threat by sending military expeditions to establish his own 'protectorates' at other points in the immediate interior, while writing a strong letter of protest to the German government. Kirk, communicating with the British Foreign Office, was strongly supportive of the sultan, and fully expected London to deal robustly on Zanzibar's behalf. But unknown to him, there had been recent shifts in British policy, and his letters were not as welcome as he might have expected.

In 1882, there had been a financial crisis in Egypt, and Britain's subsequent occupation of the country had resulted in dramatic changes in relations between the European powers. Britain's move had been a humiliation for France, and the British government found itself dependent on German goodwill for its ability to act in Cairo. Britain's interests in East Africa were far less important than its need to preserve its investment in the Middle East, and Zanzibar had become expendable. Faced with threats from Bismarck, Lord Salisbury at the Foreign Office instructed Kirk to act with caution, telling him not to communicate in any hostile way with Germans, nor permit Zanzibaris to do so. If Germany wanted a free hand in East Africa, Britain was prepared to permit this. It would even facilitate it.[13]

In Berlin, however, there was annoyance at Barghash's resistance, and blame was laid at the door of the all-powerful British consul, Kirk, who was thought to have exceeded his brief. On 5 August 1885, five German warships anchored off Zanzibar, and three days later Kirk received a telegram from London informing him that Germans had laid claim to further large swathes of inland territory, including those recently marked by the sultan's own troops. Kirk at once countered that the new German treaties were spurious – he had personally interviewed some of those who had witnessed them. He had made it clear where his loyalties lay.

In Europe, the international situation had worsened, and Britain was nervous. Continued tension over Egypt, the triumph of the Mahdi in Sudan, and threat of war with Russia over Afghanistan all persuaded the government that Bismarck's friendship was vital. Gladstone, the prime minister, even thought that German colonial expansion might be in British interests. So when the commander of the German squadron presented his demand to Barghash that there should be no further interference with German treaty making, Kirk was instructed to tell the sultan to give in gracefully.

While the German warships were in harbour, Kirk became suspicious of another ship, the *Adler*, which had held apart from the main fleet, entering and then leaving harbour without explanation. Sending out a boy to sell oranges to the men on board, he discovered that it carried an interesting passenger – Princess Salme was finally returning unannounced to Zanzibar, together with her children, including her young son. Her presence with the German fleet was clearly not a coincidence. Some years earlier she had written to her brother, bitterly castigating the British, and urging him to turn to Germany as a friend.

My brother, I wish you to understand that the English only wish to destroy your power and your name, and they only await a fitting time to seize Zanzibar ... just as lately they seized Egypt ... You in Zanzibar cannot see these things.[14]

The princess and her family had been brought along as a tentative fall-back solution. If conflict arose between Germany and Zanzibar, the German government considered it might be useful to have a male member of the ruling family, who was also a German citizen, available and on the spot. As events turned out, Salme and her family were not required.[15] Kirk was forced to act, not as Zanzibar's protector, but as the unwilling spokesman for bargains made elsewhere. Although it pained him to do so, he exercised much of his remaining credit with Barghash in persuading him his best interests lay in giving up territories he believed were his. The German fleet sailed away satisfied.

For both Kirk and Barghash it was a humiliating procedure, for it was now evident to all that Zanzibar had become pawn in a much larger game. The extraordinary political process known as 'the Scramble for Africa' was already under way. Barghash was indeed unlucky, and Kirk had been shown as compromised and undependable, whereas before he had been all powerful. He could not protect Zanzibar from those who were his own masters.

By the end of 1885, it was agreed between Britain and Germany that a delimitation commission should finally settle the extent of the Zanzibar territories in East Africa. The commission's representatives spent several months visiting the coast during the following year.[16] Barghash was never consulted at any point, and the proceedings were openly used by Germany as a means of establishing its new colony. Germany's new protectorate was authorized to cover the whole area between Portuguese East Africa and a line running from the coast to Lake Victoria through Kilimanjaro, creating the future colony of Tanganyika. Zanzibar, left only with its islands and a tiny coastal strip, had effectively been deprived of its routes to the interior, and its commercial empire was crippled.[17]

In mid-1886, Kirk was summoned to London by the Foreign Office – his personal presence there would, apparently, be useful. In reality, he was being brought home because in Africa he had been too powerful, and was identified with a policy that had been abandoned. At first, he does not seem to have suspected any subterfuge. He remained in Britain for a year, and in January was awarded the Grand Cross of St Michael and St George, but as time passed, there was no effort to return him to Africa. In early 1887, he wrote sarcastically, 'I may have to return again to Zanzibar, but my return is disliked by Bismarck and he has quite as much to say in our political appointments as our own Government.'[18] But his position in Zanzibar had become hopelessly compromised. His support for the sultan was held against him, and the Foreign Office thought him unable to fulfil their new policy. Later that year, it was arranged he should retire on grounds of ill health, and although he was only fifty-five, he never went back to East Africa.

Kirk was bitter at the way he had been treated. At the height of the crisis, he wrote:

> Why was I not told? . . . No instructions have reached me till quite lately with regard to Germany and the German policy. I have been left to follow my old and approved line of action . . .[19]

But the world had changed too quickly, and there had scarcely been time in London to absorb the suddenly shifting landscape, much less keep a distant consul informed. As the 'Scramble' gathered pace, and the frenzy of treaty making that divided up a continent took over the attentions of European chancelleries, the policies Kirk had been associated with swiftly became things of the past. His success irredeemably identified him with a weak and difficult 'native ruler', and in the new international order, native rulers were no longer honoured or required; they were merely obstacles to what was becoming a desperate land grab by the acquisitive powers of Europe. The game had moved on. Kirk, his policies and instincts had become dated and redundant.

In Britain, he felt increasingly sidelined. He was hoping for another appointment, perhaps somewhere in southern Africa, but it never happened. He attempted to keep himself active and involved in African affairs, and his advice was sought by a new generation of explorers and empire builders. Harry Johnstone and Frederick Lugard came to visit him in his house at Sevenoaks. In 1889, he was the British representative to an international conference on the slave trade in Brussels. He was a director of the Imperial British East Africa Company, and he also served as vice chairman of the Uganda Railway Committee. He maintained a correspondence with Barghash's successor in Zanzibar,[20] who wrote to him anxiously about pressure to abolish slavery entirely on the island. He did unofficial work for the Foreign Office, and he sent letters about anything to do with East Africa to anyone who mattered. In 1892, he wrote to Dyer, the Director at Kew, 'I have been engaged all the past week cramming a superficial knowledge of Africa into the minds of HM Ministers in view of the debate on the railway service vote.'[21] He was intensely interested in the Kilimanjaro expedition for the delimitation of the Anglo German frontier in the same year, and wrote strongly recommending that a naturalist be sent along to work on the botany of the area.

As ever, botany proved to be his respite. 'It makes me jealous,' he wrote in May 1892, 'to see all these expeditions got up now at public expense travelling like princes with luxuries and comfort I never had a chance of – and yet how little material they bring back.'[22] In 1894–5, he was still writing to Dyer, advising on the best kind of coffee to grow in the new protectorate of Nyasaland, and he visited Nigeria as special commissioner in 1895. In 1899, he was the guardian of the son of yet another Zanzibar ruler, Sultan Hamoud. The boy was attending Harrow school in England and, writing to the sultan, Kirk assured him that he would not hesitate to reprimand the young prince if he strayed from the course of duty.

And yet, despite his engagement and interest, throughout the correspondence of these years, during a period of intense activity in Africa, there is a nagging frustration that he had been largely forced to sit on the sidelines, away from the real action. Respected, even indulged, he was treated as yesterday's man.

John Kirk lived for another thirty-six years in retirement at his house in Sevenoaks, Kent, until his death on 15 January 1922.[23] In public, he had always underplayed his achievements. In Britain, he let Frere take most of the credit for the treaty with Zanzibar, and to his family, he would always make light of the final critical negotiations with Barghash. He had managed to persuade the sultan to agree to his terms, he joked, only by influencing him through his astrologer. And perhaps that had even played its part.

Nevertheless working in Africa had been his life, and that part had ended too soon.

EPILOGUE

It took a long time for the slave trade to be eradicated entirely from the mainland of East Africa. In northern Nyasaland, where the slavers had established one of their most profitable sources, an alliance of missionaries and commercial interests battled them for years. Victory came in the late 1890s when Cecil Rhodes provided financial and other support under the pugnacious Harry Johnstone, who took a small army up the shores of Lake Nyasa. 'Sultan' Mlozi, the last notable slaving chieftain, was defeated and publicly executed as an example to all the others, and Nyasaland was taken under British control with Johnstone as its first governor.

In a similar manner, the Germans sent General Wissmann to mainland Tanganyika, where the fight against the slavers was used as a means to further the colonial conquest. In the upper reaches of the Congo, the plantations and houses of the last Lake Arabs were finally destroyed by Belgian troops. Once King Leopold had established his right to loot and pillage his vast central African domain, he was not prepared to tolerate competition of any kind. And Frederick, later Lord, Lugard used the struggle against slavery in Uganda to justify his efficient takeover for the British Crown.

But the aftermath lingers on in all sorts of unexpected ways. People still recall stories of the ancient caravan routes from the coast. They will show you the old slaving trees that marked the staging points along the way. In northern Kenya, the Karamojo trail passes along the edge of Mount Elgon, leading from Kitale, an Arab resting place, down the escarpment to the borderlands of Northern Uganda. In the 1970s, an old woman there claimed that on dark nights she could still hear the manacled slaves singing as they went down the long road to the coast, leaving home forever.[1]

But it is, of course, by the sea, in Zanzibar and at other places along the coast, where the impact is most evident. Lamu, that little whitewashed town at the northernmost extent of Seyyid Said's dominions, is no longer an affluent place, despite being a tourist destination. It is however still a religious centre, and every year, pilgrims from across the Indian Ocean gather there for the week-long Maulidi festival, to celebrate the prophet's birthday. The crowds are enormous for such a small island, and the cultural mix is vibrant. Bajuni islanders mix with Arabs from the Comoros, Giriama people from inland and Swahilis from the coast. But generally, Lamu is poor. Exports to the Gulf consist mainly of mangrove poles for building house roofs, the wealth that used to come from ivory and slave trading has gone, and this once elegant town is decayed and run down, a small port off the main tracks. The country's wealth now lies elsewhere, in the highlands, a long way away.

There are mosques everywhere, some of them very old. But despite the Muslim character of the place, if you go to the police station, the officer lounging on the open front is a different kind of man, darker, of different build and feature. A Christian from up country, he looks at the festival preparations with boredom and the slightest contempt. This remote posting is not a popular one for his kind.

Along the narrow street, a row of old men sit on a stone bench in the shade, chatting and chewing betel nut. I started talking to one. 'They don't like us,' he said, nodding with his head in the direction of the police station. 'These up country men.'

'Why is that?'

He smiled, his face wrinkling up like an old fruit. One of his legs was drawn up under his chin, inside his long white *kanzu*. 'They haven't forgiven us, for the past. For all the years when we took them as slaves. Now they are having their revenge.'

I asked him if he'd known anyone who remembered that time, when Lamu was the last point on the route north, where the dhows smuggling slaves took on water before finally leaving for the Gulf, a hundred years and more ago.

'Oh yes,' he said. 'My grandfather knew that time. He remembered it well. He often told me about it.'

'Your grandfather?' Hoping he would say some more.

'Yes. He remembered it.'

'How did he remember it?'

The old man looked at me, sitting there on his stone bench. The others had gone, and he said nothing for a few minutes. Then he said, 'Well, you see, he too was a slave.'

SOURCES AND
ACKNOWLEDGEMENTS

There is an extensive literature on the East African slave trade, both contemporary and recent, as well as on Zanzibar itself. Early missonaries, explorers and naval officers frequently described the city, and Burton's two-volume study of Zanzibar is particularly detailed. There are also many descriptions of the slave market itself.

Records of slave trading within the Middle East during this period, however, tend to be anecdotal, given the secretive nature of the traffic and known British antagonism. Unlike the Atlantic trade, formal records were not kept. Nevertheless, there is much circumstantial evidence of East African slaves being sold throughout the region. British consuls frequently reported on the trade, and travellers, such as Burton, Snouck-Hurgronje and Burckhardt, all commented on slave trafficking in the Hijaz, and elsewhere in Arabia. Burckhardt wrote of African slave vessels coming into Jidda, and both he and Schimpfer give details on the slave-trading routes within Arabia. There are still parts of the Middle East where the local population shows evidence of years of forced migration.

Detailed accounts of relations between Said, Majid and Barghash, and the British and Indian governments are recorded in the Foreign Office archives at the Public Record Office, Kew; at the India Office archives in the British Library; and within the Zanzibar archives. I am indebted to staff in all these institutions for their help. The majority of Kirk's papers are held at the National Library of Scotland, where curators and other staff were unfailingly helpful. Other letters by him are held at the Royal Geographical Society, and in particular at Kew Gardens archives, where Michele Losse gave me constant assistance. In Zanzibar, I would like to thank Stephanie Schotz for taking the time to show me the ruins of the Seyyid's palace at Mtoni, which she is endeavouring to have restored.

Finally, I would like to pay particular thanks to two people. Firstly, to Caroline Maddox, without whose help I would never have been able to research and digest the enormous amount of archive material available on slave trading in East Africa in the nineteenth century. Secondly, and most importantly, to Christopher Fyfe. Christopher, who for many years was responsible for teaching African History at Edinburgh University, initially encouraged me to begin what turned out to be a larger task than I had ever considered. During my research and writing, he provided constant encouragement, as well as a source of new ideas and vigorous discussion. Sadly, he is no longer with us, and is missed by his many friends.

NOTES TO THE TEXT

The names of places and especially peoples (or tribes, as they were customarily referred to) are always difficult when dealing with pre-colonial African history. Thus the people whom Kirk and Livingstone called the Ajawa are today usually referred to as Yao, and I have on occasion used both names. The Maviti, also encountered on the shores of Lake Nyasa, are now more usually called the Nguni. A particularly warlike group related to the Zulu of South Africa, they had migrated north, creating considerable havoc along the way. Similarly, many Swahili words were spelt differently in the nineteenth century from accepted spelling today. I have therefore not been entirely consistent, but have tended to use contemporary forms except where they would not be comprehensible today.

During the early years of the nineteenth century, the influence of the (British) East India Company prevailed throughout the Indian Ocean, projected by the presidency in Bombay, and indeed much of India was under its control. Despite its private ownership, the Company itself was frequently referred to as the Indian government. Following the Mutiny or Indian Rebellion of 1857, however, the British Crown assumed direct responsibility for administration in India, and the Company was later dissolved. Nevertheless, strong trading links between East Africa and the subcontinent ensured the continued influence of the British

Indian Empire in Zanzibar. Terms used by Indian officers and civil servants, such as 'writer' (clerk) and 'durbar' (royal court), were frequently employed, although I have tried to keep use of these to a minimum. Reference to an 'Indian' denotes a British officer working in India.

Otherwise, the most contentious issue at the heart of this book probably concerns the debate over the numbers of slaves who were actually shipped from the East African coast into the countries of the Middle East during the nineteenth century. Until about thirty years ago, these numbers were considered to be very high, and undoubtedly evangelical and missionary rhetoric in Britain at the time tended to exaggerate them. In the late 1980s, work by Abdul Sheriff of Dar es Salaam University and others established that larger numbers than previously thought had remained working on plantations along the East African coast, and that the numbers shipped to Muslim Asia as a consequence were lower. However, it seems to me this debate has not been entirely resolved, and I have not attempted to take any view. My book mainly concerns John Kirk. His estimates of the numbers of slaves exported from Zanzibar were, as far as I am aware, the best informed at the time, and I have therefore used them.

Introduction: The Black Coast

1. *bagham*: 'This word is not pure Arabic, it is probably not to be found in any dictionary, being used in Oman for a barbarian . . . It is a term of contempt and implies that the person so named cannot speak the language . . .' Kirk to Foreign Office, 10 June 1873. FO 84.1374.
2. T.F. Buxton, quoted by Hyam in *Britain's Imperial Century 1815–1914*, p.80.
3. Farquhar to Moresby, 1822. Quoted by Coupland in *East Africa and its Invaders*, p.214.
4. New, *Life, Wanderings and Labours in Eastern Africa*, chapter 5. Hamerton thought that up to three-quarters of the population were slaves. (Memo: Relative to British Indian Subjects residing at Z. 29 January 1846. FO 54.10.)
5. Gum copal was a type of resin dug from the earth, and valuable because of its use for high-quality varnishing on coaches.

6. Burton, *Zanzibar: City, Island and Coast* Vol. 1, p.93.
7. Browne, *Etchings of a Whaling Cruise with Notes of a Sojourn on the Island of Zanzibar*, p.363.
8. Smee, 'Observations during a voyage of Research on the East Coast of Africa etc.' 1811. Appendix to Burton, *Zanzibar: City, Island and Coast* Vol. 2, p.495.
9. Devereux, *A Cruise in the 'Gorgon'*, chapter 7.
10. Report of 27 September 1840. PP on Slave Trade. FO 54.5.
11. Political agent at Aden to secretary of the Bombay government, 22 December 1841. PP on Slave Trade. FO 54.15.
12. Quoted in Bombay government to the select committee, 31 August 1841. PP on Slave Trade. FO 54.15.
13. Lord Leveson, 8 June 1841. PP on Slave Trade. FO 54.15.
14. Maddock to Willoughby, 22 March 1841. PP on Slave Trade. FO 54.15.
15. Hamerton to government of Bombay, 3 January 1842. FO 54.5.

Chapter one: The River

1. Kirk to A. Kirk, 30 January 1860. *The Zambesi Journal and Letters of Dr John Kirk 1858–1863*.
2. Ibid.
3. Murchison to Livingstone, 2 October 1855. Quoted by Blaikie in *Personal Life of David Livingstone*, p.154.
4. Livingstone to Kirk, 18 March 1858. Quoted by Coupland in *Kirk on the Zambesi*, pp103–08.
5. *The Zambesi Journal and Letters of Dr John Kirk 1858–1863*, 14–19 November 1858.
6. Ibid. 11 April 1858.
7. Kebra Basa is the contemporary spelling. Today the gorge is part of the Cahorra Bassa hydro-electric scheme.
8. *The Zambesi Journal and Letters of Dr John Kirk 1858–1863*, 4 November 1858.
9. Ibid.
10. Ibid. 1 December 1858.
11. Ibid. 2 December 1858.
12. Livingstone to Lord Malmesbury. Quoted by Coupland in *Kirk on the Zambesi*, p.136.
13. *The Zambesi Journal and Letters of Dr John Kirk 1858–1863*, 19 March 1859.
14. Ibid. 21 May 1862.

15. Ibid. 6 January 1860.
16. Ibid. 17 March 1859.
17. The Kirk Range in Malawi is still known by that name.
18. Kirk and Livingstone refer to these people as Ajawa, but I have called them Yao, which is their more usual name.
19. Over a period of time, the pattern of trade within East Africa changed. The traditional routes from the interior to the Portuguese coast were replaced by links to Zanzibar in the north, where trading conditions were better. The Portuguese slave trade was also in long-term decline, once Brazil had forbidden the importation of slaves in 1830, while the Indian Ocean trade in slaves through Zanzibar was booming. As a result, dhows were built to cross Lake Nyasa (now Lake Malawi), and the ivory and slaves were taken to the coast at Kilwa to exploit the new markets. The Yaos were the major beneficiaries of this new long-distance traffic. See Alpers, *Ivory and Slaves in East Central Africa*.
20. *The Zambesi Journal and Letters of Dr John Kirk 1858–1863*, 25 November 1858.
21. Livingstone to Kirk, 10 October 1859. Quoted by Coupland in *Kirk on the Zambesi* p 158.
22. Kirk to A. Kirk, 7 January 1861. *The Zambesi Journal and Letters of Dr John Kirk 1858–1863*.
23. Ibid. 8 January 1860.
24. Ibid. 21 November 1860.
25. Ibid. 12 November 1860.

Chapter two: The Mission

1. Devereux, *A Cruise in the 'Gorgon'*, chapter 11.
2. *The Zambesi Journal and Letters of Dr John Kirk 1858–1863*, 7 June 1861.
3. Kirk to A. Kirk, 26 June 1861. *The Zambesi Journal and Letters of Dr John Kirk 1858–1863*.
4. *The Zambesi Journal and Letters of Dr John Kirk 1858–1863*, 16 July 1861.
5. The Makololo lived in the upper Zambesi valley. Livingstone had made close friends with their chief during an earlier expedition, and following his visit with Kirk in early 1860, some returned with him, accompanying him to southern Nyasaland where they settled.
6. *The Zambesi Journal and Letters of Dr John Kirk 1858–1863*, 28 September 1861.

7. Ibid. 5 August 1861.
8. Ibid. 13 September 1861.
9. Mackenzie's journal, 16 October 1861. Quoted by Chadwick in *Mackenzie's Grave, p 61*.
10. *The Zambesi Journal and Letters of Dr John Kirk 1858–1863*, 8 November 1861.
11. Ibid. 18 December 1861.
12. Ibid. 16 January 1862.
13. Ibid. 16 January 1862.
14. Devereux, *A Cruise in the 'Gorgon'*, chapter 12.
15. Kirk to A. Kirk, 5 February 1862. *The Zambesi Journal and Letters of Dr John Kirk 1858–1863*.
16. Kirk to A. Kirk, 25 July 1862. *The Zambesi Journal and Letters of Dr John Kirk 1858–1863*.
17. *The Zambesi Journal and Letters of Dr John Kirk 1858–1863*, 28 February 1862.
18. Ibid. 4 March 1862.
19. Ibid. 5 March 1862.
20. Quoted by Coupland in *Kirk on the Zambesi*, p.229.
21. *The Zambesi Journal and Letters of Dr John Kirk 1858–1863*, 26 April 1862.
22. Ibid. 18 September 1862.
23. Ibid. 15/18/19 January 1863.
24. Ibid. 24 January 1863.
25. Ibid. 22 February 1863.
26. Ibid. 8 February 1863.
27. Ibid. 7/16 March 1863.
28. *The Zambezi Journal of James Stewart*. Quoted by Chadwick in *Mackenzie's Grave*, p.171.
29. *UMCA Report for 1862*. Quoted by Coupland in *Kirk on the Zambesi*, p.250.
30. *The Zambesi Journal and Letters of Dr John Kirk 1858–1863*, 29 April 1863.
31. Ibid. 30 April/11 May 1863.
32. Tozer, quoted by Chadwick in *Mackenzie's Grave*, p.221.

Chapter three: Cowries, Copal and Elephants' teeth

1. Kirk to Helen Cooke, 3 May 1866. KP 9942.4.
2. Burton, *Zanzibar: City, Island and Coast* Vol. 1, p.80.

3. Burton, *Zanzibar: City, Island and Coast* Vol. 1, p.82.
4. New, *Life, Wanderings, and Labours in Eastern Africa*, chapter 5.
5. Kazeh was near present-day Tabora in Tanzania.
6. Rigby report to C. Wood, 1 May 1860. FO 54.17.
7. Burton, *Zanzibar: City, Island and Coast* Vol. 1, p.80.
8. P.L. Symonds, 'Ivory and Teeth of Commerce', *Journal of the Society of Arts*, 19 December 1856.
9. Burton, *The Lake Regions of Central Africa* Vol. 2, p.408.
10. Burton, *Zanzibar: City, Island and Coast* Vol. 1, p.34. The consulate building still existed in late 2007, when it was used as a restaurant.
11. Kirk to Helen Cooke, date obscure. KP 9942.4.
12. Ibid. 23 July 1866. KP 9942.4.
13. Kirk to Hooker, 22 October 1866. DC 186. Kew.
14. Burton, *Zanzibar: City, Island and Coast* Vol. 2, p.345.
15. Kirk to Helen Cooke, 21 October 1866. KP 9942.4.
16. Kirk to Hooker, 22 October 1866. DC 186. Kew.
17. Ibid. 20 January 1867. DC 186. Kew.
18. The incident is described by Ruete in *Memoirs of an Arabian Princess from Zanzibar*.
19. Royal Geographical Society: photographs by Col. J.A. Grant.
20. Waller: evidence to 1871 committee.
21. *Bugala*: a large sea-going dhow. Literally, 'she mule'.
22. Kirk to Helen Cooke, 21 May 1866. KP 9942.4.
23. Ibid. 26 August and 1 September 1866. KP 9942.4.
24. Ibid. 23 July 1866. KP 9942.4.
25. The details of Salme's escape are recorded in KP 9942.20 and by J.M. Gray in *Memoirs of an Arabian Princess*. Seward, the acting consul, was clearly not involved. Kirk, in an early letter to Nelly, explains how Seward's wife habitually protected him from the more difficult aspects of his job, but Mrs Seward was unable to accomplish the project on her own. Foskett's notes on Kirk's papers indicate that she and Kirk worked together on the plan to smuggle Salme out of the country.

Chapter four: Azrael, Angel of Death

1. Kirk to Helen Cooke, 23 October 1866. KP 9942.4.
2. Hamerton to Bombay government, 13 July 1841. Quoted by Crofton in *The Old Consulate at Zanzibar*.
3. Hamerton to secretary of the Bombay government, 2 January 1842. PP (Enclosure 269). FO 54.5.

4. Letter from Captain Thomson. IOR/F/4/711.
5. See Ruete, *Memoirs of an Arabian Princess from Zanzibar*. The ruins of Said's palace still exist at Mtoni.
6. Hamerton to Governor in Council, July 1841. FO 54.4.
7. Hamerton to secretary of the Bombay government, 5 January 1842. PP (Enclosure 269). FO 54.5.
8. Browne, *Etchings of a Whaling Cruise with Notes of a Sojourn on the Island of Zanzibar*, p.328 ff.
9. IOR/F/4/1539.
10. Kulkarni, *the Satara Raj*; Papers relating to Committee of Inquiry, Satara 1840, and Secret Letters from Bombay; W3042,3043. BL.
11. Cogan to Palmerston, 6 May 1839. FO 54.3.
12. Cogan to Forbes, 28 October 1842. FO 54.5.
13. Cogan to Aberdeen, via Canning, 13 October 1844. FO 54.6.
14. Cogan drew expenses on behalf of the prince worth between £50,000 and £100,000 in today's money. FO 54.7.
15. Aberdeen to bin Nassir, 12 July 1842. PP FO 54.5.
16. Hamerton to Aberdeen, 31 July 1844. FO 54.6.
17. Hamerton to Aberdeen, 31 July 1844. FO 54.6.
18. Hamerton to Willoughby, 3 March 1846. FO 54.10.
19. Hamerton to India Board, 14 April 1845. FO 54.9.
20. Hamerton to India Board, 14 April 1845. FO.54.9.
21. 'Gravel': kidney stone.
22. Hamerton to Aberdeen, February 1846. FO 54.10.
23. See Pollock and Peters correspondence. FO 54.11.
24. Krapf, *Memoir on East African Slave Trade*.
25. Guillain, *Documents sur L'histoire, la Geographie et le Commerce de l'Afrique Orientale* Vol. 2, pp22–24.
26. Churchill evidence to 1871 committee; Coglan commission pp 112, 117; Sullivan, *Dhow Chasing in Zanzibar Waters*, p.78 etc.
27. Burton styled himself 'Haji Abdullah' while in the interior. Stanley, *How I found Livingstone*, p.260.
28. Burton, *Zanzibar: City, Island and Coast* Vol. 1, p.35.
29. Seward to Gonne, 14 July 1866. FO 84.1284.

Chapter five: Dates for Slaves

1. Helen Kirk's diary, 13 March 1867. KP 9942.27.
2. Kirk to Helen Cooke, 25 November 1866. KP 9942.4.

3. Helen Kirk's diary, 27 June 1867. KP 9942.27.
4. Ibid. 1 September 1867. KP 9942.27.
5. Ibid. 23 May 1868. KP 9942.27.
6. Kirk to Gonne, 6 April 1869. FO 84.1307.
7. Ibid.
8. The Rao of Kutch, an independent Indian prince, ordered that his nationals in Zanzibar should conform to the laws of British India.
9. Churchill to Gonne, 22 January 1869; and 'Notice to all Natives of India . . .' FO 84.1307.
10. Churchill to Gonne (1), 26 February 1869. FO 84.1307.
11. Churchill to Gonne (2), 26 February 1869. FO 84.1307.
12. Churchill to Gonne, 1 March 1869. FO 84.1307.
13. Helen Kirk's diary, 19 April 1869. KP 9942.27.
14. Kirk to Gonne, 12 April 1869. FO 84.1307.
15. Ibid.
16. Ibid.
17. Ibid.
18. Christie, *Slavery in Zanzibar As It Is*, p.5.
19. Chief of Beni Yaas to Sultan Majid, 1 January 1869. FO 84.1307.
20. For profits of dhow owners engaged in the slave trade, see Kirk to Derby. FO 84.1453.
21. Kirk to Gonne, 21 September 1869. FO 84.1307.
22. Ibid.
23. Kirk to secretary of state, 21 September 1869. FO 84.1307. The lady was the daughter of Suliman bin Hamed, the former ambassador and relative of the sultan. She was married to Hamed bin Suliman, another important Zanzibari. (See Chapter 12.)

Chapter six: The Tracks of Commerce

1. There are various references to the practice by travellers such as Burkhardt and Burton. For further detail see J. S. Hogendorn 'The Location of the "Manufacture of Eunuchs"', as well as Kirk to Granville, 7 April 1885. FO 84.1725.
2. Colomb, *Slave Catching in the Indian Ocean*, p.55.
3. Christie's *Cholera Epidemics in East Africa* provides a detailed description not only of the cholera epidemic of 1869, but also of the routes by which the disease travelled to reach Zanzibar.
4. Christie, *Cholera Epidemics in East Africa*, chapter 11, p.363.

5. Kirk to Hooker, 16 December 1869. DC 186. Kew.
6. Kirk to Gonne, 20 May 1870. FO 84.1325.
7. Kirk to Wylde, 3 May 1870. KP 9942.7.
8. Christie, *Cholera Epidemics in East Africa*, chapter 11, p.415.
9. Ibid. p.416.
10. Ibid.
11. In his report to Bombay (15 March 1870, ZA. AA3/33) Kirk was clear that use of water from town wells infected by sewage was the cause of the rapid spread of the disease. The association between cholera and water was established by John Snow in his work on the cholera outbreak in Soho (London) in 1855, and Kirk may have known of Snow's work.
12. Kirk to Captain Parish, 14 February 1870. ZA. AA3/33; Kirk to Gonne, 20 May 1870. FO 84.1325.
13. Kirk notebook, 22 June 1870. KP 9942.28.
14. Kirk was contemptuous of such 'evidence'. See Kirk to foreign secretary, 2 May 1870. FO 84.1325.
15. Devereux, *A Cruise in the 'Gorgon'*, chapter 5, p.69.
16. Devereux, *A Cruise in the 'Gorgon'*, chapter 8.
17. Colomb, *Slave Catching in the Indian Ocean*, p.77.
18. Devereux, *A Cruise in the 'Gorgon'*, chapter 8.
19. Ibid. Chapter 26.
20. Zanzibar court record, 1–5 May 1869. FO 84.1307.
21. The *Daphne* under Captain Meara repeatedly made arrests and burnt dhows on evidence Kirk judged inadmissible. Meara would not give up the proceeds from the dhows – he had disposed of the goods taken – and refusing to accept Kirk's judgement, took at least one appeal to London. The case took a long time to resolve but Kirk eventually won. (ZA. AA3/33.)

Chapter seven: A Discontented Man

1. Steere, *Some Account of the Town of Zanzibar*, p.6.
2. Kirk to Rigby. Quoted by Russell in *General Rigby, Zanzibar and the Slave Trade*, p.301.
3. Quoted by Reginald Foskett in introduction to *The Zambesi Journal and Letters of Dr John Kirk 1858–1863*
4. In fact, the porters had deserted Livingstone and were quite aware he was alive. They got to Zanzibar in December 1866.

5. Kirk to Rigby. Quoted by Russell in *General Rigby, Zanzibar and the Slave Trade*, p.301.
6. Kirk was paid rupees 700 p.a. plus an extra allowance of rupees 1,220, about £80, or between £1,000 and £2,000 in today's money, although that understates the value in Zanzibar. Churchill, while absent on sick leave, was paid rupees 1,400. (See ZA. AA3/33 for agency salary sheet for 1870.)
7. Kirk to Hooker, 27 April, 2 August and 13 November 1869. DC 186. Kew.
8. Ibid. 22 September 1869. DC 186. Kew.
9. Ibid. mid 1868. DC 186. Kew.
10. Kirk to secretary of state, 1 February 1870. FO 84.1325.
11. Rigby, in his lengthy report of July 1860, gives approximate numbers, but no detailed statistics. FO 54.17. Playfair, his successor, in July 1865 stated that it was 'impossible to obtain accurate statements of exports', so gave none. FO 54.22.
12. Wylde was head of the Slave Trade Department at the Foreign Office. He was succeeded by the Hon. C. Vivian in 1870. (Kirk to Hooker, 10 August 1870. DC 186. Kew.)
13. Kirk to Helen Cooke, 18 August 1866. KP 9942.4.
14. Quoted by Russell in *General Rigby, Zanzibar and the Slave Trade*, p.108.
15. FO 54.22.
16. Kirk to Rigby. Quoted by Russell in *General Rigby, Zanzibar and the Slave Trade*, p.301.
17. Ibid.
18. Kirk to Hooker, 10 August 1870. DC 186. Kew.

Chapter eight: Zealous Service

1. Clarendon to Churchill, May 1870. FO 84.1325.
2. Ibid.
3. Churchill to Clarendon, 22 April 1870. FO 84.1325.
4. Churchill to Wedderburn, 30 September 1870. ZA. AA3/33. The Mutawas were strongly in favour of slave trading for religious reasons. It was part of their antagonism towards Britain and western influence.
5. Ibid.
6. Churchill to Wedderburn, 7 October 1870. FO 84.1325.
7. KD: p.38. KP 9942/25.

8. ZA. AA3/33.
9. Churchill to Wedderburn, 8 October 1870. FO 84.1325. The defeat of the French by Bismarck's Prussian army at Sedan precipitated the demise of Napoleon III's Second Empire. The crisis removed the immediate possibility of French interference in Zanzibar.
10. Ibid.
11. Churchill to Wedderburn, 10 October 1870. FO 84.1325.
12. Churchill to Barghash, 11 October 1870. FO 84.1325.
13. Barghash to Churchill, 11 October 1870. FO 84.1325.
14. Churchill to Wedderburn, 11 October 1870. ZA. AA3/33.
15. Kirk to Hooker, 10 August 1870. DC 186. Kew.
16. Churchill to Wedderburn, 5 December 1870. FO 84.1325.
17. Barghash to Churchill, 10 November 1870. FO 84.1325.
18. Barghash to Churchill, November 1870. FO 84.1325.
19. KD: p.43. KP 9942/25.
20. Churchill to Wedderburn, 5 December 1870. FO 84.1325.
21. Wedderburn to Churchill, 3 December 1870. ZA. AA3/32.
22. Kirk to secretary of state, 12 December 1870. FO 84.1325.
23. KD: p.41. KP 9942/25.
24. Kirk to Granville, 12 December 1870. FO 84.1325.
25. Kirk to Hooker, 10 March 1871. DC 186. Kew.
26. Kirk to Wedderburn, 24 December 1870. FO 84.1325.
27. Ibid.
28. Kirk to Granville, 12 December 1870. FO 84.1325.

Chapter nine: The Gatherers of Wealth

1. *The Last Journals of David Livingstone*, pp189–90.
2. *The Last Journals of David Livingstone*, pp203, 213.
3. Brode, *Tippoo Tib: The Story of his Career in Central Africa*.
4. *The Last Journals of David Livingstone*, p.188 note.
5. Speke, *Journal of the Discovery of the Source of the Nile*, Introduction p.xxviii.
6. Brode, *Tippoo Tib: The Story of his Career in Central Africa*.
7. Kirk to Murchison, 25 September 1871. 'I can yet get no correct account of Manyema; everyone knows it, but I find no one who has been there . . . it seems to be rather a new and special line of trade.' Royal Geographical Society, Proceedings Vol. 16.
8. *The Last Journals of David Livingstone*, p.210.
9. *The Last Journals of David Livingstone*, p.318.

10. *The Last Journals of David Livingstone*, p.342.
11. *The Last Journals of David Livingstone*, p.363.
12. Stanley, *How I found Livingstone*, pp12, 14–15.
13. Kirk to Rawlinson, 15 January 1872. Royal Geographical Society, Proceedings Vol. 16.
14. Stanley, *How I found Livingstone*, p.592.
15. Livingstone to Kirk, 30 October 1871. FO 84.1357.
16. Livingstone to Murchison, 13 March 1872. Royal Geographical Society, Proceedings Vol. 16.
17. Livingstone to Waller, 8 March 1872. Waller papers, quoted by Coupland in *Livingstone's Last Journey*, p.185.

Chapter ten: Hardly to be Feared

1. Stanley, *How I found Livingstone*, p.38.
2. Stanley, *How I found Livingstone*, p.37. Burton thought that it affected up to 20 per cent of the inhabitants. 'The scrotum will often reach the knees; I heard of one case measuring in circumference 41 inches, more than the patient's body, while its length (33 inches) touched the ground. There is no cure . . .' *Zanzibar: City, Island and Coast* Vol. 1, p.185.
3. Kirk to Wedderburn, 9 March 1871. FO 84.1344.
4. Kirk to Hooker, 10 March 1871. KP. DC 186.
5. Kirk to Wedderburn, 9 March 1871. FO 84.1344.
6. KD: pp24–5. KP 9942/25.
7. Kirk to Hooker, 26 March 1871. KP. DC 186.
8. KD: p.63. KP 9942/25.
9. Kirk to Wedderburn, 9 January 1871. FO 84.1344.
10. Kirk to secretary of state, 18 April 1871. FO 84.1344.
11. Kirk to Wedderburn, 30 January 1871. FO 84.1344; Coupland, *The Exploitation of East Africa 1856–1890*, p.98.
12. KD: pp47–51, 63. KP 9942/25.
13. Kirk's report of 25 January 1872 (FO 84.1357) gives a detailed breakdown of the numbers of slaves brought into Zanzibar and exported during the previous season. The official report of the Customs House was 17,392, of which 14,392 were imported from Kilwa. However, Kirk was sure this was an underestimate due to 'the secrecy of the contraband'. Of his estimate of the total number traded (23,392), 2,000 were accounted for by deaths; just over 4,000 he put down as the normal requirements of Zanzibar, Pemba and

the immediate coast; another 7,500 were replacements for those who had died of cholera; 3,000 were for the Somali coast; and the remainder of nearly 6,800 for export to Persia and Arabia.

14. KD: p.62. KP 9942/25.
15. Kirk to Wedderburn, 8 April 1871. FO 84.1344.
16. KD: p72–3. KP 9942/25.
17. New, *Life, Wanderings, and Labours in Eastern Africa*, chapter 5.
18. Kirk to Hooker, 10 March 1871. DC 186. Kew.
19. Kirk to Hooker, 3 August 1871. DC 186. Kew.
20. Ibid.
21. KD: pp58–60. KP 9942/25.
22. Kirk to Hooker, 12 November 1871. DC 186. Kew.
23. Kirk to Hooker, 3 August 1871. DC 186. Kew.
24. Kirk to Vivian, 10 June 1871. Appendix 2, report from 1871 select committee.
25. Kirk to Hooker, July 1872. DC 186. Kew.
26. Vivian to Kirk, 12 December 1871. KP. 9942.6.
27. Kirk to Vivian, 10 June 1871. Appendix 2, report from 1871 select committee.
28. Kirk to Wedderburn, 1 January 1872. FO 84.1357.
29. Ibid.
30. KD: p.66. KP 9942/25.
31. KD: p.67. KP 9942/25.

Chapter eleven: Not Worth the Candle

1. Quotations from witnesses to the select committee can be found in the detailed report on the proceedings. (British Sessional Papers, House of Commons 1871, Vol. 12.)
2. The Niger expedition of 1841–2 was intended to contribute to the suppression of slavery in West Africa. A total of 55 out of 149 Europeans involved had died by the time it was recalled.
3. The trauma of the mutiny in India (the Indian Rebellion) had a significant impact on official attitudes towards states such as Zanzibar. Some blamed the Company for its imperious approach towards the 'position and dignity' of existing elites.
4. A figure of between one and two million pounds would be an approximate equivalent today.
5. Kaye was a notable authority on British India, writing, among other works, a history of the 'Sepoy Rebellion'.

6. 'Set a beggar on horseback and he'll ride to the devil.' The phrase refers to an undeserving person made arrogant and corrupt through great wealth.

7. 'Of all evils . . .' Thomas Fowell Buxton, the noted antislavery campaigner.

8. Frere's conviction that the growth in slave trading was a direct result of British suppression of piracy in the Indian Ocean discounted the long history of the traffic. His opinion that legitimate commerce would spring up as soon as slave trading was extinguished was the orthodox view among mid-Victorians, who believed the two were incompatible. In East Africa, at least, this was not the case. Slaves were traded alongside other products, and were regarded as just another commodity.

9. See chapter 10, note 24.

10. Surrey Chapel on Blackfriars Road, Southwark, was a Methodist and Congregational Church associated with the London Missionary Society. The Friends Meeting House, opposite Euston Station, was the London headquarters of the Quaker movement.

11. *Post*, 26 July 1872. KP 9942.51.

12. KP 9942.51.

13. *Daily News*, 2 August 1872. KP 9942.51.

14. Coupland, *Livingstone's Last Journey*, p.198, quoting *Daily Telegraph*.

15. Coupland, *Livingstone's Last Journey*, p.208.

16. *Scotsman*, 1 November 1872. KP 9942.51.

17. Ibid.

18. Royal Geographical Society, Proceedings Vol. 16 1871–2: 13 March 1872.

19. Stanley, *How I found Livingstone*, p.411–2, 430 etc.

20. Coupland, *Livingstone's Last Journey*, p.183, quoting from Stanley's Journal for March 3, 1872

21. Frere was to establish 'whether Dr. Livingstone's complaints are well founded, and whether Dr. Kirk is in any way to blame for the delays that took place in expediting the stores to Dr. Livingstone or for their plunder and failure to reach him.'

Chapter twelve: A Load Upon the Camel

1. Kirk to governor of Bombay, quoted by Crofton in *The Old Consulate at Zanzibar*, p. 52.

2. Christie, *Cholera Epidemics in East Africa*, p.7.

3. See chapter 10, note 13.

4. Kirk to secretary of state, 22 May 1872. FO 84.1357.

5. Ibid.

6. Ibid.

7. KD: p.81. KP 9942.25.

8. Elton, *Travels and Researches among the Lakes and Mountains of East and Central Africa*, p.35.

9. Bates to Kirk, 7 September 1872. KP 9942.6.

10. Oswell Livingstone to Kirk, November 1872. KP 9942.6.

11. Dawson to Kirk, 6 November 1872. KP 9942.6.

12. *Indian Statesman*, 6 July 1872. KP 9942.51.

13. *Spectator*, 27 September 1872; reprinted in Stanley's *How I found Livingstone*, p.708.

14. Badger's academic knowledge was held in great awe at the Foreign Office, giving a him a mystique that blinded officials to his poor diplomatic skills. See Frere: FO 881/2270. No. 52 p.114.

15. Granville to Frere, 9 November 1872. FO 881/2270 No. 5.

16. 'It seems to me that we may have the cares and responsibilities, if not the other attributes of a great empire, half African, half Arabian, thrust upon us, whether we will nor no . . .' Frere to Pelly, quoted by Martineau in *Life of Sir Bartle Frere* Vol. 1 p.504: 17 May 1862. Also 'We may, I believe, by an exertion of power very speedily and effectually stop the Slave Trade, but the work will only be begun unless it is followed up by a multitude of other measures having all, more or less, for their result, if not their immediate object, the civilization of the Continent.' Frere to Granville: FO 881/2270 No. 126 p.254.

17. Gavin, *The Bartle Frere Mission to Zanzibar*, note to p.147.

18. *Letters of Lord Acton to Mary Gladstone*, p.14, and note: 1 June 1880. The context was Frere's controversial actions in South Africa.

19. Frere to Granville, 14 January 1873. FO 84. 881/2270. No. 44.

20. An Anglo-French declaration of 1862 undertook to respect Zanzibar's independence.

21. Kirk knew better than to criticize Frere's methods openly, although privately he expressed doubts (see Kirk to Hooker, 2 April 1873, DC 186.) He also thought much of the blame for the mission's failure was due to the unwise reliance on Badger. (Kirk to Wylde, 13 May 1878. KP 9942.7.)

22. The failure of the slave population of Zanzibar to reproduce was one reason Zanzibaris advanced for the need to import. It was suggested

that slave mothers, not wishing to bring up their children in servitude, chose to abort their babies.

23. Badger: 17 January 1873. FO 84. 881/2270. No. 83 Incl. 7.
24. Badger: 19 January 1873. FO 84. 881/2270. No. 83 Incl. 8.
25. Frere to Badger, 21 January 1873. FO 84. 881/2270. No. 83 Incl. 11.
26. Badger: 25 January 1873. FO 84. 881/2270. No. 83 Incl. 16.
27. Frere: 27 January 1873. FO 84. 881/2270. No. 83 Incl. 18.
28. Ibid.
29. Ibid.
30. Ibid.
31. Badger: no date. FO 84. 881/2270. No. 83 Incl. 19.
32. Interview, Frere and Barghash. FO 84. 881/2270. No. 83 Incl. 21.
33. Elton, *Travels and Researches among the Lakes and Mountains of East and Central Africa*, p.39.
34. Kirk: FO 84. 881/2270. No. 83 Incl. 24.
35. Ibid.
36. Ibid.
37. Barghash to Frere, 11 February 1873. FO 84. 881/2270. No. 83 Incl. 26.
38. Pelly: 13 March 1873. FO 84.1390.
39. Frere: 27 March 1873. FO 84.1390.
40. Ibid.

Chapter thirteen: Not Without Emotion

1. Livingstone mentions the young elephant on its journey to the coast. (*The Last Journals of David Livingstone*, p.415.) On arrival in Bombay, it was much admired, but by October the governor did not know what to do with it. The chief minister of the nizam of Hyderabad collected elephants, and Sir Philip gave it to him as a present while he was travelling in the nizam's territory. (KP. 9942.8 Aug/Oct 1873.)
2. Gavin, *The Bartle Frere Expedition and Zanzibar, 1873*, p.144.
3. Westerners living in Zanzibar generally felt that slaves were not badly treated by their owners, although crime at almost every level of society was punished often with great cruelty. The British press, eager to find examples to illustrate the evil of the sultan's rule, used every incident to fuel antislavery feeling. The *Illustrated Missionary News* in particular was at the forefront of this sensationalist reporting. 'The soldiers had strung a man up by the hand to the

flagstaff in the market place, and were beating him to death . . . What a sight! There was the victim as described, hanging by his hands . . . His veins were bursting, and his flesh was deeply lacerated; he was gasping for breath. Seeing us he turned his eyes upon us and groaned . . .' (*Illustrated Missionary News*, 1 January 1873, p.2.)

4. See FO 88/1270 (correspondence concerning the Frere mission, numbers 3 and 4) for the flexibility Frere was given in the negotiations.

5. For example, letters of 2 April and 15 August 1873. KP. 9942.8.

6. Frere: 1 February 1873. FO 84.1389.

7. Kirk was confirmed as political agent on 18 March. Frere had been quick to understand the difficulty of his position. (Frere to Wodehouse, 30 January 1873. FO 84.1389.)

8. Captain Frederic Elton, who had been employed by the Natal government as a 'frontier agent', was taken on as assistant political agent and vice consul. Frederic Holmwood, 'a young English gentleman of apparently good education who has been travelling for his amusement', was to assist in the office and courtwork.

9. Coupland, *The Exploitation of East Africa 1856–1890*, p.200; and Gavin, *The Bartle Frere Expedition and Zanzibar, 1873*, p.145.

10. As early as 1868, Kirk had written to Wylde saying he thought force was not the complete answer. (Kirk to Wylde, 26 October 1868. KP.9942.7.)

11. Kirk to Frere, 3 April 1873. FO 84.1374.

12. From December to May each year, there was a closed season for the shipping of slaves along the coast. It had been introduced by Majid some years earlier as a partial concession to the British, but had had little effect.

13. Kirk to secretary of state, 1 May 1873. FO 84 1374.

14. KD: p.57. KP 9942.25.

15. Kirk to Foreign Office, 27 May 1873. FO 84.1374.

16. $116 had been received in duties as against $8,290 for the previous year. (Kirk to Foreign Office, 31 May 1873. FO84.1374.)

17. Elton, *Travels and Researches among the Lakes and Mountains of East and Central Africa*, p.54.

18. Kirk to Foreign Office, 26 May 1873. FO 84.1374.

19. For detail on the French consul's offer to Barghash, see Kirk to Wylde, 3 July 1873; and Kirk to secretary of state, 2 July 1873. FO 84.1375.

20. Kirk to Foreign Office (no. 49), 5 June 1873. FO 84.1374.
21. Kirk to Wylde, 3 July 1873. FO 84.1375.
22. Kirk to Foreign Office (no. 49), 5 June 1873. FO 84.1374.
23. Barghash Proclamation, 8 June 1873. FO 84.1374.
24. Kirk to Granville, 10 June 1873. FO 84.1374.

Chapter fourteen: The Kisiju Road

1. Kirk to Foreign Office, 9 March 1875. FO 84.1416.
2. Kirk to Wylde, 3 July 1873. FO 1375.
3. Kirk to Hooker, 15 November 1873. DC 186. Kew.
4. Kirk to secretary of state, 3 July 1873. FO 84.1375.
5. Kirk's memo on the Somali slave trade, 31 May 1873. FO 84.1374.
6. Kirk to secretary of state, 3 July 1873. FO 84.1375.
7. Prideaux to Foreign Office, 17 February 1874. FO 84.1398.
8. Elton, *Travels and Researches among the Lakes and Mountains of East and Central Africa*, pp82–3.
9. Elton, *Travels and Researches among the Lakes and Mountains of East and Central Africa*, p.86. Elton made detailed maps of the slave routes from Kilwa south west to Lake Nyasa, where the main hunting grounds were. In 1876, he travelled through Mozambique to Nyasaland, met some of the Yao slaving chiefs, returning to East Africa overland. Before reaching Zanzibar, however, he contracted malaria and died, and his journals were published posthumously.
10. Wylde to Kirk, 11 February 1876. KP. 9942.7.
11. Kirk to Hooker, 28 February 1875. DC 186. Kew.
12. *The Times*, 10 June 1875.
13. '*The Lament of Noor-ud-Deen*' was originally written in Arabic. Mrs Phillips set it to music, and Badger provided the English translation.
14. *The Times*, 26 June 1875.
15. *The Times*, 30 June 1875.
16. Not surprisingly, Barghash was a little confused by the proliferation of Stanleys he came across. Kirk had to point out that Stanley of Alderley, while related to the Earl of Derby (whose family name was Stanley), was a very different person. Dean Stanley, the eminent churchman and theologian, was from yet another family, and none of them were related to the most famous Stanley of all, the explorer.
17. There is a suggestion in Salme's book (p.271) that even at this stage, Bismarck had shown interest. In 1874 there were repeated attempts

by Salme to establish contact with her brother, using the assistance of the German consular service, and with the backing of, among others, the Duke of Saxe Coburg. Barghash rejected all approaches. (See Prideaux to foreign secretary, 21 November 1874. FO 84.1400.)

18. *The Story of Bibi Salimah*, p.4. KP. 9942.20.

19. She had been found in the Langham Hotel by the brother of Colonel Playfair, a previous agent in Zanzibar, who was an MP. He invited her to stay in his house in Kensington from where he also took up her cause. He claimed he was constantly blocked from all contact with Barghash by the prevarications of the Reverend Badger. (Playfair letters: June 1875. KP 9942.20.)

20. Ruete, *Memoirs of an Arabian Princess from Zanzibar*, pp269–74; for a description of Salme in London, see Russell, *General Rigby, Zanzibar and the Slave Trade*, p.309.

21. See *New York Times*, 28 July 1873. Nevertheless, Frere seemed to have learnt the wrong lessons from his Zanzibar mission. In 1877 he was sent to South Africa as High Commissioner. Confronted with the threat of Cetshwayo's Zulus, he sent them an ill-judged ultimatum, launching the Anglo Zulu War in December 1878. The disastrous battle of Isandlwana, in which the British army was all but wiped out, caused Frere to be censured by the House of Commons, and he was recalled in August 1880. His reputation never recovered. He died in 1885, and there is a statue of him on the Thames Embankment.

22. Kirk to Derby, 21 February 1876. FO 84.1452.

23. Prideaux (reporting Elton), 8 January 1874. FO 84.1398.

24. Kirk to Wylde, 3 May 1876. KP. 9942.7.

25. Kirk to Foreign Office, 9 March 1875. FO 84.1416.

26. Kirk to Derby, 21 February 1876. FO 84.1452.

27. Ibid.

28. Kirk to Derby, 8 January 1877. FO 84.1484.

29. Kirk to Wylde, 6 April 1877. KP. 9942.7.

30. Ibid.

31. Kirk to Derby, 5 February 1877. FO 84.1484.

32. Kirk to Derby, 26 February 1877. FO 84.1484.

33. Ibid.

34. Kirk to Derby, 24 August 1877. FO 84.1486.

35. Kirk to Wylde, 27 May 1880. KP. 9942.7.

Chapter fifteen: Barghash the Unlucky

1. Kirk to Granville, 23 November 1884. Quoted by Coupland in *The Exploitation of East Africa 1856–1890*, p.387.
2. Kirk to secretary for foreign affairs, 2 December 1873. FO 84.1376.
3. Kirk to Wylde, 16 April 1879. KP 9942.7.
4. Report on Dar es Salaam, 17 February 1874. FO 84.1398.
5. Among the Yao chiefs whom Kirk mentioned as continuing to send thousands of slaves to the coast was Makanjira, a predecessor of the chief mentioned in the Prologue. (See 20 July 1876. FO 84.1454, and 5 November 1877. FO 84.1486.) Kirk, Livingstone and Elton all met this man.
6. Kirk to Derby, 24 August 1877. FO 84.1486.
7. Cameron to Derby, quoted by Coupland in *The Exploitation of East Africa 1856–1890*, p.267.
8. Thomson, *To the Central African Lakes and Back* Vol. 1 p.11.
9. Kirk to Wylde, 3 May 1876. KP 9942.7.
10. Kirk to Salisbury, 8 March 1880, quoted by Coupland in *The Exploitation of East Africa 1856–1890*, p.346.
11. KD: p.90. KP 9942.25.
12. Brode, *Tippoo Tib: The Story of his Career in Central Africa*.
13. See Coupland, *The Exploitation of East Africa 1856–1890*, p.412 etc.
14. '*The Story of Bibi Salimah*'; KP 9942.20.
15. For German plans to use Salme as a justification for force, see Gray, *Memoirs of an Arabian Princess*. Salme did come on shore, and paraded about town, causing some embarrassment, but her brother pointedly refused to meet her. Her son, Rudolf Said Ruete, wrote to Kirk on his eighty-ninth birthday in 1921 from Switzerland. His mother was then living with her daughter in Jena, and in 1922 a new sultan awarded her a pension. She died in her eightieth year in February 1924.
16. The British representative on the commission was the future Lord Kitchener.
17. The agreement was finalized in October 1886, leaving the sultan with the islands of Zanzibar, Pemba, Mafia and Lamu, as well as a strip of land ten miles deep along the coast. The territory inland was divided between British and German 'spheres of influence'. Germany leased from the sultan the port of Dar es Salaam, and in 1890, finally purchased the strip of Zanzibar coastline adjoining its own territory. Zanzibar itself became a British protectorate.

18. Kirk to Dyer, 1 April 1887. Kew English Letters 1866–1900. Quoted by Coupland in *The Exploitation of East Africa 1856–1890*, p.481.
19. Kirk to Hill, 7 August 1885. Quoted by Coupland in *The Exploitation of East Africa 1856–1890*, p.435.
20. Barghash died on 27 March 1888, and was succeeded by Seyyid Khalifa, one of his younger brothers.
21. Kirk to Dyer, 6 March 1892. Z. Cultural Products. Kew.
22. Kirk to Dyer, May 1892. Z. Cultural Products. Kew.
23. Kirk is buried beside his wife in the churchyard of St Nicholas's, Sevenoaks. His funeral service was conducted by the Canon of Zanzibar on 19 January 1922. Nelly died in 1914.

Epilogue

1. Livingstone recorded how, to his surprise, the slaves would often sing as they walked, manacled and yoked, to the coast. He was told that they rejoiced at the idea 'of coming back after death, and haunting and killing those who had sold them'. *The Last Journals of David Livingstone*, p.245.

BIBLIOGRAPHY

Unpublished and archival sources

Admiralty Records, British Library, London
A number of these (notably ADM 1/216, 1385, 1418, 2188, 2269, 3290 and 3409) contain material relevant to Zanzibar's early history.
Archives of the Royal Botanical Gardens, Kew, Surrey
Several volumes contain correspondence between J.D. Hooker and Kirk, notably Directors' Correspondence (DC) Vols 41, 60, 90, 126, and 186. Others covering the Zambesi Expedition and Zanzibar Cultural Products are of interest.
British House of Commons Sessional Papers 1871, Vol XII (I)
Report from the Select Committee on the Slave Trade (East Coast of Africa) together with the Proceedings, Minutes and Appendix, including the Muscat Zanzibar Commission of 1860.
Cambridge University Library, Cambridge
Sir John Milner Gray papers on Zanzibar (RCMS 126 section K), and James Augustus Grant photos of Zanzibar (Y3047C).
Department of Archives, Zanzibar (ZA)
Vols AA1–AA9 cover consular and general correspondence for the period, although much of this is duplicated in the Foreign Office records.
Foreign Office Records, Public Record Office, Kew, Surrey
FO 54, Vols 1–24: these contain much of the consular correspondence relating to Zanzibar (and Muscat/Oman) until the late 1850s.
FO 84: this long series concerning the slave trade contains some 35 volumes of letters (between 540 and 1,486) with specific relevance to East Africa and Zanzibar.

FO 881.2270: this has correspondence relating to the Frere Mission to Zanzibar.

India Office Records (IOR), British Library (BL), London

The series L/P and S/9 (Vols 12, 37, 40–3 and 48–50) contain correspondence of relevance to Zanzibar.

The series IOR/F4 contains material relevant to Zanzibar's early history, notably files 257, 343–4, 617, 711, 746, 783–5, 913, 1350, 1419, 1435, 1475 and 1539.

National Library of Scotland, Edinburgh

The Papers of Sir John Kirk (KP) (Acc. 9942) comprise 65 files of correspondence, notebooks and journals (both Kirk's and his wife's). Some also contain contemporary newspaper cuttings and photographs, many taken by Kirk himself.

British Parliamentary Papers (PP)

A number of these specific to the East African Slave Trade are reprinted in FO files. PP LXI and LXII for 1873–4 cover the Frere Mission to Zanzibar.

Royal Geographical Society (RGS), London

Vol 16, covering Proceedings for 1871–2, has correspondence between the RGS and Kirk.

Published sources and bibliography

Acton, J.E.E., *Letters of Lord Acton to Mary Gladstone*, Macmillan, London, 1913.

Alpers, E.A., *The East African Slave Trade*, East African Publishing House, Nairobi, 1967.

Alpers, E.A., *Ivory and Slaves in East Central Africa*, University of California Press, California, 1975.

Bayly, C.A., *The Birth of the Modern World: 1780–1914*, Blackwell, Oxford, 2004.

Beachey, R.W., *A Collection of Documents on the Slave Trade of Eastern Africa*, Rex Collings, London, 1976.

Beachey, R.W., *The Slave Trade of Eastern Africa*, Rex Collings, London, 1976.

Bennett, N.R., *Mirambo of Tanzania*, Oxford University Press, London, 1971.

Bennett, N.R., *A History of the Arab State of Zanzibar*, Methuen & Co., London, 1978.

Bennett, N.R., *Arab versus European*, Holmes & Meier, New York, 1986.

Blaikie, W.G., *Personal Life of David Livingstone*, John Murray, London, 1910.

Boteler, T., *Narrative of a Voyage of Discovery to Africa and Arabia performed by HM ships Levin and Barracouta from 1821 to 1826*, Richard Bentley, London, 1835.

Brode, H., *Tippoo Tib: The Story of his Career in Central Africa*, Longmans Green, London, 1907.

Browne, J.R., *Etchings of a Whaling Cruise with Notes of a Sojourn on the Island of Zanzibar*, Harvard University Press, New York, 1846.

Browne, W.G., *Travels in Egypt, Syria and Africa in 1793*, Cadell & Davies, London, 1799.

Burckhardt, J.L., *Travels in Nubia*, John Murray, London, 1819.

Burckhardt, J.L., *Travels in Syria and the Holy Land*, John Murray, London, 1822.

Burckhardt, J.L., *Travels in Arabia: Comprehending an Account of Those Territories in Hedjaz which the Mohamedans Regard as Sacred*, Henry Colburn, London, 1829.

Burton, F.R., *Personal Narrative of a Pilgrimage to al-Madinah and Mecca, Vols 1 & 2*, Tylston and Edwards, London, 1893.

Burton, R., *Lake Regions of Central Equatorial Africa*, Journal of the Royal Geographical Society, London, 1859.

Burton, R.F., *The Lake Regions of Central Africa, Vols 1 and 2*, Longman Green, London, 1860.

Burton, R.F., *Zanzibar: City, Island and Coast, Vols 1 and 2*, Tinsley Brothers, London, 1872.

Burton, R.F., *First Footsteps in East Africa*, Tylston and Edwards, London, 1894.

Cameron, V.L., *Across Africa, Vols 1 & 2*, Daldy, London, 1877.

Cannadine, D., *Ornamentalism: How the British Saw their Empire*, Penguin, London, 2001.

Chadwick, O., *Mackenzie's Grave*, Hodder & Stoughton, London, 1959.

Chambers, J., *Palmerston, the People's Darling*, John Murray, London 2004.

Christie, J., *Slavery in Zanzibar As It Is*, Harrison & Sons, London, 1871 (see *The East African Slave Trade*, Fraser, Tozer & Christie).

Christie, J., *Cholera Epidemics in East Africa*, Macmillan & Co., London, 1876.

Clarence Smith, W.G., *The Economics of the Indian Ocean Slave Trade in the 19th Century*, Frank Cass & Co., London, 1989.

Clarence Smith, W.G., *Islam and the Abolition of Slavery*, Oxford University Press, London, 2006.

Colley, L., *Captives: Britain, Empire and the World 1600–1850*, Jonathan Cape, London, 2002.

Colomb, P.H., *Slave Catching in the Indian Ocean*, Dawsons, London, 1873.

Cookey, S.J.S., *Tippu Tib and the Decline of the Congo Arabs*, Tarikh, London, Vol. 1, no. 2, 1966, pp58–69.

Cooper, F., *Plantation Slavery on the East Coast of Africa*, Yale, London, 1977.

Cope Devereux, W., *A Cruise in the 'Gorgon'*, Bell and Daldy, London, 1869.

Coupland, R., *Kirk on the Zambezi*, Oxford University Press, London, 1928.

Coupland, R., *The British Anti Slavery Movement*, Thornton Butterworth, London, 1933.

Coupland, R., *East Africa and its Invaders*, Oxford University Press, Oxford, 1938.

Coupland, R., *The Exploitation of East Africa 1856–1890*, Faber, London, 1939.

Coupland, R., *Livingstone's Last Journey*, Collins, London, 1947.

Crofton, R.H., *The Old Consulate at Zanzibar*, Oxford University Press, London, 1935.

Desmond, R., *Kew: The History of the Royal Botanic Gardens*, Harvill, London, 1998.

Elmslie, W.A., *Among the Wild Ngoni*, Oliphant Anderson & Ferrier, London, 1901.

Elton, J.F., *Travels and Researches among the Lakes and Mountains of East and Central Africa*, John Murray, London, 1879.

Farrant, L., *Tippu Tip and the East African Slave Trade*, Hamish Hamilton, London, 1975.

Feierman, S., *The Shambaa Kingdom*, University of Wisconsin Press, Madison, 1974.

Foskett, R. (ed.), *The Zambesi Doctors: David Livingstone's letters to John Kirk 1858–1872*, University Press, Edinburgh, 1964.

Foskett, R. (ed.), *The Zambesi Journal and Letters of Dr John Kirk 1858–1863*, Oliver and Boyd, Edinburgh, 1965.

Fraser, H.A., Tozer, W.G. & Christie, J., *The East African Slave Trade*, Harrison & Sons, London, 1871.

Freeman-Grenville, G.S.P., *The East African Coast*, Clarendon Press, Oxford, 1962.

Freeman-Grenville, G.S.P., *The French at Kilwa Island*, Clarendon Press, Oxford, 1965.

Gavin, R.J., *The Bartle Frere Expedition and Zanzibar, 1873*, Historical Journal Vol. 2, Cambridge, 1962.

Gavin, R.J., *Seyyid Said*, Tarikh, Historical Society of Nigeria, Nigeria, 1965 (Vol. 1).

Ghaidan, U., *Lamu: A Study of the Swahili Town*, The East African Literature Bureau, Nairobi, 1975.

Gilbert, E., *Dhows and the Colonial Economy of Zanzibar 1860–1970*, James Currey, Oxford 2004.

Gobineau, A. de, *Trois Ans en Asie*, B. Grasset, Paris, 1905.

Grant, J.A., *A Walk Across Africa: or Domestic Scenes from My Nile Journal*, William Blackwood & Sons, Edinburgh, 1864.

Gray, J.M., *Memoirs of an Arabian Princess*, Tanganyika Notes and Records, Dar es Salaam, 1954.

Gray, J.M., *The French at Kilwa in 1797*, Tanganyika Notes and Records, Dar es Salaam, 1962 (nos 58, 59, pp172–3).

Gray, J.M., *A History of Zanzibar from the Middle Ages to 1856*, Oxford University Press, London, 1962.

Gray, J.M., *The Recovery of Kilwa by the Arabs in 1785*, Tanganyika Notes and Records, Dar es Salaam, 1964 (March) (no. 62, pp20–4).

Gray, J.M., *A French account of Kilwa at the end of the 18th Century*, Tanganyika Notes and Records, Dar es Salaam, 1964 (September).

Gray, R. & Birmingham, D. (eds), *Pre-Colonial African Trade*, Oxford University Press, Oxford, 1970.

Guillain, C., *Documents sur L'histoire, la Geographie et le Commerce de l'Afrique Orientale, Vols 1–3*, Arthus Bertrand, Paris, 1857.

Hakan Erdem, Y., *Slavery in the Ottoman Empire and its Demise*, Macmillan Press, London, 1996.

Hall, R., *Empires of the Monsoon*, HarperCollins, London, 1996.

Hinde, S.L., *The Fall of the Congo Arabs*, Methuen & Co., London, 1897.

Hitti, P.K., *History of the Arabs*, Macmillan, London, 1937.

Hogendorn, J.S., *The Location of the 'Manufacture of Eunuchs'* (see *Slave Elites in the Middle East and Africa*).

Hyam, R., *Britain's Imperial Century 1815–1914*, Batsford, London, 1976.

Jeal, T., *Livingstone*, Heinemann, London, 1973.

Jeal, T. *et al*, *David Livingstone and the Victorian Encounter with Africa*, National Portrait Gallery, London, 1996.

Jiddawi, A.M., *Extracts from an Arab Account Book 1840–54*, Tanganyika Notes and Records, Dar es Salaam, 1951.

Johnston, H.J., *The Story of my Life*, Bobbs-Merrill, Indianapolis, 1923.

Judd, D., *Empire – the British Imperial Experience*, Harper Collins, London, 1996.

Keay, J., *The Honourable Company: A History of the English East India Company*, Macmillan, New York, 1991.

Kelly, J.B., *Sultanate and Imamate in Oman*, Oxford University Press, London, 1959.

Kelly, J.B., *Britain and the Persian Gulf 1795–1880*, Clarendon Press, Oxford, 1968.

Krapf, J.L., *Memoir on East African Slave Trade*, Church Missionary Intelligencer, London, 1853.

Krapf, J.L., *Travels, Researches and Ministry Labours during an 18 years residence in East Africa*, Trubner, London, 1860.

Kulkarni, S.A., *The Satara Raj*, Mittal Publications, New Delhi, 1995.

Lewis, B., *Race and Slavery in the Middle East – an Historical Inquiry*, Oxford University Press, Oxford, 1990.

Livingstone, D., *Missionary Travels and Researches in Southern Africa*, John Murray, London, 1861.

Livingstone, D. & C., *Narrative of an Expedition to the Zambesi*, John Murray, London, 1865.

Livingstone, D., *The Last Journals of David Livingstone, Vols 1 and 2*, Jansen McClurg, Chicago, 1875.

Lombard, M., *The Golden Age of Islam*, Markus Weiner, Princeton, 1975.

Lovejoy, P., *Transformations in Slavery: a History of Slavery in Africa*, Cambridge University Press, London, 1983.

Lugard, F.D., *The Rise of our East African Empire, Vols 1 and 2*, W. Blackwood & Sons, London, 1893.

Lyne, R.N., *Zanzibar in Contemporary Times*, Hurst & Blackett, London, 1905.

Mackenzie, D., *A Report on Slavery and the Slave Trade in Zanzibar, Pemba and the Mainland of the B P of E Africa*, Anti Slavery Reporter, London, 1895 (S 4, Vol. 1).

Martin & Ryan, *A Quantitive Assessment of the Arab Slave Trade of East Africa 1770–1896*, Kenya Historical Review, 1977 (Vol. 5).

Martineau, J., *Life of Sir Bartle Frere, Vols 1 & 2*, John Murray, London, 1895.

Mason, P., *The Men who Ruled India*, Rupa, Delhi, 1985.

Maurizi, V. (Sheikh Mansur), *History of Seyd Said*, Oleander Press, New York, 1984.

Mauss, M., *The Gift*, Routledge, London, 1990.

McLynn, F., *Stanley: The Making of an African Explorer*, Scarborough House, London, 1990.

McLynn, F., *Hearts of Darkness: The European Exploration of Africa*, Pimlico, London, 1992.

Meirs, S., *Britain and the Ending of the Slave Trade*, Africana Publishing Corporation, London, 1975.

Miers S., Kopytoff I. (eds), *Slavery in Africa: Historical and Anthropological Perspectives*, University of Wisconsin Press, London, 1977.

Middleton, J., *Zanzibar, its Society and its Politics*, Oxford University Press, London, 1965.

Middleton, J., *The World of the Swahili*, Yale University, London, 1992.

Miles, S.B., *The Countries and Tribes of the Persian Gulf*, Harrison & Sons, London, 1919.

Moorehead, A., *The White Nile*, Hamish Hamilton, London, 1960.

Murray, S.S., *A Handbook of Nyasaland*, The Crown Agents, London, 1932.

New, C., *Life, Wanderings, and Labours in Eastern Africa*, Hodder & Stoughton, London, 1873.

Nichols, C.S., *The Swahili Coast: Politics, Diplomacy and Trade on the East African Littoral 1789–1856*, Africana Publishing Corporation, New York, 1971.

O'Connor, D.P., *The Zulu and the Raj – the Life of Sir Bartle Frere*, Able Publishing, New York 2002.

Ogot, B.A. (ed.), *Zamani*, East African Publishing House, Nairobi, 1968.

Oliver, R., *The African Experience*, Weidenfeld, London, 1991.

Oliver, R. & Mathew, G. (ed.), *History of East Africa, Vol. 1*, Oxford University Press, London, 1963.

Owen, I.R., *The Ivory and Teeth of Commerce*, Journal of the Society of Arts, December, 1856 (Vol. 5, no. 213, pp65–8).

Owen, W.F., *Narrative of Voyages to Explore the shores of Africa, Arabia, and Madagascar, Vols 1 & 2*, J. & J. Harper, New York, 1833.

Packenham, T., *The Scramble for Africa*, Weidenfeld & Nicolson, London, 1991.

Page, M., *The Manyema Hordes of Tippu Tip*, International Journal of African Historical Studies, Boston, 1974 (Vol. 7, pp69–84).

Prior, J., *Narrative of a Voyage in the Indian Seas in the Nisus Frigate*, Richard Phillips, London, 1819.

Raby, P., *Bright Paradise: Victorian Scientific Travellers*, Chatto and Windus, London, 1996.

Randsford, O., *Livingstone's Lake*, John Murray, London, 1966.

Reader, J., *Africa: A Biography of the Continent*, Hamish Hamilton, London, 1997.

Rice, P.C., *Amber: the Golden Gem of the Ages*, Kosciuszko Foundation, New York, 1944.

Roberts, A., *Tanzania before 1800*, East African Publishing House, Nairobi, 1968.

Roberts, E., *Embassy to the Eastern Courts of Cochin China, Siam, and Muscat, 1832–4*, Harper and Brothers, New York, 1837.

Robinson, R. & Gallagher, J., *Africa and the Victorians*, Macmillan, London, 1967.

Ross, A.C., *David Livingstone: Mission and Empire*, Hambledon & London, London 2002.

Ruete, E., *Memoirs of an Arabian Princess from Zanzibar*, Markus Wiener, New York, 1989.

Ruschenberger, W.S.W., *Voyage Round the World: including an Embassy in Muscat and Siam in 1835*, Carey, Lee and Blanchard, Philadelphia, 1838.

Russell, C.E.B., *General Rigby, Zanzibar and the Slave Trade*, Allen & Unwin, London, 1935.

Said, E., *Orientalism*, Routledge & Kegan Paul, London, 1978.

Said-Ruete, R., *Said b.Sultan (1791–1856) Ruler of Oman and Zanzibar*, Alexander-Ousley, London, 1929.

Schimpfer, *Memo on the East African slave trade*, Appendix to Sullivan: *Dhow Chasing* (see above).

Segal, R., *Islam's Black Slaves: the Other Black Diaspora*, Atlantic, London 2001.

Sheil, M.L., *Glimpses of Life and Manners in Persia*, John Murray, London, 1856.

Sheriff, A., *Slaves, Spices, and Ivory in Zanzibar*, James Currey, Oxford, 1987.

Sheriff, A., *The History and Conservation of Zanzibar Stone Town*, James Currey, London, 1992.

Sirhan Ibn Sa'id ibn Sirhan, *Annals of Oman*, Oleander Press, New York, 1984.

Snouck-Hurgronje, C., *Mekka in the latter part of the 19th century*, Luzac & Co., London, 1931.

Snow, J., *On the Mode of Communication of Cholera*, John Churchill, London, 1855.

Speke, J.H., *Journal of the Discovery of the Source of the Nile*, Blackwood, London, 1863.

Speke, J.H., *What led to the discovery of the source of the Nile*, Blackwood, London, 1864.

Stanley, H.M., *How I found Livingstone*, Sampson Low, London, 1872.

Stanley, H.M., *Through the Dark Continent*, Harper & Brothers, New York, 1879.

Stanley, H.M., *Slavery and the Slave Trade*, Harpers New Monthly Magazine, March 1893.

Steere, E., *Some Account of the Town of Zanzibar*, Bell & Daldy, London, 1869.

Sullivan, G.L., *Dhow Chasing in Zanzibar Waters*, Sampson Low, London, 1873.

Thomas Baines: An Artist in the Service of Science in Southern Africa, Christie's Publications, London.

Thomson, J., *To the Central African Lakes and Back, Vols 1 and 2*, Sampson Low, London, 1881.

Toru, M. & Philips, J.E. (eds), *Slave Elites in the Middle East and Africa*, Kegan Paul, London 2000.

Turley, D., *The Culture of English Anti Slavery 1780–1860*, Routledge, London, 1991.

Valentia, G.A., *Voyages and Travels to India, Ceylon, the Red Sea, Abysinnia and Egypt, Vols 1–3*, W. Miller, London, 1809.

Vansina, J., *Paths in the Rainforest*, James Currey, London, 1990.

Wallis, J.P.R., *The Zambezi Journal of James Stewart*, Chatto and Windus, London, 1952.

Walvin, J., *Black Ivory: Slavery in the British Empire*, HarperCollins, London, 1992.

Wellsted, J.R., *Travels in Arabia*, John Murray, London, 1838.

Wright, M., *Strategies of Slaves and Women*, James Currey, London, 1993.

INDEX

Wylde, Henry 133, 153, 277,
  289, 293, 299

Yao Ajawa tribe 41, 48–9, 51,
  56, 58, 216, 234, 297

Zambesi expedition
  (1858–60) 29–31, 32, 33–4,
  35–8, 40–5
  (1861–63) 46–9, 50–68
Zanzibar and East Africa
    16–17, 25, 41, 68, 71,
    72–9, 113–15, 136–9,
    145–7, 177, 306–10
  cholera epidemic 127,
    130–6, 149, 199, 233
  cyclone hit 231–3, 235–6,
    245, 250
  and Germany 301–4, 308
  slavery 6–10, 11–25, 70, 74,
    76–7, 79–80, 81–2, 90–1,
    92–3, 94–6, 98–9, 100,
    102, 104, 105–6, 108, 109,
    110, 111–12, 114, 117,
    119, 120–4, 127, 128,
    133–6, 139–41, 146, 148,
    151–3, 159–60, 162, 164,

    174, 196, 199–200, 206–7,
    208, 209–26, 229, 233–5,
    241, 243–53, 256, 257,
    258–60, 262–74, 285,
    286–93, 295–7, 308
  Treaty of 1845 9–10, 23, 102,
    104, 105, 212, 261–2
  Vice Admiralty court 10,
    139, 143–4, 149, 234–5,
    260
  see also Barghash, Sultan;
    British government in
    London; Churchill,
    Henry; Dhamji, Ludda;
    dhows; East India
    Company; Frere, Bartle;
    Hamerton, Atkins; ivory;
    Kirk, John; Kirk, Nelly;
    Majid, Sultan; Rigby,
    Christopher; Royal Navy;
    Said bin Sultan, Seyyid;
    slaves
Zanzibar, Sultan of see
    Barghash, Sultan; Majid,
    Sultan; Said bin Sultan,
    Seyyid